ANSWER WISELY

© Edward Gross Co., Inc. *From a Painting by C. Bosseron Chambers.*

CHRIST THE KING

ANSWER
WISELY

By MARTIN J. SCOTT, S. J., *Lecturer on Religion,*
College of St. Francis Xavier, New York

LOYOLA UNIVERSITY PRESS, CHICAGO, ILLINOIS

1943

Imprimi Potest:

　　JOSEPH A. MURPHY, S. J.

　　　　Provincial of the New York-Maryland Province

April 4, 1938

Nihil Obstat:

　　AUSTIN G. SCHMIDT, S. J.

　　　　Censor Deputatus

June 20, 1938

Imprimatur:

　　✠ GEORGE CARDINAL MUNDELEIN

　　　　Archbishop of Chicago

June 23, 1938

PREFACE

THIS BOOK IS INTENDED for more mature students who are about to go forth into the world as champions of Catholic Action. As such they will be called upon to answer wisely the questions of sincere inquirers and the charges of hostile critics. Surrounded as they are by agnostics and materialists who know nothing of God's governance of His world and who depend upon reason alone for the solution of all life's problems, they must be prepared to prove that the Catholic church, still possessed of the revealed truth entrusted to her keeping by her divine Founder and still guided and protected by the Holy Spirit, has a positive, a true, and a complete answer for every question or problem pertaining to man's destiny in heaven and the right ordering of his life upon earth.

The topics taken up are those that are most important because of the conditions that prevail in society today. For the most part they have to do with the divinity of Christ and the claims of His Church, with the nature of the soul and the purpose of life, with the means that must be employed if one is to live as a generous and loyal Catholic, and with some of the outstanding problems created by the false philosophy of the day. Whenever possible use has been made of the encyclicals of the present Supreme Pontiff, who in majestic language has reiterated the truths taught centuries ago by Christ Himself and by St. Peter, whose successor he is.

In the Points for Discussion that follow the chapters

the chief objections of unbelievers and opponents are stated. All are answered in the chapters themselves. It is the student's task to frame for himself a short and convincing answer which will expose the fallacy and satisfy any honest mind.

M. J. S.

FEAST OF ST. BARNABAS
June 11, 1938

TABLE OF CONTENTS

ANSWER WISELY

THE Church today stands in need of an educated laity. To rightly carry on her work of spreading the kingdom of God and restoring Catholic life in the family and in society, there must be those of the laity who will co-operate in the apostolate of the hierarchy. This is designated 'Catholic Action' by the Holy Father. That it fills a definite and important place in the work of the Church there can be no doubt. An educated laity is a most powerful means to bring the truths of the Gospel to the attention of non-Catholics.

The non-Catholic inquirer will naturally turn to his Catholic neighbor for information on points of Catholic doctrine; he will naturally look to the layman who is associated with him in business and social life to explain the position of the Church on controverted points, and to make clear the Catholic side of historical and doctrinal questions. These inquirers, however well-meaning, will rarely come to a priest for their information. They will probably admit that they could expect from the priest a kind and courteous welcome, but nevertheless some natural shyness holds them back. If the Catholic layman does not answer their questions they do not seek further. The Catholic layman can guide them to the truth.

CHAPTER I

RELIGION

No OTHER SUBJECT has received from mankind the attention given to religion. The greatest minds of every epoch have devoted their earnest efforts to its study. Pagan as well as Christian scholarship has made it the principal object of keenest inquiry. Not only scholars but people generally have regarded religion as the most vital of all concerns. Now more than ever has religion come to the fore as a subject of study.

Materialism in its various phases is a challenge to religion of whatever sort. Materialism is a denial of the very basis of religion; namely, a personal power behind the forces of nature. Religion is the relationship between a personal Creator and a rational creature; that is, between God and man. If there is no personal God with whom personal relationship is possible there can be no religion.

Materialism is a doctrine which proclaims that everything is matter only, that man is simply a compound of physical and chemical elements, that there is no such thing as a spiritual substance, and that man is but a high-grade animal for whom the grave is the final end.

Materialism is the basis of modern atheism, communism, and all the -*isms* which deny that there is a personal power above and outside the universe. Materialism is also the basis of the various -*isms* which proclaim that man has no spiritual soul nor free will, nor existence after

1

death. In due course it will be shown that there is a personal God, Creator and Ruler of the world, with whom man, who has a rational soul, is capable of relationship.

Religion is natural or supernatural, according to its origin.

Natural religion is that whose truths and duties may be known by the sole reasoning of man, and whose rites and worship are those of man's own creation.

Supernatural religion is that whose origin is from a source superior to human nature, and whose worship is ordained by a power higher than human. Christianity proclaims that it is a supernatural religion revealed to mankind by Jesus Christ, the Son of God.

Christ is accordingly the most momentous factor in the history of mankind. If He is what Christian belief affirms, He bears a personal relation to each one of us individually; and this relationship is such that it signifies more than anything else in the whole world. Hence the fierceness of the controversy now raging about Christ. He cannot be ignored. His claims are of such a nature that we must either admit or reject them. He means everything or nothing to us. We may believe in other persons without being necessarily affected by our belief. But we cannot believe in Christ without either living by His divine law or defying His divine authority. If people could believe in Christ without the obligation of living by His precepts, few would deny Him.

An infidel is one who does not believe that Christ is God. Those who deny altogether that there is a God are atheists. Deists are those who believe in God, but not the God of revelation. They admit the existence of a supreme being, but not the God of Christianity. Agnostics are those who affirm that there may or may not be a God, but that at all events He is unknowable by man. These erroneous tenets will be refuted in their proper place.

One reason for the denial of God as made known by revelation is the existence of evil in the world. The God of revelation is a good God, our Father in heaven. The existence of evil seems to be incompatible with goodness, and hence the objection to the God of Christianity. The existence of evil is a mystery. Whether we believe in God or not, evil remains a mystery. Christianity, however, gives the most satisfactory view regarding the existence of evil.

Before man passes judgment on the Creator, he should know the Creator's purpose not only here but in the eternal hereafter. God may permit evil in the present life for the sake of everlasting good hereafter. A man often submits to a painful surgical operation for the sake of permanent benefit. This life is but a moment compared to eternity, and the good God may permit evil here in order that eternal good may result. If a person who did not understand life-saving tactics saw a life-saver knock a drowning person unconscious, he would judge it an act of cruelty, whereas it was the means of saving the life of the struggling man.

We cannot pass judgment on the acts of God unless we know not only the present but the future also. Since we do not know the future, we should realize that God, who in His goodness, wisdom, and power created the world, rules it wisely and with paternal goodness. We can affirm no contradiction nor incompatibility between the existence of evil and a good God because we have not the complete data of time and eternity before us. Although the existence of evil is a mystery to man, Christianity gives the only right view regarding it.

Atheism, agnosticism, materialism, and communism in the face of evil offer nothing but desperation. Christianity divinely assures man that suffering may be converted into eternal welfare; that affliction, injustice, and the various vicissitudes of life may become wings raising mortals to the realm of glorious immortality. There are some people, however, who declare that religion is not necessary, that man is capable by himself of knowing and doing everything necessary in order that he may fully realize his destiny. The answer to this is that man from the beginning has been groping sadly with regard to the truths most essential for the guidance of the human race in matters of religion and morality. Also, man relying solely on his own powers has fallen at times to the level of the brute creation.

When a person has youth, health, wealth, and friends, he may think that religion is not necessary. But people are not always young, healthy, and surrounded by friends. Moreover, in the hour of temptation which at times comes to everyone, unless man has something superior to himself to aid him, he is almost certain to fall. When we consider the vicissitudes of life, man's limitations, and the proneness to error which characterizes him, it becomes evident that religion which guides him aright and gives the means to follow the guidance is necessary for the attainment of his destiny.

Considering life as a whole, religion is as necessary as food. We must realize that any view of life which leaves out eternity is false. Without religion man is only too apt to close out the eternal and most important part of his career. Unless a traveler knows his destination and tends towards it, he will not ordinarily reach it. Moreover, it is not enough to know the destination; the traveler needs, besides, help and sustenance on the way. The true religion not only points out our destination and the way to it, but moreover furnishes all the aids necessary for reaching it. Without revealed religion it is possible to know, in a more or less obscure way, what the end of man is, and with difficulty to be able to reach it. But by Christian revelation the end of man is *definitely* known and the means for attaining it are *abundantly* supplied.

Considering man's weaknesses, his tendency to evil, and the liability of his intellect to err, religion, which gives strength, fortitude, and definite guidance, is necessary for the generality of mankind. If, with religion, it is no easy matter to keep in the right way, we may be sure that without it, most people are in danger of taking the easy and broad path which leads to destruction.

Since, therefore, religion is such a vital matter we should be vitally interested in it.

At present there is a wave of irreligion sweeping over mankind to their temporal and eternal detriment.

The Son of God became man in order that the children of men might become the children of God. Christ established His Church to continue to the end of time the mission which He inaugurated while on earth. We are members of that Church, and as such we should endeavor to know its teaching, not only for our own benefit but also for that of those with whom we associate.

"The Church today stands in need of an educated laity. To rightly carry on her work of spreading the kingdom of God and restoring Catholic life in the family and in society, there must be those of the laity who will co-operate in the apostolate of the hierarchy. This is designated 'Catholic Action' by the Holy Father. That it fills a definite and important place in the work of the Church there can be no doubt. An educated laity is a most powerful means to bring the truths of the Gospel to the attention of non-Catholics.

"The non-Catholic inquirer will naturally turn to his Catholic neighbor for information on points of Catholic doctrine; he will naturally look to the layman who is associated with him in business and social life to explain the position of the Church on controverted points, and to make clear the Catholic side of historical and doctrinal questions. These inquirers, however well-meaning, will rarely come to a priest for their information. They will probably admit that they could expect from the priest a kind and courteous welcome, but nevertheless some natural shyness holds them back. If the Catholic layman does not answer their questions they do not seek further. The Catholic layman can guide them to the truth."

It is the purpose of this course in religion to show the reasonableness of the Catholic religion, and to equip young men and women to meet the difficulties and inquiries which are bound to confront them in their everyday life. A right understanding of Catholicism will enable laymen to be effective in what is termed Catholic Action, which means co-operating with the hierarchy in spreading the knowledge of Christ and His Church.

The prime purpose of Catholic Action is spiritual. It is to promote effectively the cause of Christ by external activity. It is a crusade to do something which will influence others to know more about Christ and His Church, to increase respect for His religion, and to win sympathy and love for Christ Himself.

Catholic Action is not restricted to the ideal of an exemplary private life. The force of good example is indeed of immeasurable value in drawing others to Christ's service, and is an essential part of any effective apostolate; but it does not exhaust the meaning or scope of Catholic Action.

Catholic Action is a true apostolate in which Catholics of every social class participate by being united in thought and action around those centers of sound doctrine and social activities sanctioned by episcopal authority. In particular, Catholic Action embraces every social activity sponsored by ecclesiastical superiors, such as pious sodalities, spiritual retreats, organizations such as the Holy Name Society, the Legion of Decency, parish welfare associations, parochial schools, Catholic education, Catholic publications, and movements for social betterment and decency and for upholding moral standards regarding divorce, birth control, mercy killing, and so forth. In a word, Catholic Action means being actively interested and engaged in whatever cause the hierarchy champions. Catholic Action is just what the word implies —activity under episcopal leadership. If the bishop directly or indirectly leads a movement, Catholic Action implies supporting that movement.

It is thus seen that religion is not confined to one's own welfare, but is, moreover, a matter of concern for all those who are of the brotherhood of Christ, and for those who are outside and who may be brought in. Moreover, true religion implies in its adherents the endeavor to have its standards of creed and conduct made as universal as possible. The adherents of error display an earnestness in its propagation which often puts to shame the adherents of truth. The activities, for instance, of communists in spreading their false and ruinous doctrines might well serve as a spur to Catholics to engage earnestly in the cause of divine truth, which is theirs.

This course in religion is devised in order to make Catholic young men and women crusaders for Christ and His Church. The world at large is weary of the theories which have plunged it into confusion and despair, and will eagerly listen to sound principles of creed and practice if properly and tactfully presented.

Catholicism is divinely true. It has stood the test of time. Too many persons know only a caricature of Christ's religion. With the present hunger for religious truth, the educated Catholic layman has a splendid opportunity of doing something personal for Christ and making Him and His Church better known and loved.

It is an honor to be allowed to do something personal for a worldly monarch, but a much greater honor to do something personal for Christ, the King of Kings, the Lord of time and eternity.

SUMMARY

Religion has claimed the most serious consideration in every epoch of history.

The greatest minds of every generation have devoted their efforts to its study.

Religion is at present of most vital concern, for it is challenged by materialism, which in its various forms is a denial of the very basis of religion; namely, a personal power behind the forces of nature.

Religion is natural or supernatural according to its origin.

Christianity proclaims that it is a supernatural religion revealed to mankind by Jesus Christ, the Son of God.

Christ's divinity is the basis of Christianity and hence He is the most important person in history. He cannot be ignored but must be accepted as God or rejected as an impostor.

An infidel is one who denies that Christ is God.

An atheist denies the existence of God altogether.

A deist believes in a supreme being but not in the God of revelation.

An agnostic holds that God is unknowable.

One reason for the denial of God is the existence of evil.

Christianity alone gives a satisfactory view of the mystery of evil. Man has not the data of time and eternity to form a judgment on God's providence.

Considering man's weaknesses, his tendency to evil and liability to error, and the vicissitudes of life, religion is necessary for mankind.

Catholic Action is the co-operation of laymen with the hierarchy in spreading the knowledge of Christ and His Church. It is a crusade to influence others to know and live by Catholic standards. It embraces every activity sponsored by ecclesiastical authority.

A good knowledge of religion as outlined in this course will equip one for effective service in the cause of Christ.

POINTS FOR DISCUSSION

1. There are so many contradictory religions that we are justified in rejecting religion altogether.

2. Religion takes for granted a personal God, but there is no such being.

3. Religion owes its origin to human invention.

4. Christianity is not a supernatural religion, but the invention of designing men.

5. Christ was a great and good man, but not God.

6. One religion is as good as another.

7. Voltaire and other infidels were men of keen intellect. They rejected the divinity of Christ for sound reasons.

8. God is unknowable, hence religion does not concern man.

9. The God of Christianity is declared to be good, but the evil in the world is proof that He is not good.

10. Some of the most successful men have practiced no religion, hence religion is not really necessary.

11. We are not concerned with the salvation of others, but only with our own.

CHAPTER II

JESUS CHRIST

CHRIST IS TRUE GOD as He claimed to be. By the term 'God' we mean the intelligent first cause of all things, the personal creator and ruler of the world, self-existing—that is, eternal, uncaused. That there is such a supreme being will be shown when we come to consider the existence of God.

Christ claimed to be God in the true sense; that is, to be the creator and ruler of the universe. His claim to be God Almighty was the most stupendous ever made in the annals of mankind. In appearance Christ was like other men, yet He affirmed that He was their creator and ruler and judge. Are we to accept His claim? Are we to honor Christ as God or brand Him a liar or lunatic? This is the crux of the Christian inquiry.

If Christ is God His religion is divine; and we know that in accepting it, and living by it, we are believing and living as God ordains. On the other hand if Christ be not God, Christianity is a fraud, an imposition, a delusion, and the sooner it is abolished the better. The line is sharply drawn: Christ is or is not God.

In passing, let it be said that no institution based on a false foundation could survive through the centuries as the Catholic church has done.

Christ distinctly proclaimed that He was God. Are we to accept His claim? It is one thing to make a claim, quite another to substantiate it. Christ made divine

11

claims.[1] Divine claims must be supported by divine evidence. Did Christ furnish divine evidence for His divine claim? When a person makes a claim, two things must be looked into before accepting it: (1) the character of the claimant and (2) the evidence for the claim.

With regard to Christ's character, even His opponents admit that mentally and morally He was the most perfect being that this world has known. The most perfect being is neither a fraud nor a fool. Christ accordingly is to be believed, since the most perfect being is neither deceived nor a deceiver.

Christ, however, was not content with merely declaring that He was God, but proceeded to confirm His claim by deeds possible to God alone. A miracle is a visible fact outside the course of nature and possible to divine power alone. Christ, realizing the stupendous nature of His claims, knew that He must do the works of God in order to be believed.

The Jews had the sublimest conception of God, yet here before them stood a man like themselves, who affirmed solemnly that He was God Almighty! No wonder they were astonished and accused Him of blasphemy.

Christ made allowance for their attitude, knowing that it was based on reverence for Jehovah. And so when His claims met with their rejection, He said in effect to them: "I know you are shocked because I declare that I am God, but if you do not believe Me, believe the works which I do, which are possible to divine power alone. Divine power is not exercised to confirm a false claim, otherwise God would be approving falsehood.

---

[1] John 10:30; Matthew 28:19; John 9:35-38; John 5:23; John 17:5. Chapter IV shows that the Gospels are a true historical document.

"Accordingly, I proceed to do what divine power alone can effect."

Before their eyes He gave sight to the man born blind, cleansed the leper, gave hearing and speech to the deaf and dumb, made the cripple sound, multiplied the loaves and fishes, ruled the raging elements, and raised the dead to life. All these things He did merely by His will power. His word alone gave sight to the blind and life to the dead.[1]

There are many wonderful things done today by scientific methods, and sometimes these wonders are termed miracles. But they all have a natural explanation, they require materials and time, and they make no claim to supernatural power. Christ's miracles were instantaneous, without the employment of material means, and performed as evidence of supernatural confirmation of His claims.

Since Divine Power could not approve error, and since Divine Power approved Christ's claims, He is what He declared Himself to be, the true Son of God.

Saints, it is true, have performed miracles, but not by their own power nor as evidence of their divinity, but always in the name and by the power of God.

It is important to understand that Christ's miracles were divine evidence for divine claims. Christ performed many miracles, which could not be wrought by natural power or forces. He raised Lazarus from the dead instantly and by a sole command, saying to the corpse of four days, "Lazarus, come forth." And the dead obeyed

---

[1] Christ's miracles were performed as divine confirmation of His claims. "The works themselves which I do give testimony of Me that the Father hath sent Me" (John 5:36).

the voice of the Creator, sprang to life, and came forth from the tomb (John 11:43).

Just before He performed this miracle Christ made it a distinct proof that His mission was divine, saying to His heavenly Father in hearing of the multitude: "That they may believe that Thou hast sent Me" (John 11:42).

Another manifestation of divine power was Christ's command of the natural elements, when by His own authority He said to the tempest that was engulfing the vessel: "Peace, be still," and a calm instantly rested on the raging sea (Mark 4:39).

On another occasion Christ by a word only gave sight to the blind man who cried out for mercy. Jesus said: "What wilt thou that I do to thee?" But he said: "Lord, that I may see!" and Jesus said to him: "Receive thy sight." And immediately he saw and followed Him, glorifying God (Luke 18:41-43).

Other notable miracles of Christ were the multiplication of the loaves and fishes, the raising to life of the dead son of the widow of Naim, the cleansing of the lepers. In fact, every page of the Gospels is a record of deeds possible to divine power alone, both with regard to the deeds themselves and the manner in which they were performed.

Christ accordingly substantiated His divine claims by divine evidence, and having done so, must be believed on His word only, for God can neither deceive nor be deceived.

Christ, besides presenting the divine evidence of miracles for His claims, also furnished the divine evidence of prophecy. Prophecy is not calculation. An astronomer can foretell an eclipse and a scientist can predict the exact consequences of a combination of forces. This is possible on account of the regularity of nature's laws. No one but God, however, knows the future of those beings whose actions are not determined by fixed laws.

Man alone of all visible creation is not determined by fixed laws. No man can foretell, even regarding himself, what will happen a week or a year from now. Of course he plans, and counts on carrying out his plans, but they may entirely miscarry. Shrewd persons sometimes predict the future of human events, but more often they go awry. God alone knows for certain the future regarding mankind. The foretelling of the future regarding events dependent on human action is possible to divine foreknowledge alone.

Prophecy is the foretelling of an event not naturally knowable. Christ furnished the divine evidence of prophecy to confirm His divine claims. He foretold, among other things, His passion, death, and resurrection; the destruction of Jerusalem; the perpetuity of His Church. None of these things was naturally knowable.

God's foreknowledge does not *determine* man's actions, but simply *knows* them. An example may help us to understand this. An aviator in an airplane two miles up can see, with a powerful glass, miles and miles of the country below. A traveler going along an unknown road in that country can see just so far before him and behind. The aviator sees the road from beginning to end. Now, because the aviator knows the turns, ditches, and hills of the road, he knows that the traveler will turn and descend and climb as he goes on his way. But that knowledge does not determine the traveler's turns, descents, and ascents.

In a somewhat similar manner God, who knows all things, knows what man will *freely* do. A mother knows that a child will eat ice cream if offered it, but the child does not eat the cream because of the mother's knowledge.

God would not be God if He were ignorant of the future, for He would be dependent on it, whereas He is dependent on nothing, being infinitely perfect, as we shall see in due course.

Christ's miracles and prophecies are, therefore, divine evidence for His divine claims. He claimed to be God in the true sense, hence He is God. Time and again Christ declared He was the true Son of God, the Father Almighty.

On a certain occasion He said: "I and the Father are one." The Jews accused Him of blasphemy for this, and threatened to stone Him "because that Thou, being a man, makest Thyself God" (John 10:30-33). To which Jesus replied: "Do you say: Thou blasphemest, because I said I am the Son of God? If I do not the works of My Father, believe Me not; but if I do, though you will not believe Me, believe the works, that you may know and believe" (John 10:36-38).

When Jesus sent His apostles forth to preach His kingdom on earth, He commanded them to baptize in the name of the Father and of the Son and of the Holy Ghost. He said in the *name*, not the *names*, because God is one supreme being, although there are three persons in God. This is the mystery of the Trinity.

When Jesus said, "I and the Father are one," He did not say one person, which would be a contradiction, but one nature, one supreme being, God.

This leads us to the second matter of our consideration, that Christ is true man. It seems strange that we have to prove that Christ was true man. At present many persons declare He was man and man only. But in the early centuries there were those who asserted that Christ was man in appearance only. They had no doubt at all that He was God, but they denied that He was man in the complete sense—that is, possessing all the faculties of a human being, such as mind, will, and so forth.

Unless Christ was truly human, He could not have suffered and died on the cross, as in fact He did, in order to redeem mankind. Christ could not have suffered mental anguish and corporal pain unless He had a real human soul and body.

When it is said that God became man, the meaning is not that He ceased to be God and was changed into man, but that being God from all eternity He in the course of time assumed human nature. Christ was God from eternity, and man from the time He was born of the Virgin Mary.

Perhaps an example will help us to understand somewhat this mystery of the incarnation.

Suppose a king desired to improve the condition of his lowly subjects, and for that reason put aside his royal garments and dressed himself as a beggar and lived among beggars in order the better to realize their condition and to help them.

It is true to say that while among these unfortunates, and sharing their lot, he was a beggar. But he was also truly a king, a king as well as a beggar. He did not cease to be king by becoming a beggar, but only assumed an added state of existence.

In some such way, but with a substantial difference, God became man. When the Son of God became man He assumed human nature by substantially uniting it to the divine, so that the one person Christ was divine and human. This union was not incidental nor temporary but substantially real, somewhat the same as the union of soul and body in man.

Christ as the Son of God is the equal in all things to the eternal and almighty Father. As man He is inferior to the God-head just as His human is inferior to His divine nature.

This explains how it is that Christ, at times, speaking as man, says that He does the will of His Father in heaven.

In the agony in the Garden of Gethsemane He cried out: "Not My will but Thine be done." And on the cross, dying for our redemption, He said: "My God, why hast Thou forsaken Me?" and again: "Father, into Thy hands I commend My spirit."

The Trinity and the incarnation are mysteries. The human intellect is incapable of comprehending them. We accept them not because we understand them, but because we understand that Christ who revealed them is God, who can neither deceive nor be deceived.

This brings us to the third part of our consideration, that Christ is our redeemer.

Almighty God could have effected the restoration of fallen mankind in any way He willed, but having willed that it was to be by human reparation, it was necessary that it should be by man. But man of himself could not offer adequate reparation for an offense against the infinite majesty of God.

Thus it was that the Son of God deigned to become man and as such be our redeemer.

As man Christ could atone for sin, and as God-Man He could offer atonement of infinite value.

Christ might have redeemed us by any single human act, but He chose the way of suffering in order to win our love and loyalty. He sacrificed His life in order that we might have everlasting life. Christ became man in order that the children of men might become the children of God.

"As many as received Him, He gave them power to be made the sons of God" (John 1:12).

Christ although a historical personage is more than that. There is a personal relationship between Him and each one of us. He lives today in the hearts of millions who are living for Him and if need be ready to die for Him. He is truly the King of Kings, and what is more, He is our brother, and entitles us to look up to the Creator of heaven and earth and address Him as our Father.

SUMMARY

I. Jesus Christ is true God as He claimed to be. By the term 'God' is meant the creator and ruler of the world, the personal first cause of all things.

Christ confirmed His divine claims by the divine evidence of miracles and prophecies, and by His character.

Christ's character was absolutely perfect, mentally and morally.

The most perfect being is neither a liar nor a lunatic, therefore Christ is to be believed.

Besides, He furnished divine evidence for His claims.

A miracle is a visible fact outside the ordinary course of nature and possible to divine power alone. Christ performed many miracles, and said: "If you do not believe Me believe the works that I do." (Resurrection of Lazarus, calming the tempest, sight to the blind.)

Prophecy is the foretelling of an event not naturally knowable.

Christ foretold His passion, death, resurrection; destruction of Jerusalem; perpetuity of His Church.

II. Christ was perfect man.

If not really man He could not have suffered pain of mind and body.

The incarnation means that the Son of God became man by assuming human nature to the divine, forming the one person Christ, who was God from all eternity and man from His birth of the Virgin Mary. The two natures were substantially united somewhat as the soul and body in man.

III. Christ is our redeemer.

Redemption means the atonement for man's transgressions against God and restoration to heavenly inheritance.

Jesus said: "The Son of man is . . . come . . . to give His life a redemption for many" (Matthew 20:28).

On the cross Jesus offered Himself as a victim for our redemption, fulfilling what He said at the Last Supper: "This is My blood of the new testament which shall be shed for many unto remission of sins" (Matthew 26:28).

POINTS FOR DISCUSSION

1. God is a pure spirit, but Christ was a being of flesh and blood, hence He was not God.

2. If Christ was God, He would have prevented the Jews from crucifying Him.

3. Christ's divine claims rest on miracles. But miracles are incompatible with nature's fixed laws, and therefore impossible.

4. Miracles are no proof of divinity, otherwise the saints who worked miracles would be divine.

5. Christ was the friend of sinners, but God hates sin.

6. Prophecy is given as evidence of Christ's divine claims, but prophecy is clever human calculation.

7. God is infinite, therefore He could not become a finite being such as man.

8. God cannot die, but Christ died on the cross.

9. If Christ was God, He should have prevented the sin of willful murder by the Jews, but instead He deliberately co-operated with them in their sin by knowingly delivering Himself into their hands.

10. If Christ redeemed mankind, all mankind will be saved, and there is no need of anything further on our part.

11. Redemption by Christ was not necessary, for man could redeem himself by repenting of his sin.

CHAPTER III

PERSONAL DEVOTION TO CHRIST

DEVOTION MEANS SERVICE AND SACRIFICE for the sake of a person or a cause. An incident which happened in the life of Father DeSmet, the Jesuit missionary among the Rocky Mountain Indians, will serve to show what is meant by devotion.

In the early days of his missionary labors Father DeSmet was the only priest for all the Indian tribes in the West. He passed from tribe to tribe, and sometimes an interval of several years elapsed before he returned to a tribe. Before leaving a place, he always designated the most worthy and capable Indian to act as catechist during his absence.

On his return to a tribe of Sioux Indians after a long absence, Father DeSmet arranged to hear their confessions. The catechist, whose Christian name was Joseph, made everything ready and gathered together the penitents.

The missionary heard the confessions of all who came, but noticed that the catechist himself did not come. After waiting some time, he went out to see if there were any more to be heard. The only one he saw nearby was Joseph. He asked him if all had gone to confession, to which Joseph replied that all had gone who intended to go. The priest then said: "But you have not been to confession, Joseph?" "No, Father," he said; "I do not intend to go."

The priest thought that Joseph did not understand, and said again: "You have not gone to confession, have you, Joseph?"

Again Joseph said that he did not intend to go. Seeing, however, a look of consternation on the priest's face, he quickly said: "Father, didn't you tell us that the Son of God became man for our sake?" The priest nodded assent. "And that Jesus so loved us as to die on the cross to save us?" Again the priest bowed assent. "Well, Father, if an Indian suffered torture for me, do you think I could do anything to offend him? You told us that sin offends God, that it is the only thing that offends Him. And so, Father, I made up my mind never to sin, to endure any pain or loss rather than offend God, and that's why I am not going to confession. I have nothing to confess."

Father DeSmet relates that he threw his arms around the Indian and realized he was embracing a saint. That Indian was devoted to Christ. Rather than offend Him he would be willing to be cut, burned, or killed.

This Indian was not an educated man, but he understood that devotion to Christ meant avoiding what offended Him and doing what pleased Him.

Devotion to a person, as we know, implies being interested in what concerns him and doing what may help him in his aims.

Devotion to a person or cause may not infrequently demand sacrifice and require hardship. This is the reason why devotion is so highly appreciated and so splendidly rewarded. Provided it be shown in a worthy cause or for a deserving person, there is nothing more praiseworthy than devotion.

Devotion to Christ is devotion to the noblest and most deserving being that the world has known. There are many reasons why we should be devoted to Christ, chief among them being the following:

1. The Son of God became man in order that man might become a partaker of the divine nature (2 Peter 1:4). This means that Christ has made us heirs to the heavenly kingdom and to participation in the happiness and glory of God Himself (John 1:12).

We would, no doubt, be devoted to a monarch who adopted us into the royal family and endowed us with the wealth of princes. Christ has done more than that by conferring on us adoption into the divine family.

2. Christ merits our devotion because of His devotion to us, shown by service and sacrifice throughout His life. From the cradle to the cross His career was one long manifestation of love for mankind.

On Calvary He gave the supreme proof of His love for us by sacrificing His life in order that we might live forever in God's own home. "Greater love than this no man hath, that a man lay down his life for his friends" (John 15:13).

No person in the annals of mankind so merits devotion as Christ merits ours, for the life which He laid down for us was the most precious that this world has known.

3. Another reason for our devotion to Christ is that He instituted the Eucharist as a perpetual memorial of His devotion to us.

In leaving us a token of His love, He was satisfied with no souvenir but Himself. The Eucharist is the miracle of Christ's love, by which He abides with us sacramentally. "This is My body which is given for you" (Luke 22:19).

Christ gave us His body not only when He sacrificed Himself on the cross, but also when He instituted the Mass as the renewal of that sacrifice, and as the means of giving us Himself in Holy Communion.

By these and other titles Christ merits our devotion, a return of love for love, our best service and greatest sacrifice.

But why does Christ want our love and devotion? He is infinitely happy. What can we give Him that He does not possess? Christ wants our devotion not for His sake but for ours. If we are devoted to Christ in this life, we shall share His happiness and glory forever in the life beyond.

God is goodness itself. Now it is the nature of goodness to share what it has with others. God desires to make mankind partakers of His happiness. He does this in proportion as man becomes capable of sharing it. Good and evil cannot associate. Nothing defiled can enter heaven. If we love God we shall be good, for love is the most powerful motive known to man, and also the most agreeable. Fear can make us do disagreeable and difficult things, but love can make us do things that are seemingly impossible.

It is because the love of God, shown by devotion to Christ, is the surest means of attaining eternal companionship with Him that He wants our love. God wants our love in order to crown it.

It is the characteristic of goodness to impart itself to others as far as possible. Man, although not altogether good, is nevertheless sufficiently so to urge him to communicate what he can of himself to those who are receptive.

An incident in the life of Michelangelo will serve to illustrate this trait.

After this consummate artist had finished his masterpiece in marble, the famous statue of Moses, he stood contemplating it for a while. He had worked long and hard on it and as he gazed enraptured on it, he suddenly exclaimed: "Speak, Moses!" He had given the statue everything but life, and would have given that also if he could. He had communicated to his creation everything in his power, and regretted that he could give no more.

This urge to bestow oneself on one's creation comes from the Creator, who desires to bestow His happiness on His masterpiece, man, the only visible creature capable of sharing it.

God wants our devotion and love because it is the most effective means of making us become partakers of the divine nature.

The love and devotion we should have for God is not sentimental nor emotional, but the will to do what pleases Him. It does not consist in feelings, but in doing God's will regardless of our feelings.

Love is of two kinds, emotional and preferential.

Emotional love comes to us through the senses, and manifests itself in our sensitive nature, causing ardent sentiments of desire and affection for the beloved object. This is the love a person has for a friend whose countenance he can behold, the grasp of whose hand he can feel, and the sound of whose voice he can hear. Sight, feeling, and sound reach us through the senses, and create those agreeable emotions which constitute love. This is not the love God expects from us, for we do not see Him nor touch Him nor hear His voice.

There is, however, another kind of love which comes to us through the intellect and manifests itself mainly in our will. The love we have of honor, of liberty, of justice comes to us from the esteem in which we hold these things. This is called preferential love because it makes us prefer honor, justice, and liberty to whatever would cause their loss, no matter how otherwise desirable.

This is the love we should have for God, preferring to lose everything rather than His friendship. It is supernatural, based on God's goodness and love for us.

This preferential love may or may not be accompanied by sensitive fervor. Some of the greatest saints never experienced emotional ardor in their devotions. On the other hand, there have been saints who experienced such sensitive love that they were wrapt in ecstasy.

The generality of mankind, however, must be content with preferential love, which shows itself in the firm will to do or suffer anything rather than offend God. Christ said: "If you love Me keep My commandments" (John 14:15). That is the test.

Sometimes very holy people are troubled because they do not experience joyous transports in their devotions such as they read about in the lives of some of the saints. Such ecstasies and raptures are experienced by very few.

True love of God consists in doing one's duty in one's station of life regardless of whether one finds pleasure or pain in so doing.

St. Thomas More furnishes us a good example of the kind of love of God which every Christian is bound to have to a greater or less degree. St. Thomas More was the chancellor of England and next in power and prestige to the King. He was the most esteemed man of the realm and throughout Europe. On account of his high standing the King wanted his approval of his marriage with Anne Boleyn.

In order to get More's approval he heaped honors and emoluments on him, but to no purpose. Finally the King had the saint thrown into prison and sentenced to death for his refusal to approve the marriage. While in prison More's daughter Margaret was sent to him by the King in order to win him over to the royal wishes. Margaret was tenderly loved by her father and it was thought he could refuse her nothing.

Here was a struggle between the tenderest human love and the love of God. Perhaps no father had greater love for his daughter than More had for Margaret. She pleaded with him to yield to the King's wishes, and told him that all his honors would be restored to him if he would do so. If he refused he was to be executed and his family thrown into poverty and disfavor.

Every human sentiment and worldly advantage urged him to give in. On the other hand, if he yielded he would offend God. It was the most sacred human love contending with conscientious duty; the tenderest natural feelings pleading against devotion to Christ. Because More truly loved God he preferred to sacrifice human love and worldly advantages rather than offend God. His devotion to Christ enabled him to triumph over every natural inducement.

The next day More was led out to execution, and when his head fell, England lost her noblest son, but heaven welcomed a devoted subject of the King of Kings. For all eternity St. Thomas More will share the glory and happiness of the Lord he so faithfully served and loved during the period of mortal life.

Some people think that piety consists in feelings and sentiments of devotion, and in frequent external religious practices. These and similar religious manifestations may or may not accompany piety. Some of the most pious people experience little or no fervor or sentiment in their religious duties, but, nevertheless, perform them faithfully. It is fidelity to God's law that constitutes true devotion to Christ, regardless of whether or not one experiences delight or weariness in its performance.

It cannot be stated too strongly nor too plainly that piety does not consist in feeling pious, nor in joyous sentiments in devotional practices, but in the will to do God's will.

Feeling, emotion, and sentiment are frequently temperamental and have no essential place in devotion. If some people find delight in devotional exercises, well and good. But those who do not experience pious sentiments but nevertheless perform their devotions faithfully are truly pious, often more so than those who are demonstrative by nature.

Now that we realize the kind of love God's service calls for, we will consider the various degrees of love or devotion.

There are three degrees of love of God.

First, the observance of the commandments, which is of obligation for all and necessary if we would arrive at eternal salvation.

Second, the practice of the counsels of perfection, which characterizes those who are not satisfied with doing merely what they are obliged to do.

Third, the heroic degree, which they practice who aim at the highest virtue possible in imitation of their leader and model, Christ.

We shall consider briefly these three degrees of the love of God.

1. THE OBSERVANCE OF THE COMMANDMENTS. Christ solemnly affirmed that salvation was impossible without keeping the commandments. "If thou wilt enter into life keep the commandments" (Matthew 19:17). And again: "If you love Me keep My commandments" (John 14:15).

This degree of love means preferring every loss or pain rather than commit mortal sin. The avoidance of mortal sin is the first and necessary degree of the love of God.

"What shall it profit a man if he gain the whole world and suffer the loss of his soul?" (Mark 8:36).

2. THE PRACTICE OF THE COUNSELS. The second degree of the love of God is the practice of the counsels of Christ. To those who were not content with obligatory service to God, Christ said: "If thou wilt be perfect . . . follow Me" (Matthew 19:21). Following Christ means living by the counsels of perfection, consisting mainly in the three characteristic virtues of Christ's life, poverty, chastity, and obedience.

Those who dedicate their lives to the practice of these virtues may be in any career of life, but are notably found in the religious orders of men and women, who bind themselves by vow to observe these three virtues. Monks, religious brothers, and nuns consecrate their lives by these three vows to service and sacrifice in the cause of Christ and His Church.

We may be sure that God will not be outdone in generosity, and that these generous souls will rejoice forever in the home He has prepared for those who greatly love Him.

3. THE PRACTICE OF HEROIC VIRTUE. The third or heroic degree of the love of God consists in seeking to know and do what is most acceptable to God whether or not it be a matter of commandment or precept.

Those who practice this degree are notably the saints, not only those who are canonized, but those also who in every age and part of the world, whether as religious, seculars, or civilians, dedicate themselves to sublime efforts and sacrifice for the sanctification of souls and the extension of God's kingdom on earth.

Very often this degree of love calls for the loftiest heroism, as we see in the case of the martyrs and missionaries.

Christ Himself gave us the example of this degree of love by laying down His life in torture that we might have everlasting life. "Greater love than this no man hath, that a man lay down his life" (John 15:13). Not only they lay down their life who suffer martyrdom, but also that countless army of Christ's lovers who endure a bloodless martyrdom in various walks of life by fidelity and devotion to Him.

Devotion to a worthy human cause or person is praiseworthy; devotion to a divine person and cause is sublime. No person or cause on earth has such claims to our devotion as Christ, who became man in order that we might become partakers of divinity.

Devotion to Christ is not only a duty but a privilege. It is certainly an honor to do something acceptable to the Creator of heaven and earth, the King of Kings, the Lord of time and eternity.

SUMMARY

Devotion means service and sacrifice for a person or cause.

Christ has greater claims to our devotion than any person or cause on earth.

1. He became man in order that we might be made partakers of divinity.

2. From the cradle to the cross He proved His love for us by service and sacrifice.

3. By the Eucharist He left us a perpetual memorial of His love for us and His devotion to us.

Gratitude demands a return of love for love. By devotion to Christ we make this return of love.

Why does God want our love?

Not for Himself, for He is infinitely happy. He can gain nothing by our love, except the manifestation of His external glory.

God wants our love for our own sake, in order to crown it with everlasting happiness.

If we love God we have the greatest and most agreeable motive for doing His will.

If we do His will here we shall enjoy His glory and happiness hereafter.

Fear can make us do difficult things, but love enables us to do the seemingly impossible.

There are three degrees of love or devotion.

First, the observance of the commandments. This degree is necessary for salvation. It means the will to avoid all mortal sin.

Second, the observance of Christ's counsels. This degree consists in the imitation of Christ by the vows of poverty, chastity, and obedience in the religious state, or by striving for perfection in one's state of life—especially by avoidance of venial sin.

Third, the heroic degree, doing what is most acceptable to God whether or not it be enjoined by command or counsel. This often demands heroism such as the sublime deeds of saints.

POINTS FOR DISCUSSION

1. Christ has no need of our devotion, for as God He is perfectly happy.

2. God can have no desires, since He wants for nothing; hence He does not desire our devotion.

3. We show our devotion to Christ by keeping the commandments, hence that is all that is necessary.

4. A faithful Catholic is one who avoids mortal sin. If a person is a faithful Catholic, he fulfills his duty.

5. If a man saves his soul, he attains his final end. He can save his soul without devotion to Christ.

6. Devotion is a matter of gratitude, but we show our gratitude by keeping the commandments.

7. Devotion is all right for saints, but very few aim at being saints.

8. Devotion is all right for people not occupied with the cares and business of life, but for active people of the world devotion is out of the question.

CHAPTER IV

THE GOSPELS

THE GOSPELS ARE ONE of the most important credentials of Christianity, containing as they do the record of the life and teaching of Jesus Christ.

The Church existed before the Gospels, and it was she who gave us the Gospels. Although the Church does not depend on the Gospels alone for the proof of her divine origin or authority, nevertheless because she has put her seal on them, she stands or falls with them.

It is because the Church is identified with the Gospels that those who endeavor to discredit Christianity assail the Gospels. If it could be established that the Gospels are not a true historical record, the Catholic church, which upholds them as divinely true, would be in error, and consequently not a divine institution.

In brief, the Catholic church and the Gospels stand or fall together.

The opponents of Christianity have leveled their heaviest artillery against the Gospels, because if this record can be shown to be untrue, Christ would be an imposter and Christianity a delusion.

If the truth of the Gospels can be impugned, the divinity of Christ and the divine establishment of the Catholic church are but a fable, or rather a perversion of history, an egregious imposition on mankind.

This explains the rabid and persistent attacks on the genuineness and truth of the Gospels.

It may be said, in passing, that the result of all the assaults on the Gospels has been to make them stand out as the truest historical record in the annals of mankind. The very attacks on the truth of these sacred volumes has led to the most thorough examination into everything pertaining to them. The greatest scholars of the world have investigated the monuments and documents of early Christian days in order to find some historical data inconsistent with or contradictory to the Gospel story, but only to find added confirmation for its trustworthiness.

A special school of thought known as rationalism has set itself the task of destroying supernatural religion, and has expended its most virulent efforts at discrediting the Gospels. Rationalists are those who affirm that we should not believe in anything not knowable by unaided reason.

Since Christianity is a revealed religion, given to mankind by Jesus Christ the Son of God, and since it proclaims truths not attainable by reason alone, it is opposed by rationalists.

But before Christ gave us His religion, He proved by divine evidence that He was God. We know that God can neither deceive nor be deceived. Consequently we believe Christ, even though what He proclaims is above our understanding. It is not above our understanding, however, to know that God cannot teach what is false.

When, therefore, Christ proclaimed that He was divine, and the approval of God Almighty confirmed Him and His mission, we know that His doctrine is divinely true, even if it is above our comprehension.

The incarnation, the Trinity, and the Eucharist are mysteries of faith which we believe on God's word. They are above but not contrary to reason. Every day multitudes of intelligent people believe things they do not understand, but which they accept on the authority of astronomers, scientists, and specialists in various departments of knowledge. This is not unreasonable, for it is highly reasonable to believe in experts.

If we believe these authorities because they are experts in their departments, we should much more readily believe Christ, who is eternal truth, divine authority.

If rationalists wish to discredit Christianity let them prove that Christ is not God. They are welcome to use all the reason the Creator has given them to investigate Christ's divine claims.

But to start out on the principle that supernatural religion is false, and then deny Christianity because it is supernatural, is to follow a procedure which is far from rational.

After this digression let us return to the matter of the Gospels.

The Gospels are a brief narrative of the deeds and teaching of Christ. They were written by four persons known as evangelists. Two of these, Matthew and John, were apostles; the other two, Luke and Mark, were secretaries of apostles.

The writers of the Gospels, therefore, were either apostles who were eye-witnesses of what they narrate, or companions of apostles who were eye-witnesses of the events recorded.

The evangelists had nothing to gain by narrating the Gospel facts, rather everything to lose, for they suffered persecution, exile, and death for proclaiming the Gospel truths. No one willingly dies for falsehood, but champions of truth gladly seal their testimony by their blood.

The Jews themselves never denied the Gospel facts, although it would have been the most effective means of discrediting Christianity.

They imprisoned the apostles for proclaiming the Gospel facts, scourged them, and commanded them not to preach them, but never denied the facts. If the Jews who were on the ground could not discredit the Gospel facts, it is certainly too late in the day to attempt to do so now.

Unless the Gospels were a true record the facts would have been denied at the time they were declared, for multitudes were living at that time who had seen and heard Jesus. Moreover, a great multitude of Jews were converted to Christianity by the facts recorded in the Gospels, and very many of these converts willingly suffered scourging, imprisonment, and death for the faith they embraced.

We may be sure that these converts from Judaism thoroughly investigated the Gospel claims before embracing a religion which demanded such great sacrifices without giving any worldly inducements for its acceptance.

People do not willingly accept and adhere to a cause which brings them privation and suffering unless the truth of it is compelling.

Neither the preachers of the Gospel nor those who accepted it had any motive for preaching or believing it except the fact that the events were as proclaimed.

If the Jews could have pointed out a single false statement of fact in the Gospels they would have done so, and by so doing would have discredited the record. But being unable to do so, they had recourse to intimidation, persecution, and calumny in order to offset in some way the marvelous number of conversions from Judaism to Christianity.

St. Peter's first sermon in the very city where Christ was crucified converted thousands of Jews to the worship of the Crucified as God. Unless the Gospels were a true record of facts the conversion of these Jews was a greater miracle than any recorded in the Gospels.

We must remember that so many Jews became Christians that the Jewish authorities instituted the first Christian persecution. They began it in Jerusalem and afterwards extended it to neighboring cities and eventually to Rome.

To sum up: The Gospels were written by those who lived at the time that the facts recorded took place; they were addressed primarily to people living at or near the date of the facts narrated; the writers were eye-witnesses, had every opportunity of being well informed on what they described; they had no motive for deceiving; a close study of what they wrote gives evidence that they wrote simply to convey to others what they saw and heard; and finally, what they describe could not have been recorded by anyone unless the things narrated were actual occurrences.

The invention of a character like that of Christ's, and of discourses such as those recorded of Him, would be beyond the power of the combined genius of Homer, Dante, and Shakespeare. Yet the evangelists were very ordinary men, chiefly of the peasant type, and absolutely incapable of the sublime portraiture of the Gospels unless they were merely setting down facts as seen and heard.

The chief point is that the evangelists had no motive for deceiving. Moreover, if they wanted to deceive, they could not have done so, for there were too many living witnesses of all that they narrated.

Rousseau has well said that men may deceive in order to gain something or to escape punishment or disgrace, but not to incur loss, opprobrium, punishment, and death. The evangelists suffered chains, scourging, exile, and death for their testimony. We may well believe such witnesses.

The Gospels are the truest book in the world, and the more the light of investigation is thrown on them the more they stand out as divinely true. Harnack, the prince of rationalists, after trying for thirty years to discredit the Gospels, finally declared that no one with pretense to scholarship can now question the genuineness or authenticity of the Gospels.

It may be asked, Why does such a man not become a Christian? The reason is prejudice. He interprets the Gospel facts to suit his preconceived theory that the supernatural must be rejected. Rationalists are far from being rational.

The early Christians were as critical and as great lovers of life as rationalists of today, yet they accepted the Gospel facts and died for them. They were on the ground, they could examine the things recorded, and they believed even though belief cost them their life.

The Gospels were written in the first century and within the lifetime of those who were witnesses to the facts recorded. The Gospels of Matthew, Mark, and Luke were written before the year A. D. 70; that is, before the destruction of Jerusalem, which they foretold. St. John's Gospel was the last written, which was before the end of the first century.

The Church not only gave us the Gospels, but preserved them intact and transmitted them down through the centuries.

It may be well to call attention to the fact that no book now in existence existed in the time of the Caesars. Every book now extant is a copy of the original or a copy of a copy. The oldest book in the world today is a Bible whose origin dates from about the year A. D. 350.

If it were not for the Church, in whose monasteries ancient manuscripts were copied and preserved, there would not be in the world today one book from classical antiquity. Unless the Church from the beginning had exercised special care in the copying and transmission of manuscripts, we should not now possess any document of early Christianity. The monasteries preserved for the world the written records of the past.

Those who assail the Catholic church overlook the fact that without her aid they would not now possess the storehouse of classical learning in which they glory, and which they too often use to attack the mother that gave them their intellectual equipment.

The Gospels proclaim a revealed religion, a religion not man-made, but one whose author is the eternal Son of God.

Revelation proclaims the fatherhood of God, the brotherhood of man, the Trinity, the incarnation, the Eucharist, the universal judgment, and a future eternal life.

None of these things could be definitely and certainly known by human reason alone, and some of them, even after revelation, are incomprehensible; as, for instance, the Trinity and the Eucharist. These are mysteries of faith, which are believed on the sole word of the one who revealed them, Jesus Christ, eternal truth.

It is not unreasonable to believe that God who gave us our reason will not ask us to believe what is against reason. Christ's word alone suffices for belief, since we know from reasonable inquiry that He is what He claimed to be.

St. Augustine said that he would not believe that Christianity was a divine religion if it taught only what could originate in a human mind. The truths of the Gospel are such that they never could have been conceived by a human intellect. Every other religion teaches only what human reason can evolve, which is sufficient proof that they are only human religions. Christianity alone teaches truths too sublime to be creations of the human mind.

Revelation means declaring something otherwise hidden. A man reveals his thoughts by speech. Our thoughts would always remain our own, hidden from others altogether, unless we made them known. A telescope reveals the glory and magnitude of the firmament, which otherwise would be unknown to man.

Night reveals the starry heavens, which would be invisible if it were always daylight. Jesus Christ, the eternal Son of God, revealed to mankind things about God, ourselves, and the hereafter which we should not otherwise know. By reason we could know that there is a God, Creator of the world, but not that He is our Father. By reason we could know that man's soul is immortal, but not that it was destined for eternal membership in the divine family.

The Gospel contains the revelation of Jesus Christ, which is the basis of His supernatural religion. All those who for one reason or another do not want to accept a supernatural religion are opponents of the Gospels.

Some persons are opposed to the Gospels because of pride of intellect. They do not want to submit their reason to any higher authority.

Others deny the Gospels because belief in them implies living as the Gospels teach, and since the Gospels inculcate a high standard of morality, and impose moral and intellectual restraints, they try to find some excuse for rejecting them.

Man wants to be a law to himself, to do as he wishes. The Gospels declare that man must submit to God's law or else incur the penalty of God's judgments. If the Gospels did not demand conduct in conformity with the sublime truths they reveal, very few if any would question their veracity.

The Gospels are the best life of Christ. There are other lives, inspired by Christian devotion and keen scholarship, which clarify the Gospel facts by contemporary history and literary criticism.

Among those lives in English may be mentioned Coleridge and Maas, and in French, Didon and Fouard, in excellent English translation. Recent lives are by Grandmaison, Prat, Goodier, and O'Brien.

Christ is the light of the world. The Catholic church is the institution He founded to enlighten mankind, and the Gospels are the documentary evidence of His divine mission.

The Gospels are as true as God.

SUMMARY

The Gospels are a brief record of the life and teaching of Jesus Christ.

The Church existed and was widely established before the Gospels were written; consequently her origin or authority does not depend on them.

Since, however, she has put her seal of approval on them, she is identified with the Gospels and stands or falls with them.

Those who aim at discrediting the Catholic church try to discredit the Gospels. But although they have used every means to find a flaw in them, they have succeeded only in confirming their historical truth.

The Gospels were written by the four evangelists: Matthew and John, who were apostles; and Mark and Luke, who were companions of apostles.

The Gospels of Matthew, Mark, and Luke were written before the year 70, and that of John before 100.

Reasons why the Gospels are true:

1. The evangelists were either eye witnesses or companions of eye-witnesses of what they relate.

2. They had no motive for deceiving; they gained nothing, but suffered imprisonment and death for preaching what they recorded.

3. They could not have deceived if they had wished, for multitudes who lived with Christ were living when the Gospels were written.

4. The Jews never denied the Gospel facts, but tried to suppress them.

5. The conversion of such great multitudes of the Jews to Christianity would have been impossible unless the Gospel facts were true.

6. The evangelists could not have invented Christ's character nor His doctrine.

7. No merely human pen could have given us the Gospels unless the things recorded were actual occurrences.

Christianity is a revealed religion given to mankind by Jesus Christ, the Son of God.

We believe revelation not because we understand it, but on the sole word of God, who is eternal truth. He who gave us our reason will not ask us to believe what is against reason.

POINTS FOR DISCUSSION

1. The Gospels are not a historical record, but a fabrication to glorify Christianity.

2. The Gospels were written in order to enable the apostles to obtain ascendency over the people and to establish the Church.

3. The Gospels were written long after the events therein recorded, and are a mixture of fact and legend.

4. The evangelists contradict one another, and evidently were not present at the events they narrate.

5. The evangelists were interested parties who profited by the glorification they conferred on Christ. Hence they are not reliable historians.

6. The people living at the time the Gospels were written were credulous and superstitious. The evangelists took advantage of this state of mind to impose the Gospels on them.

7. If the Gospel facts were true, the Jews would have become Christians.

8. The Jewish leaders were not fools. If the Gospel facts were true, they would not have rejected Christ.

9. If rationalists declare that the Gospels are genuine, why do they not become converted and cease to try to discredit Christianity?

CHAPTER V

THE FOUNDATION AND MISSION OF THE CHURCH

CHRIST DELIVERED A REVELATION to mankind declaring what we are to believe and what we are to do in order to attain eternal salvation. This revelation was thenceforth to constitute mankind's true religion. Christ was in the world for a few years only, yet He came for all mankind to the end of the world. In order to perpetuate His mission He established a society which He called His Church, which He promised by His divine authority would exist until the end of time and teach religious truth without error. "To His Church the only begotten Son of God entrusted the perpetuation down the ages of the divine and lofty task which He had Himself received from His Father" (Leo XIII, Encyclical *Immortale Dei*).

Christianity is not a school of philosophy, but the authoritative teaching of Jesus Christ, the Son of God.

A body of teaching does not preserve itself. Even if written in books or carved on stone, it would not for that reason preserve itself. Books are lost or perish with time, stone disintegrates or may be demolished by vandals. No document ever given to mankind is its own interpreter. The most carefully composed legal documents have been subjected to various and even contradictory interpretations. The Constitution of the United States was most carefully worded, yet its framers, realizing the possibility of various interpretations, made the Supreme Court of the United States its sole interpreter.

45

To perpetuate His mission, to preserve and transmit His revelation, Christ founded an organic body, a visible society called His Church.

A church in order to serve its purpose must be visible and recognizable. "Only a visible church can be the stay and maintenance of truth" (Newman, *Via Media* I, 193).

Christ began the establishment of His Church almost from the beginning of His public life. After a night of prayer He chose a small band of companions whom He called apostles. They were asked to give up their homes and possessions for the mission which He was to assign to them. He trained them in His virtues and spirit, and taught them the doctrine which He came to impart to mankind. The chief of this band was Simon, whose name Christ changed to that of Peter, which in the language then spoken (Aramaic) signified a rock. Upon the foundation of Peter, as a living rock, Christ erected the divine structure which He called *His* Church because it was of His building, and of which Peter was to be the head.

"And I say to thee that thou art Peter; and upon this rock I will build My Church, and the gates of hell shall not prevail against it. And I will give to thee the keys of the kingdom of heaven. And whatsoever thou shalt bind upon earth, it shall be bound also in heaven: and whatsoever thou shalt loose on earth, it shall be loosed also in heaven" (Matthew 16:18-20).

This Church, with Peter as its head, was to be the perpetuation of Christ's mission to the world. The apostles were sent the same way as Christ had been sent by His Father: "As the Father hath sent Me, I also send you" (John 20:21). "Go ye into the whole world and preach the Gospel to every creature" (Mark 16:15). "He that heareth you, heareth Me" (Luke 10:16). The commission to go forth in His name and with His authority was given in the most solemn manner: "All power is given to Me in heaven and in earth. Going, therefore, teach ye all nations" (Matthew 28:18-19).

The Church was commissioned to bring to men not only a knowledge of Christ's doctrine, but also the means of salvation instituted by Him. "He that believeth and is baptized shall be saved" (Mark 16:16). He gave its ministers power to forgive sin: "Receive ye the Holy Ghost. Whose sins you shall forgive, they are forgiven them" (John 20:22-23). Furthermore, Christ commanded them to perpetuate the sacred rite which He instituted the day before He sacrificed His life for us on the cross. "This is My body which is given for you. Do this for a commemoration of Me" (Luke 22:19).

To His Church, accordingly, Christ committed the mission which He inaugurated while on earth. And since He came for all mankind to the end, He endowed His Church with perpetual life: "And behold I am with you all days, even to the consummation of the world" (Matthew 28:20). And because He was always to be with His Church as her invisible head, He said: "If he will not hear the Church, let him be to thee as the heathen and publican" (Matthew 18:17).

We see therefore Christ's purpose in founding His Church. The Son of God became man in order to be our teacher and guide, and to impart to us a new and supernatural life in preparation for our life with God hereafter. He might have remained always on earth, He might have devised various other means for His mission to mankind. But in point of fact He established a Church, a visible and perpetual society, to speak in His name and with His authority.

In a word, Christ made His Church His representative on earth. In appointing her to this sublime office He took means to make sure that the Church which He instituted to represent Him should not *misrepresent* Him. By conferring infallibility on her He guaranteed her against false doctrine in faith or morals. The Church of Christ speaking authoritatively, or the pope defining doctrine 'ex cathedra' has God's guarantee that she will not mislead mankind with regard to creed or conduct.

The pope is infallible only when as head of the Church, and speaking as Christ's vicar, he proclaims the true meaning of a doctrine of revelation. On matters not relating to religion his pronouncements are worth only so much as they merit by the reasons and evidence presented for them. But as Christ's vicar, speaking by virtue of his sublime office, he is guaranteed against religious error, regardless of whether or not he is a good or bad man.

Infallibility is conferred on the office, on the head of the Church as such, not on the individual in his personal capacity.

Besides confiding His doctrine to the Church, Christ also constituted her the perpetual means of continuing His ministry.

Jesus not only taught the saving truths of eternal life, but also instituted visible channels of grace, called sacraments, which were to help the faithful to practice His precepts and attain everlasting happiness. The preaching of Christ's doctrine and the administration of His sacraments necessarily require a visible ministry; hence the corporate organization instituted by Him to perpetuate

His mission was a visible Church. This fact is emphasized because the Reformation is based on the false affirmation that Christ did not establish a visible Church.

By giving to Peter alone the keys of the kingdom of heaven, Christ clothed him alone with supreme authority. For this reason the pope, Peter's successor, is called the vicar of Christ. 'Vicar' means one who rules in the person of another. The pope, therefore, as vicar of Christ, is the visible head of Christ's kingdom on earth, the Church, of which Christ Himself is the invisible head. This supreme authority was recognized from the very day of Pentecost, when the Church began her active ministry. While Christ was on earth He was the shepherd of the little flock which constituted the infant Church. Shortly before He left this earth for His heavenly home, He designated Peter as chief pastor to shepherd the flock which He was leaving, charging him to feed His lambs and sheep (John 21:15-17). By appointing Peter the shepherd Christ made him responsible for the fold.

No one but God Almighty could found a perpetual and infallible society. The existence of the Catholic church today is proof that her founder was divine, for no merely human society could endure throughout the centuries as the Catholic church has done.

The Catholic church is what is called a corporate society; that is, a unified organization like the human body, all of whose members are controlled by the head. The Catholic church is the only corporate society in the world today that existed in the days of the Roman Empire.

The Jews, as a race, existed even before the Church, but the Jews are not a corporate society, since they have no head, no ruler, no high priest. They are not even a nation, for they have no national home.

The existence of the Catholic church today is a miracle, the fulfillment of Christ's prophecy, and living proof that His other promises will be fulfilled.

We say that the existence of the Catholic church today is a miracle, and a brief consideration will show it to be so.

Decay is the law of everything natural. The tendency of everything is to grow weaker with age. Even granite disintegrates with time. But the Church, because she is not merely natural but also supernatural, grows stronger rather than weaker with age. Today she is the only universal corporate society in the world. Moreover, although she embraces the whole world, she is the most unified, the most authoritative, and the most vigorous corporate society in the world. Unless the Church was a divine institution she had perished long ago. Her existence today is as great a miracle as the resurrection.

The Catholic church, like her Founder, is both divine and human. She is divine in her constitution, human in her members. Although her members pass away generation after generation, she lives on. Although her members fail at times to live up to her lofty standards, she never lowers these standards, but like her Founder is the light of the world.

Although the world persecutes her as it did her Founder, she makes no compromise with its sinful demands. Alone of all institutions she proclaims today the doctrine whole and entire that her Founder entrusted to her.

The Church is the guardian of a sacred trust given

her by Christ, and as the guardian of that trust, she has gone on century after century, refusing to surrender or compromise it despite every human inducement and threat.

It is true that not all her members are a credit to her. Sins and scandals have tainted even those in high places. But Christ foresaw and foretold that scandals would come. He compared the Church to a field in which only good seed was sown, but in which weeds also sprung up. Although Christ foretold scandals, He also warned against them, threatening dire punishment for the offenders.

Christ was the light of the world, but not all who beheld that light followed its guidance. The Church also is the light of the world, even though that light often shines in vain for some of her own members. Christ pointed out the way to eternal life, but did not compel anyone to follow it. God gave man free will and does not *compel* service. The Church like her Founder guides man to eternal welfare, but if they refuse to follow her guidance, she can but deplore it and pray for them.

Pentecost was the birthday of the Catholic church. On that day the Holy Spirit descended upon the apostles, and they went forth to preach Christ crucified and risen from the dead. In a second of time the apostles were transformed from illiterate and timid men into the greatest missionaries this world has known. No natural power can explain the instant transformation of the apostles. It was the power of God, the same power which has abided with the Church ever since and will so abide unto the end. "Behold I am with you all days, even to the consummation of the world" (Matthew 28:20).

The mission of Christ's Church is to rear the children of men to become the children of God.

Like Christ she is in the world but not of the world. She came forth from God and will lead to God all those who faithfully follow her guidance.

It is because the Church is like Christ, the religious Teacher of mankind, that she is so solicitous for Catholic education. Pope Pius XI in his encyclical on education specifies the reasons why Catholic education is so necessary, especially in our time. The following summary gives the main reasons why Catholics should esteem and support religious teaching as an essential part of the education of youth:

1. Catholic education aims: (a) at securing the supreme good, namely, everlasting possession and enjoyment of God; (b) at the maximum welfare of society.

2. The right to educate youth rests primarily with the family, which was instituted by God for the generation and formation of offspring.

3. The Church was commissioned by her divine Founder to teach religious truth to mankind, hence it is her right and duty to insist on religious education.

4. The duty of the state is to protect the rights of her citizens. In proportion as the state co-operates with the Church will the general welfare be secured.

5. Since the purpose of Catholic education is to form a true Christian, it is an important factor of Catholic Action.

It will be seen from the above résumé that Catholic education is a matter of special concern to all true children of Holy Mother Church.

Catholics are called upon to make great sacrifices

for Christian education, but the cause is one which abundantly justifies whatever sacrifices it may entail.

In the present era Catholic education is one of the most necessary means for the maintenance and extension of Christ's Church.

SUMMARY

Christ came for all mankind to the end of time, yet He was with us but a few years.

The means He instituted to perpetuate His mission was the foundation of a kingdom He called His Church, and with which He promised to abide until the end of the world.

Christ came to redeem mankind and to teach them the way and give the aid to eternal welfare.

He made His Church the custodian of His doctrine and the minister of His sacraments.

Since a fallible Church could not represent the infallible Christ, He made her infallible in matters of revelation.

The Church is infallible, but her members are not impeccable.

The Church will last until the end of the world, but her members will pass away every generation.

Christ made Peter the rock basis of His Church. He made him the visible head of the Church of which He Himself is the invisible head. By giving to Peter the keys of the kingdom of heaven He made him His vicar on earth.

Christ was the light of the world, and He made His Church the light of the world. The Church like Christ cannot teach error of creed or conduct.

The pope is infallible when, speaking as Christ's vicar, he defines a doctrine of revelation. As an individual the pope may err. His pronouncements merit only as much as the reasons he advances.

The Church is divine in her constitution, human in her members.

A true definition of the Church is to say that she is the continuation of Christ in the world, carrying on the mission He inaugurated while on earth.

Decay is the law of everything natural, but the Church, because she is supernatural, grows stronger rather than weaker with age.

The Church is the only corporate society in the world today that existed in the time of the Caesars.

The perpetual existence of the Church is as great a miracle as the resurrection.

POINTS FOR DISCUSSION

1. Christ's religion does not need a visible Church, since His teaching is contained in the Bible and all who believe and live by the Bible are members of His Church.

2. The Bible is the word of God, and that is sufficient for salvation.

3. Christ established His Church for all mankind to the end of the world. The Catholic church is not Christ's Church, since it does not embrace all mankind.

4. The Church cannot be infallible, since infallibility is incompatible with human liability to error.

5. Papal infallibility is impossible, for a pope is a fallible human being.

6. A pope, out of malice, could proclaim false doctrine, and thus discredit the Church.

7. The Catholic church has abounded in scandals, hence cannot be the Church of Christ.

8. No church that is intolerant can be the church of the merciful Christ. The Catholic church has been notably intolerant.

9. The perpetuation of the Catholic church is due to political cleverness, not to divine assistance.

10. The Catholic church is arrogant, claiming that she

alone is the Church of Christ, to the exclusion of all others.

11. Why is the Church so solicitous for education?

12. Religious education should be *imparted in the church and not in the school.

CHAPTER VI

LOYALTY TO THE CHURCH

WHAT PATRIOTISM IS TO COUNTRY, that, loyalty is to
Church. Patriotism is devotion to an earthly power, loyalty to the Church is devotion to the kingdom of God on
earth.

Patriotism shows itself by service and sacrifice for the
welfare of one's country. A patriot does not measure his
service to his country by what he *must* do but by what
he *can* do. He is not content with merely avoiding viola-
tions of his country's laws, but does all in his power to
have law and order respected.

If his country needs his services he does not wait until
he is forced to come to her aid, but volunteers as soon as
he knows her danger. If his country stands in need of his
financial aid, he is ready to give it even though it entail
great sacrifice.

Moreover, a patriot will not stand by idly if his country
is defamed, but will uphold her good name at any cost.
Should anything of a nature destructive to his country's
welfare come to his notice, a patriot will do all in his
power to ward off the peril.

If, moreover, a project for his country's good is presented, the patriot will not hesitate to add his support
to it.

In brief, patriotism consists in voluntarily doing for
one's country what is not of strict obligation. In every
nation there are multitudes of people who are not content

with doing only what they must do under penalty of fine or imprisonment.

The kingdom of God, Christ's Church, has her patriots —legions of men and women who desire to show their devotion to the cause of Christ by doing all in their power to advance its interests.

First there are the heroic patriots of the Church, not only the great saints who are solemnly venerated, but also that great army of religious men and women who consecrate themselves by vow to service and sacrifice in the crusade which the Church is making for the welfare of mankind both here and hereafter.

Besides this army of consecrated lives there are the countless men and women in every walk of life who by word, deed, and example make the Church better known, served, and loved.

These legions of lay people do not weigh their duty by what they must do, but by what they can do.

In the first place, they are faithful to their ordinary duties as Catholics, the observance of the commandments of God and of the Church. Any devotion that does not include a practical Catholic life as a foundation cannot be regarded as loyalty to the Church. Attendance at Mass, due reception of the sacraments, and due support of the Church are taken for granted in every Catholic worthy of the name. The fulfillment of these obligations constitutes the minimum of loyalty to the Church.

Without this degree of loyalty a Catholic is rather a detriment than a help to the cause of Christ.

Presupposing, therefore, the observance of the ordinary duties of religion, what distinguishes the loyal Catholic?

A loyal Catholic should be well informed on the doctrine and devotions of his Church. Great harm has come to the Church from the religious ignorance of some of her subjects. We do not refer to the ignorance of the uneducated, who on account of circumstances have not had the opportunity of being well informed, but to the ignorance of those who are qualified to be well informed.

There are Catholics who are well informed on nearly every timely subject except their religion. If they are asked about politics, business, the theater, or any other topic of the day, they can give reasonable information on it. But if asked about a doctrine or practice of their Church, they are too often silent or confused, or give an answer which misrepresents Catholicism.

In doing this they not only reflect discredit on the Church, but not infrequently discourage an earnest inquirer from embracing the faith.

Very few non-Catholics come in contact with official Catholicism. They seldom have occasion or inclination to meet a clergyman or a nun. If the Catholic layman does not enlighten them on matters of inquiry, they ordinarily go no further.

Loyalty to Church, therefore, implies in Catholics a sufficient knowledge of the teaching and history of the Church to answer the ordinary questions concerning these matters. Any Catholic who has the opportunity of knowing his religion and neglects it, can hardly be called loyal to the Church.

A loyal Catholic, besides making himself well-informed about the Church, will also be actively interested in the organizations she sponsors. Not every organization or society appeals to everyone, but in the Church there is a sufficient variety of activities to provide something in which every loyal member can become interested.

There are some persons who feel aversion to activity in almost any kind of organization. But this does not excuse them from giving assistance to these Church activities in one way or another.

If one cannot actually join a society, one can aid its activities by financial contribution.

Loyalty to country is shown not only by enlisting in her service but also by contributing to her support. Taxes are an obligatory levy on citizens, payable by all alike, but patriotic citizens, besides paying taxes, also contribute voluntarily when their country stands in need of their aid.

The Church appeals not only for enlistment in her activities, but also for support of them, and the loyal Catholic will respond in one way or another.

Loyalty to the Church, moreover, includes thinking with her even on matters not strictly of creed.

In her wisdom, guided by the Holy Spirit, the Church knows what is for the best interests of the faithful. When, for example, she insists on the necessity of religious education, it is because experience has shown that ordinarily the neglect of religious education in youth leads to the loss or serious impairment of faith in manhood.

Even with all the safeguards of faith the dangers to it are many and great. If one really knows the Catholic religion, one has the best possible equipment for facing the specious objections and alluring inducements of the paganism which characterizes the modern world.

Loyalty to the Church means not only highly

esteeming religious schools, but also helping to support them.

The Church takes a firm stand, not only on the question of Catholic education, but on whatever concerns the family, society, and state. The loyal Catholic will be desirous of co-operating with the Church in her stand regarding marriage, birth control, amusements, vicious literature, destructive communism, and other dangers to Church, family, and society. This co-operation is termed Catholic Action.

Now more than ever the world needs sound principles of creed and conduct.

A spirit of modified paganism has possessed the modern world, and will rush it to destruction unless counteracted by the saving truths of revelation. The loyal Catholic will realize that in upholding the Church he is obeying the voice of God, who abides with her and whose voice she is.

The Church, like Christ, is the light of the world, and loyalty to her means making the journey of life on the road which leads to real welfare here and eternal happiness hereafter.

It is not easy, of course, to follow the guidance of the light of truth. Human nature is very human. It has its weaknesses and its evil tendencies. Above all it is selfish, and wants to be a law to itself. It balks at Christian restraint, forgetting that even in worldly matters restraint is the law of success.

In business, in sports, and in matters pertaining to health restraint is absolutely essential unless one is prepared to lose the desired goal.

The most important goal in life is the attainment of

salvation. We must be ready and willing to practice restraint for this glorious attainment.

Loyalty to the Church certainly imposes restraint, and the sacrifice, often, of what costs dearly.

The requirements of God and the Church may at times bear hard on some people, but so do the laws of one's country. Taxes are a dreadful burden at times and not infrequently cause actual impoverishment. But taxes must be paid no matter what the sacrifice.

Traffic rules may at times cause very great hardship to individuals, but laws are made for the general welfare, and if they come hard on an individual there is no help for it. If a man is hurrying in an automobile to catch a boat or train to miss which will cause him great financial loss, and he is suddenly stopped by the traffic officer and arrested for speeding, it is certainly a hardship for him, but the traffic laws, nevertheless, are for the general welfare, and save countless lives.

The Catholic church legislates for the whole world and for eternal welfare.

The loyal Catholic will bear this in mind when there is question of divorce, birth control, and other matters which may at times demand heroic sacrifice in order to comply with the laws of God and the Church.

Assuredly, there are conditions when the Church's laws on divorce, birth control, and other matters make compliance very hard, but service which does not demand sacrifice does not call for loyalty. If a man is unhappily married and has the opportunity of contracting what seems to be a happy marriage, it is not easy to bow to the requirements of the matrimonial bond and renounce what seems to be a happy future.

But it is just such compliance with the laws of God that constitutes loyalty. Patriotism often demands from citizens sacrifices which require heroic renunciations. Surely the kingdom of God may expect of its subjects loyalty at least as great as that which citizens give to the state.

Catholic education is another matter which demands loyalty, often of a high degree.

The support of parochial schools imposes a heavy burden on pastors and on the people. Yet if the Church, especially in this country and at the present time, does not provide a thorough religious education for all her children, she may find that the coming generation will not be church-goers.

Not only parochial schools, but higher education also, makes heavy demands on Catholics. As things are now there are few free Catholic high schools and colleges. Parents consequently who desire higher education for their children must make great sacrifices in order to send them to a Catholic high school or college.

Again we must refer to the patriotism of citizens, who to comply with their country's needs often submit to very severe exactions.

If loyalty to the Church made no demands on one's comfort and income it would not be the splendid virtue that it is. Everyone would be loyal to a cause if it cost nothing. What costs little or nothing, however, is of little worth. Loyalty is of such great value because it sometimes costs much. Kings and rulers munificently reward loyal subjects. Christ, the King of Kings, will surely appreciate loyalty to His kingdom on earth, the Church.

He so loved the Church as to give His life for it. He

regards as done to Himself whatever we do for His Church. Certainly, if we could do something for Christ in person, we should consider ourselves honored and fortunate, no matter how hard the task. Loyalty to the Church is loyalty to Christ Himself, and whenever we are called upon for service or sacrifice for religion we should regard it as a personal request from Christ, as indeed it is.

Today more than ever Catholics need to show loyalty to the Church. All kinds of false and destructive theories seek to undermine not only the Church but civilization as well. These false doctrines are alluringly presented, but if, as loyal children of the Church, we always accept her divinely inspired guidance, we have nothing to fear from them. The test of loyalty is in the hour of need. Soldiers on parade make an imposing spectacle, but it is the battlefield, not the parade, that shows the brave and loyal soldier. The Church is ever at war with evil. Her children are always exposed to the fire of the enemy. The loyal Catholic will gladly do all in his power that the cause of Christ may triumph.

We know that eventually success will crown the Church's efforts, but meanwhile it depends on loyal Catholics to keep the standard of Christ aloft. Loyal Catholics are the chivalry of Christianity.

SUMMARY

What patriotism is to country loyalty is to the Church.

One who is loyal to country is ready to serve her and make sacrifices for her.

Loyalty to the Church means first of all being a practical Catholic, especially by fidelity to Mass and the sacraments.

A loyal Catholic does not, however, limit his duty to what is

of obligation, but seeks to promote the welfare of the Church
by activity in whatever tends to make her better known, loved,
and served.

He should be well informed regarding the teaching and practices of his faith, and be able to give a satisfactory answer to
objections or inquiries.

As one's country may require sacrifices of her subjects, so
the Church may at times require sacrifices of her children.

Her teaching on marriage, education, birth control, divorce,
and so forth, is God's teaching.

The Church laws may bear hard on certain individuals, but
so does every law that is for the general welfare, as taxes,
traffic regulations, quarantine, and so forth.

A loyal Catholic will bear with fortitude whatever inconvenience or burden the observance of the Church's laws may
entail.

A patriot is concerned for his country's welfare and honor.
A loyal Catholic will be concerned for the fair name of the
Church, and besides will co-operate with her efforts to pre-
serve and extend the kingdom of God.

This co-operation is termed Catholic Action, and should
enlist every Catholic worthy of the name.

Loyalty to country is devotion to an earthly power. Loyalty
to the Church is devotion to the King of Kings.

Loyal Catholics are the chivalry of Christianity.

POINTS FOR DISCUSSION

1. Loyalty is not due to a tyrannical government. The
Catholic church is notably tyrannical, especially regarding marriage.

2. Church dignitaries are often arrogant and unreasonable. Loyalty to an institution with such representatives is out of the question.

3. The Catholic church has no right to interfere with
natural rights. By her legislation on mixed marriages the

Church interferes with the natural right of marrying a person of one's choice.

4. The Church's legislation on birth control is unreasonable and cruel, especially in our time, when it is hardly possible to provide for large families.

5. The Church forbids divorce, even if one party to the union becomes insane or is imprisoned for life. This is cruel legislation and unworthy of a Christian church.

6. The Church is a money-grabber. She charges for baptisms, funerals, marriages, and even for attendance at Mass.

7. Young persons get all the religious instruction they need at home, Sunday school, and Sunday Mass. Attendance at Catholic schools is not at all necessary.

8. Christ was born in a stable and lived a life of poverty. The pope, Christ's vicar, should not live in luxury and pomp.

9. The Church has one law for the rich, another for the poor—witness the granting of divorce to the wealthy.

10. The Church is always asking for money.

CHAPTER VII

EARLY PERSECUTIONS AND THE MARTYRS

LOYALTY TO CHRIST AND HIS CHURCH has been a characteristic virtue of Christians from the very origin of Christianity. Christ foretold that His followers would be persecuted by the world, even as He Himself was persecuted.

Adversity proves friendship, and persecution tests the loyalty of the adherents of a cause.

The first Christians were put to a most severe test of loyalty, and in great numbers gave proof of their devotion and fidelity to Christ. In point of fact, the loyalty of the early Christians is something naturally unexplainable, something which can be accounted for only by the special assistance of God.

One of the supplementary proofs of the divinity of Christianity is the testimony which the martyrs bear to it. The number of martyrs in the early Church, the manner in which they met death, the cruelty of their torments, their constancy under threats and promises, the absence of human encouragement and inducement, and the final triumph of their cause—all these attest that some power more than human sustained them and the cause for which they made the supreme sacrifice.

The word 'martyr' means *witness*. In the beginning of Christianity a martyr was one who witnessed to Christianity by confessing openly that Christ was God and that His religion alone was divinely true. Gradually the term martyr was restricted to those only who confessed Christ by shedding their blood.

During the first ages of the Church to be a Christian meant, ordinarily, to incur contempt and hostility. The price paid for conversion to the religion of the Crucified was so great that none but a divine religion could justify or exact it. The first Christians were converted Jews. The Jews as a race regarded their converted brethren as the adherents of an imposter and betrayer of the messianic promises. The pagans considered the Christians the enemies of the human race and abominable to the gods.

It is safe to say that no undertaking in the history of mankind faced such tremendous external obstacles as Christianity met with in its very infancy.

When we consider the stern morality inculcated by the religion of Christ, the absence of worldly or natural motives, the dreadful penalties visited on its adherents, and the persistence of the assaults on the followers of the Crucified, we must conclude that no merely human enterprise could have survived these internal and external obstacles.

For three centuries persecution assailed the Church, taking toll of millions of lives by the most dreadful tortures that the mind of brutal man could devise. Under the persecution of Diocletian, one of the ten major persecutions, it is calculated that two millions of Christians were violently put to death. This, which was the last of the major pagan persecutions, was so dreadful and extensive that the Emperor boasted that the very name of Christian was forever obliterated, and he, moreover, had a medal struck to commemorate the end of Christianity.

Both Jews and pagans did all in their power to crush

what they termed 'the abomination of the Nazarene.' The Jews regarded Christ as the enemy of their race, since He destroyed their hope of a glorious Messias who would free them from the Roman yoke and make them the dominant people of the world. In the eyes of the Jews, to be a Christian meant the abandonment of the Messianic promises and despair of Israel's salvation.

The scribes and Pharisees by their perverted interpretation of Scripture had flattered the people's pride and fed them on false hopes of grandeur.

The Messias whom they led the people to expect was to renew the glorious reign of Solomon and make the Jewish race lords of the world. They persisted in confounding the eternal and spiritual kingdom of the Messias with a temporal and material kingdom. When Christ declared that His kingdom was not of this world, the Jewish leaders would have nothing to do with Him except to endeavor to exterminate Him and His followers.

The same culpable blindness which closed the eyes of the Jewish leaders to the Scriptures, which portrayed the Messias as a suffering redeemer and not as a military conqueror, also closed their eyes to Christ's resurrection and its significance.

In spite of the resurrection, which on the first day of St. Peter's preaching of it converted thousands of Jews to the worship of Christ as God, the ruling element of the race raged against Christ and His followers. St. Stephen was stoned to death; the apostles were imprisoned and scourged, and one of them, James, was martyred in the very city where Jesus was crucified. Beginning at Jerusalem, the Jewish leaders carried their persecution to neighboring towns and cities.

Conversion to the religion of Christ in the beginning was so impeded and punished by the Jews that it is astonishing that anyone of the Jewish race became a Christian.

Yet all the first Christians were converted Jews. It was these converted Jews, driven from Jerusalem by persecution, who served to establish the religion of the Crucified in various parts of the Roman Empire.

The rapid spread of Christianity in Rome itself alarmed the Jewish leaders, and caused them to send thither persecuting zealots to stir up Roman opposition to the religion of Christ. But the Jews in Rome were not allowed to persecute Christians as they had done and were doing in Judea. The Roman law protected all religions and worships.

In order to bring about Roman opposition to Christianity, it was necessary to turn the Roman rulers against the new religion.

The fiery Jewish zealots spread false reports to the effect that the Christians were enemies of the human race, that they killed and ate infants at their orgies, that they sought to undermine the state, and devised other calumnies calculated to incite people and ruler against the new worship.

It was the same diabolical propaganda that the Synagogue had employed to discredit Christ among His own people and to bring about His condemnation.

The storm of Roman persecution was not long delayed. The followers of the Crucified were about to exhibit in their own lives the truth of Christ's prophecy: "You shall be witnesses unto Me in Jerusalem, and in all Judea and Samaria, and even to the uttermost part of the earth" (Acts 1:8). The Christians of the Roman Empire were about to witness unto Christ by the shedding of their blood.

It was during the lifetime of the apostles that the sword of pagan persecution first smote the infant Church.

The Church was surely an infant in comparison with the colossal pagan giant that sought her life; and had it not been that God preserved her, no power on earth had enabled her to survive. Both St. Peter and St. Paul fell victims to the first pagan persecution inaugurated by Nero, A. D. 64.

Altogether there were ten major persecutions from Nero (A. D. 64) to Diocletian (A. D. 303). In all the history of mankind there is no record of such prolonged and intense persecution as that carried on by the pagan Roman Empire against the adherents of Christ's religion. Those persecutions were called 'major' which were decreed by the Emperor and extended throughout the Empire.

The sufferings inflicted on the martyrs defy description. Paganism had brutalized its votaries, and brutality characterized the persecution of the Christians. When we reflect that little children and delicate women endured indescribable tortures with courage and calmness that amazed rough soldiers hardened to pain and privation, we may conclude that they were sustained by a power more than human.

Sometimes groups of Christians were slaughtered wholesale by the sword; or put aboard leaky vessels which were towed out to sea, there to sink; or assembled in large buildings which were securely barred and set on fire. Some were crucified, some were clothed with animal skins and thrown into the arena to be devoured by wild beasts. Some were covered with pitch and set on fire, in order to illumine the night and make a spectacle for the heartless populace.

Others were sewn or tied in sacks with serpents and thrown into the sea; others had their hands cut off, others their feet; some had their eyes dug out, others had their tongues plucked out; others had their limbs stretched so as to cripple them for life; some were tied to the heels of vicious horses which were then lashed to a furious pace; some had red-hot irons applied to various parts of their bodies. Others were buried alive; some pierced to death by stencils; maidens were brutally treated and strangled; mothers were obliged to witness the torture of their children and to be cruelly put to death themselves.

These torments were endured willingly. Those being led to torture were offered every worldly inducement to renounce by word or gesture the religion of Christ. But Christ was for them more than the whole world, and for love of Him they went to death praying for their tormentors, and with such peace and composure that their very executioners were often converted to their victim's religion.

The heroism of the martyrs contributed greatly to the spread of Christianity, so much so that it gave rise to the statement that "the blood of martyrs is the seed of Christians."

Historians are not agreed as to the number of martyrs from Nero to Diocletian, but it is estimated that it reached seven or eight million. It must be borne in mind that the martyrs were of all races and conditions and ages. They were not sustained by patriotism nor by approving onlookers, nor by any other natural sentiment which sometimes makes heroes out of ordinary mortals.

It is the absence of every worldly or natural motive and support that constitutes the martyrs an argument for the divinity of the cause for which they suffered and to which they witnessed unto blood.

Not only did the martyrs show no resentment toward their torturers, but on the contrary they prayed for them after the example of their Master on Calvary. And as the patient sufferings of Christ on the cross converted the thief on His right, changing him from a reviler into a defender, so did the meekness, patience, and forgiveness of the martyrs convert to the faith many of those who had been their executioners.

The testimony of the early Christian martyrs has so favorably impressed the world with the divinity of Christ's religion that its opponents have done everything in their power to discredit their testimony. Gibbon wrote the *Decline and Fall of the Roman Empire* mainly in order to assign natural motives for the establishment of Christianity. Moreover, it is claimed by the enemies of Christianity that the number of martyrs was greatly exaggerated, and that they were put to death not for religious but for political reasons.

With regard to the number of martyrs we have the testimony of pagans themselves that it was a countless multitude. Pliny states that the Christians filled the Empire. Diocletian boasted that he had annihilated them. This in itself is sufficient evidence that the great number which historians have from the beginning assigned to the martyrs has justification.

When rationalists were finally convinced that the martyrs were numbered by millions, they shifted their attack by saying that the martyrs were slain because they were fanatics, dangerous to the state. But fanatics do not go to torture and death like the martyrs, who forgave and prayed for their tormentors, and suffered with such composure and resignation that their very enemies were often converted.

Finally, rationalists declare that the martyrs were hostile to the state, and that they suffered as enemies of law and order. But nowhere, even amongst pagan authors, is any other charge made against the martyrs except their religion. Justin, Tertullian, and other Christian champions openly reproved the pagan authorities for putting to death peaceful citizens who were devoted to the Empire.

Roman law permitted any and every religious worship. Even the Jews, who did not worship idols, were privileged by law to practice their religion. Rome boasted freedom of worship and tolerated every cult under the sun.

Why, then, did she not tolerate Christianity?

It was because superstitious pagan worship was declining before the might of Christian truth; and not being able to oppose it by argument, its votaries had recourse to violence.

The Christians were the best citizens of the Empire in everything that made for good citizenship. As soldiers, rulers, fathers, husbands, wives, mothers, sons, and daughters they were unsurpassed. Hence it was that Tertullian declared: "Either the Christians are guilty or innocent. If guilty, why do you not prosecute them as other criminals in your courts of justice? If innocent, why do you punish them?"

The Christians were persecuted for one reason only, for confessing Christ.

The death of Christ on Calvary, which seemed to His persecutors the end of His career, was rather its beginning. From the seed of Calvary the Church of Christ was born. Likewise from the soil made fertile by the blood of martyrs Christianity arose to renewed life, and eventually became the dominant religion of the greatest empire that the world has known.

In the providence of God the persecutors of Christianity have furnished a convincing argument for its divinity. No religion that was not true, no religion that was human only, could have survived the repeated and continuous efforts of the mightiest power on earth to crush it. But instead of destroying the infant religion of Christ, persecution caused it to wax strong and to develop into mature growth and strength.

The Roman world was astounded at the close of the last persecution to find itself Christian. The religion which Diocletian had proclaimed annihilated became the religion of the Empire when Constantine, by the Edict of Toleration in 313, granted complete religious liberty to Christians.

SUMMARY

The rapid spread of Christianity alarmed both the Jews and Romans.

The first persecution of Christians was by the Jews of Jerusalem, who did all in their power to destroy the Church of Christ. The Jews regarded Christian converts as traitors to their race and betrayers of the Messianic promises.

St. Stephen was the first martyr. St. James, Bishop of Jerusalem, was also martyred.

The persecuted Christians fled from Jerusalem to neighboring cities and to Rome.

The second persecution was by the pagan Roman Empire.

In all, there were ten major persecutions beginning A. D. 64 under Nero and ending A.D. 303 under Diocletian. Major persecutions were those decreed by the emperor and extending throughout the Empire.

Paganism was the state religion of Rome, and its worship of idols was a state function. Idolatry and Christianity were incompatible, and when the Jews declared that Christians were the enemies of the gods, the Empire decreed their extinction.

But the blood of martyrs became the seed of Christians. After three centuries of persecution the Roman Empire found itself Christian.

Some of the distinguished martyrs were: Ignatius, Bishop of Antioch; Polycarp, disciple of St. John; Agatha, Agnes, Cecilia, and Lawrence.

Rationalists in their endeavor to discredit the martyrs deny the large number of the martyrs and, moreover, affirm that they were put to death because they were dangerous fanatics or hostile to the state.

Pagan historians furnish proof of the large number of the martyrs and that they were good citizens.

That they were not fanatics is shown by the calm manner in which they went to torture and death and by their forgiving and praying for their enemies.

The Christians were the best citizens of the Empire. The only crime of the martyrs was their fidelity to Christ.

POINTS FOR DISCUSSION

1. The martyrs were fanatics, hence their constancy is no argument for Christianity's claims.

2. The martyrs were sincere, but so were the sacrificial victims of idolatry.

3. The Jews were justified in persecuting converts to Christianity because they were traitors to their race.

4. The Romans persecuted Christians because they defied the authority of the state.

5. The number of martyrs has been greatly exaggerated in order to furnish an argument for Christianity.

6. The conversion of the Roman Empire to Christianity was due to political, and not to religious, motives.

7. It is only interested Christian writers who are authority for the rapid and extensive spread of early Christianity.

8. Mohammedanism spread rapidly and extensively, but that is no argument for its supernatural character.

9. The early converts to Christianity were mostly from the lower classes, who hoped to gain by a religious revolution.

CHAPTER VIII

The Growth of the Early Church

THE CHURCH FOUNDED BY CHRIST began as an institution on the day of Pentecost, when the Holy Ghost, as promised by Christ, descended upon the apostles and in an instant changed them from ordinary men into the greatest missionaries this world has known.

Pentecost was the birthday of the Catholic church. From the cenacle the apostles went forth and preached Christ crucified and risen from the dead. The first sermon made three thousand converts. In the very city where Christ was crucified as a malefactor, He was worshiped as God by multitudes of the very people who had seen or shared in His condemnation. Unless the resurrection was a fact, the establishment of Christianity was a greater miracle than the resurrection itself.

It was because so many Jews became Christians that the leaders who had crucified Christ sought to destroy His religion. These leaders rejected Christ because if He prevailed they and their worldly ambitions would fail.

Despite persecution, however, the Church spread rapidly throughout the Roman Empire. She was a perfectly organized society with a supreme head and devoted bishops, priests, and people. The chief characteristics of the early Church were its visible organization, its authority, its unity of belief, and the loyalty, charity, and sublime fortitude of the faithful.

In the very first century Pope Clement exercised universal authority, even though St. John the Apostle was then living. This is evidence that the successor of St. Peter has been from the beginning the head of the Church. After three centuries of persecution the Church had her resurrection from the catacombs to the splendor of public worship.

Even worse than persecution was the scourge of heresy, which not only threatened the integrity of the faith, but also caused dreadful dissensions which would have wrecked any merely human organization. The Church survived persecution and heresy because her invisible head, Christ, was with her as He had promised.

Heresy is the denial of a doctrine revealed by Christ and entrusted to His Church for transmission.

Heresy served to bring out Christian dogmas more clearly and definitely by stating their meaning in unmistakable terms. It also raised up champions of the faith known as fathers and doctors of the Church.

Besides these expositors of creed, there were noble champions of the Church called apologists, who defended, explained, and justified Catholic doctrine and practice to the pagan world. In religion the word 'apologist' is a technical term for one who expounds and upholds Christian belief. It does not imply what is ordinarily conveyed by the English word; namely, excuse or regret. The apologists were among the most learned and esteemed citizens of the Empire, and most of them laid down their lives in torture for the faith they championed.

The greatest change effected in the history of mankind was the transformation of pagan into Christian Rome. If, previous to the event, anyone had predicted it, he would have been regarded as one bereft of reason. If, moreover, the means employed for the establishment of Christianity were taken into consideration, no one of sound mind would entertain the remotest idea of its possibility.

From the natural standpoint the establishment of Christianity was an impossibility. Neither human genius nor human resources could have effected the revolutionary change among mankind which was brought about by the religion of Jesus Christ. When all the facts are weighed it is evident that what St. Augustine said represents the verdict of everyone who is logical and open to conviction: "The establishment of Christianity without miracles would be the greatest of all miracles."

In order to better realize the significance of what the Church had to contend with from its very beginning, let us consider briefly the conditions and obstacles in the way of its early growth.

1. THE JEWISH ORIGIN OF THE CHURCH. At the time of Christ the Jews were held in contempt by the Romans. That the worship of a despised race should not only be adopted by its haughty conquerors, but moreover be allowed to supplant its own is unique in the annals of mankind.

2. THE WORSHIP OF CHRIST CRUCIFIED. The second obstacle to the growth of the early Church was that it prescribed the worship as God of one crucified as a traitor to Rome and His own race. That a person hated and persecuted by the chief priests and leaders of His own people, and moreover condemned by a Roman tribunal as a malefactor and put to death by the punishment assigned to slaves, should displace the cherished pagan deities of the dominant race of mankind, is something unex-

plainable unless Christ rose from the dead and was truly God.

3. THE BELIEF IN ONE GOD. Another fact that makes the triumph of the Church remarkable is that the worship of Christ entailed belief in one only God.

From time past reckoning pagans believed in and worshiped a multitude of deities. Idolatry was ingrained in the people, almost second nature to them. Yet they abandoned the traditional and congenial worship of their indulgent deities for that of one only God, whose worship entailed austere morality. Such a change of worship, with the naturally inadequate means employed, proclaims it the work of God, and puts the divine seal on the Church of Christ.

4. DOGMAS INCOMPREHENSIBLE TO HUMAN UNDERSTANDING. What adds to the significance of this change of religion is that Christianity proposed for belief dogmas which were beyond the power of the human intellect to understand. It was faith opposed to pagan pride of intellect. The dogmas of the Church were not proposed for debate but for acceptance, because they were the revelation of God Himself. It was thus necessary for the proud pagan philosophers to sacrifice their reason on the altar of God's word.

Christ first established that He was divine, and then spoke with divine authority and demanded acceptance of what He said because He was God who could neither deceive nor be deceived.

Unless the Church had furnished divine credentials for her claims the proud intellects of Greece and Rome had never bowed down in submission to the religion of the Crucified.

5. THE AUSTERE MORALITY OF CHRISTIANITY. When we add to the incomprehensibleness of dogmas the austerity of Christian morality, we are confronted with a combination of obstacles altogether too formidable for a human undertaking to surmount. It is almost impossible for us who live in an environment created by centuries of Christian morality to comprehend the degraded and vicious conditions into which idolatry had plunged its votaries. Vice which must now hide its head was then open. Every vice had its own deity, in worshiping which the vice which it symbolized, whether of lust, drunkenness, or cruelty, was indulged in.

No reasonable being would predict that the stern morality of the cross would replace the indulgent rites of Jupiter and Venus. Yet the cross of Christ supplanted the gods of marble which everywhere adorned the temples of profligate deities.

6. THE CHURCH'S CLAIM TO AUTHORITY. Before the advent of Christianity, pagan rulers recognized no authority above their own. The emperor was a law to himself; in fact he was worshiped as a deity. Christianity proclaimed that rulers as well as subjects were amenable to a power above. The Church, instead of being a tool of those in power, was a divinely authoritative voice which spoke to mankind with the sanction of omnipotence.

Pagan rulers recognized in this doctrine an encroachment on their unlimited exercise of power, and resented it by proscription, torture, exile, and death. The Church, however, triumphed over pagan absolutism and eventually numbered these mighty monarchs among her docile children.

7. THE DOCTRINE OF HUMAN EQUALITY. The brother-

hood of man proclaimed by the Church was another obstacle that impeded the growth of the early Church.
Pagan masters had the right of life and death over their
slaves. The Church proclaimed that slaves as well as
masters had human rights. She declared that one man
may owe service to another, but that master and servant
owed service to the Creator, and that to take the life of
a slave was murder as much as to take the life of an
equal. The haughty Roman magnates resented any restriction on their authority, and violently assailed the
Church in consequence. By degrees, however, the Church
succeeded in making these bitter opponents her loyal and
devoted children.

8. THE CHURCH'S ATTITUDE TOWARD WOMAN. The attitude of paganism towards women was another great obstacle to the growth of the early Church. Women were
regarded as not only inferior to men, but mostly as
chattels or instruments of lust. In the history of mankind
nothing has done more for civilization than the respect
for women inculcated by Christianity.

The Church had to overcome man's hitherto unchal-
lenged lordship over woman, and to change him from
master into her companion and protector. When pagan
civilization was at its highest, the condition of woman
was lowest. Hardly anything was a greater obstacle to
the growth of the Church than the traditional attitude
of man towards woman. The Church, by the veneration
paid to the Mother of Jesus, gradually restored woman
to the position of honor which is her due and which she
has since held in Christendom.

9. THE REJECTION OF IDOLATRY. Idolatry was the
great obstacle to the establishment and spread of Chris-

tianity. It was in the very weave and texture of the social, military, and governmental life of the Roman Empire.

Family duties, military undertakings, and governmental procedure were intimately associated with idolatrous rites. The life of the people was bound up with pagan deities and temples, elaborately served by priests and priestesses.

Pagan worship flattered the pride and indulged the grossest passions of the people. Vice was glorified, or rather deified, by idolatrous worship. Chaste Christianity gradually triumphed over this vile monster of paganism. Where the impure rites of Venus once held sway, the chaste Mother of Christ was venerated by countless youths and maidens consecrated to lives of purity.

Never in the history of the world was there such an array of obstacles against an undertaking as that which confronted the Church in her infancy. No cause, humanly speaking, could have surmounted these obstacles, even with every support of genius and material resources. The Church overcame them all without the aid of worldly influence, or the power of wealth, or the force of arms. The only means she employed to gain the Christian victory was the preaching of Christ crucified and risen from the dead.

Unless, therefore, the resurrection was a fact, it could not have changed the pagan Roman Empire into the seat of Christendom. It was the most stupendous change in the history of mankind and has no explanation except the power of God.

Not only Christian but pagan witnesses testify to the wide and rapid growth of the early Church.

Pliny, governor of a Roman province, reporting conditions to the Emperor, speaks as follows of the progress of Christianity in the first century: "The contagion of Christian superstition is not confined to the cities; it has invaded the villages and the country, and has taken possession of persons of every age, rank, and sex. Our temples are almost entirely abandoned, and the religious ceremonies neglected" (Epist. 97).

Tertullian, in the second century, in his defense of Christianity addressed to the Roman Emperor, states: "If we were to withdraw from you the Empire would be a desert" (Apolog. C. XXXVII).

The rapid and wide growth of the Church has been a matter of very great wonder to students of history. It held out no worldly inducements, catered to no human weaknesses; it neither flattered the pride, nor indulged the passions, of man. Besides, of all men in the world, naturally speaking, the apostles were the least qualified for such a momentous undertaking as the establishment of Christianity.

Either they were transformed and aided by the Holy Ghost or not. If they were, it was supernatural concurrence and puts the seal of divinity on the Church of Christ. If the apostles were not transformed and aided by the Holy Ghost, the establishment of Christianity by them would have been more wonderful than the miracles which they recorded.

Those who deny the supernatural must explain how these peasants succeeded so marvelously in their stupendous undertaking.

The hostile Jewish Synagogue was amazed at the persuasiveness and eloquence of these unlettered fishermen. The Jewish leaders could not understand how these ordinary men, without preparation of any kind, had become such eloquent preachers of a cause which apparently had terminated forever on Calvary.

Not only was the Synagogue astonished at the intellectual change in the apostles, but also at their wonderful moral transformation. Previously they were timid, but after Pentecost they displayed such heroic courage and constancy as to completely astound their persecutors.

In the Acts of the Apostles we read that when the apostles were summoned before the Jewish Council the chief priests, "seeing the constancy of Peter and of John . . . wondered" (Acts 4:13).

And well might they have wondered, for they beheld the power of the Holy Spirit in these ambassadors of the crucified and risen Christ.

The apostles were the first of a long line of champions of the Church of Christ.

Orators like Ambrose and Chrysostom, theologians such as Gregory, Basil, Augustine, and Athanasius, scholars like Tertullian, Origen, and Jerome, these and countless others proclaimed, explained, and justified the religion of the cross and were greatly instrumental in making Christianity triumph over paganism.

The main reason for the triumph of the Church, however, was its divinity. All the power on earth could not have effected the establishment of Christianity unless its founder was God and its doctrine divinely true.

The triumph of the Church of Christ was that of truth over error, morality over vice, spiritual values over material, and eternal interests over temporal.

It was because the Church of Christ had a message from God to man that she prevailed over the allurements of the world, and led mankind to look beyond the passing present to the eternal future. It was because the Church was divine that she not only survived the assaults of the world, but moreover emerged from the conflict stronger rather than weaker.

After three centuries of assaults from without, and heresies and human frailties from within, the Catholic church found herself firmly established throughout the civilized world.

The Church was then, as she is today, a miracle. Unless she was divinely sustained she had perished long ago; but because Christ is with her, she will carry on to the end of time the mission confided to her by the Lord of time and eternity.

SUMMARY

The Church founded by Christ began as an institution on the day of Pentecost, when the Holy Ghost, as promised by Christ, descended upon the apostles and in an instant changed them from ordinary men into the greatest missionaries this world has known.

Pentecost was the birthday of the Catholic church.

From the cenacle the apostles went forth and preached Christ crucified and risen from the dead.

St. Peter's first sermon made three thousand converts in the very city where Christ was crucified.

Despite persecution by the Jews and Romans, the Church spread rapidly throughout the civilized world.

She was a perfectly organized society, with a supreme head and devoted bishops, priests, and members.

The chief characteristics of the early Church were its visible organization, its authority, its unity of doctrine, and the loyalty, charity, and sublime fortitude of the faithful.

In the very first century Pope Clement exercised universal authority, even though St. John was then living. This is evidence that the successor of St. Peter was head of the Church from the beginning.

Heresy threatened the integrity of the faith and also caused bitter persecution of the faithful.

Heresy caused the Church to define more clearly the dogmas of the Church, and also raised up noble defenders of the faith, known as fathers and doctors of the Church.

Apologists explained and upheld the faith against pagans.

The main obstacles to the growth of the early Church were:

1. The Jewish origin of the Church.
2. The worship of Christ crucified.
3. The belief in one God.
4. Dogmas incomprehensible to human understanding.
5. The austere morality of Christianity.
6. The Church's claim to authority.
7. The doctrine of human equality.
8. The Church's attitude toward woman.
9. The rejection of idolatry.

Never in the history of the world was there such an array of obstacles to an undertaking. No merely human cause could have overcome them.

The Church, divinely sustained, triumphed.

After three centuries of persecution the Church found herself firmly established throughout the civilized world.

Her rapid and extensive growth was possible to supernatural power alone.

POINTS FOR DISCUSSION

1. The early Church was not a visible organization, but a body of believers in Christ.

2. The early Church was not authoritative, otherwise it would have prevented heresy.

3. From the disputes among the apostles themselves it is apparent that there was not unity of doctrine in the early Church.

4. The early Church could not have been a visible or-

ganization since it had no permanent or public place of administration.

5. The Roman Empire permitted every form of religion. It had a temple to the deities of all nations. The Jewish origin of Christianity was therefore no obstacle to its establishment.

6. The Greeks and Romans believed in one supreme deity, Zeus or Jupiter. Hence the doctrine of one god was no obstacle to the pagans.

7. Mysteries were always attractive to the pagan mind, hence the mysteries of Christianity were rather a help than a hindrance to its establishment.

8. The absolutism of pagan rulers was a help instead of a hindrance to Christianity because Christianity restricted tyrants and favored the people.

CHAPTER IX

The Church and the Barbarians

As the Roman Empire weakened, the barbarians entered in droves.

By the term 'barbarians' Rome signified those peoples outside the domination and influence of the Roman Empire. Specifically, these barbarians were Goths, Vandals, Huns, and Lombards.

The Goths were a Teutonic people, probably Scandinavian in origin, but dwelling about the Baltic Sea at the time that they entered into Roman history. They were known as Ostrogoths (those of the east) and Visigoths (those of the west). The Dniester River was the line separating these two divisions of the Goths.

The Vandals had their origin in Silesia and were a kindred people to the Goths.

The Huns were a Turanian race from Tartary and northern Asia.

It was the pressure of the Huns on the Goths that brought about the Gothic invasion of the Roman Empire.

The Great Wall of China held back the Huns from pushing eastward and left them no outlet except to the west. It was Hun pressure that forced the Goths into Moesia and led to the battle of Adrianople and the Gothic wars with Rome.

The home of the Lombards was Pannonia, whence they gradually approached the fertile fields of Italy.

These four barbarian peoples, at one time or another,

89

invaded the Roman Empire, and if it had not been for the Church would have destroyed civilization in Europe.

The Goths were the first to encroach on Roman territory, their first invasion occurring while the Empire was pagan. Later, in the fourth century, they were allowed to settle in Moesia on condition that they embrace Christianity.

They agreed, and missionaries were sent to them in 360 from the Eastern Empire, whose capital was Constantinople.

At this time the Empire was divided into the two major divisions of 'east' and 'west,' in order better to defend itself against barbarian invasion. Unfortunately, the Eastern Empire had come under the influence of Arianism, a heresy which denied the true divinity of Christ. As the missionaries to the Goths were Arians, these Goths became Arians. They carried their Arianism into Italy, France, Spain, and Africa, causing at times persecution and very severe conflicts with orthodox Christians. Eventually they were converted to true Christianity.

Arianism was a dreadful blight on early Christianity, and unless the Church had been divinely founded and sustained she had not survived this ordeal.

Arianism falsely proclaimed that Christ was not of the same nature as God, that He was not eternal but created in the course of time, and that consequently the Son is a creature, and not divine by nature, but by grace, and therefore not true God.

This heresy caused persecution by Arian rulers and wrought untold harm to the Church, but in the end served to establish definitely the true divinity of Christ.

The Huns swept down from Asia, conquered the Ostrogoths, and drove the Visigoths into conflict with the Romans.

Under Alaric the Goths made their way to Rome itself, which they eventually took by assault. This was the beginning of the end of the Roman Empire. The Goths passed into various parts of the Empire, leaving no barrier between the Huns and the Romans.

The Eastern Empire felt the first shock of the Hun invasion. Attila became sole monarch of these barbarians in 447 and proceeded to lay waste the Roman territory up to the gates of Constantinople. In 452 Attila invaded Italy and conquered everything before him, and was on his way to attack Rome when Pope St. Leo, heading an embassy from the city, entreated him to desist from further conquest and to live in peace with the Empire.

This was one of the most dramatic events of history, bringing the spiritual power of Christianity, so weak in material strength, face to face with the mighty barbarian conqueror. Strange to relate, the conqueror yielded to the defenseless pontiff and turned his powerful hosts homeward.

After the Huns came the Vandals under King Genseric. They ravaged Gaul, then crossed the sea to Africa, took Carthage, and ruined that province of the Empire. They next advanced on Rome, and Pope Leo again went forth to meet a conquering foe, but could do no more than dissuade him from destroying the churches and from slaughtering the citizens.

It was because of the needless ruin everywhere caused by the Vandals that wanton destruction to this day is called 'vandalism.'

The final barbarian invasion of the Empire was by the Lombards under their King Alboin in 568. No effective resistance was offered them, and town after town fell into their hands until they came to Pavia, which withstood a siege of three years before yielding to the invaders, and which after capture became the capital of the Lombard realm.

In brief, the invasions of the barbarians swept like a tidal wave over Europe, leaving disorder, destruction, and misery in their wake.

Rome, abandoned by the emperors at Constantinople, had little or no protection against rapine and injustice except in the Church. As a consequence the prelates of the Church gradually became temporal as well as spiritual rulers. The pope became the real protector of the Western Empire, and later, in 755, was made head of the Italian states by Pepin, King of the Franks. This was the beginning of the temporal power of the papacy, originating in the need of the times.

Gradually the Church converted the barbarians and made of them the Christian nations of Europe.

A notable factor in the conversion of the barbarians and the preservation of civilization was the work of the monastic institutions, especially the Benedictines. This order takes its name from St. Benedict, the organizer of monasticism in the Western Empire.

Monasticism, derived from the Greek word μόνος, which means *alone,* is the state of life of those who dwell in seclusion, apart from people engaged in the ordinary life of the world. The dwelling place of these people, isolated from the world, is called a monastery, and those who live therein are known as monks, friars, nuns, or in general as religious. They are subject to a fixed rule and bind themselves by vow to a life of holiness by the practice of poverty, chastity, and obedience, after the example of Christ's life of service and sacrifice for mankind.

Unless the nature of monasticism be understood, it would hardly be possible to understand the heroic labors of the monastic orders for the conversion of the barbarians and the preservation of civilization.

Monks, although living secluded from the world, are not without influence on it. Personal holiness is not the only object of the monastic life. If stress is laid on personal holiness, it is because in proportion as a person is holy he will be able to labor effectively for the glory of God and the welfare and salvation of mankind. Persons animated by merely human or natural motives could never have achieved the marvelous results accomplished by the monastic orders during the centuries of barbaric spoliation and degradation.

The monastic orders may engage in any kind of work compatible with a life of prayer and sacrifice. It was thus that the monks taught the barbarians agriculture, architecture, road-building, and various trades which transformed them from nomads into permanent dwellers. Monasteries were centers of civilization, the universities of the period, wherein art, literature, and science were preserved and transmitted.

Agriculture ranked first among the various forms of monastic external labors. In the early stages of barbaric invasion the monasteries were built in inaccessible places in order to escape destruction by the half-savage hordes which laid waste everything in their path. Gradually the monks cleared forests, drained marshes, bridged rivers, and built roads, until almost imperceptibly the desert places became a farm or garden. By degrees people clustered about these monastic lands and were taught the occupations in which the monks themselves excelled.

The half-savage barbarians, together with the people ruined and dominated by them, came by degrees to look upon the monasteries as their greatest benefactors.

Many monastic sites thus developed into the modern cities of Europe.

It was to the monasteries that all who sought an education applied for instruction. The monks opened schools wherein was taught everything known to art, science, and culture generally. If it were not for the monks, hardly anything of classic literature or ancient culture would have been preserved to posterity. Some people who use their education in the endeavor to discredit the monks forget that without the monks the universities of today might never have been.

In the monasteries the learning of antiquity was preserved and transmitted. It may not be generally known that there is not now in the world one book that existed in the time of the Caesars. Every book of classic antiquity is a copy of the original or a copy of a copy. The oldest book in the world is a Bible which dates from the fourth century. The literature of antiquity was preserved and transmitted to modern times by the labors and skill of the monks.

In the monastery was a room called the *scriptorium,* in which the monks sat at desks while a reader on a platform slowly dictated from a classic volume or from the Bible. The monks wrote what was dictated, and each page as finished was compared with the page dictated, and if correct, received a mark to certify that it was a true copy.

A hundred monks thus copying from dictation would be able to reproduce a hundred copies of the book. Each letter of every word had to be carefully printed by hand on parchment, which was afterwards assembled to form a book or codex.

It is readily seen that before the invention of modern mechanical printing a book was a rare and valuable possession. It would take a copyist several years, working steadily every day, to produce a book like the Bible. Since books were scarce, very few people could read. In fact, many rulers and even some kings could not read. Learning was confined for the most part to the clergy, since they alone had books. It was on this account that the secretaries of the nobility were largely from the clerical ranks, and hence they were called 'clerks.'

Besides books, the art and science of antiquity were conserved in the monasteries and passed on to posterity.

It must not be thought, however, that the monastic orders limited themselves to learning and industry. They performed works of charity towards the poor, the sick, and the traveler. They propagated Christianity and strengthened faith by their example, preaching, and missions. By prayer and self-denial they called down God's blessing on those for whom they labored, and whom they heroically served. In point of fact, they gave mankind the highest example of social service that the world has known.

At one time the order of Benedictines had thirty thousand monasteries, and each one of them was a school, a dispensary, a library, a hospice, and a sanctuary. It may readily be seen what a tremendous agency monasticism was for the spiritual and material welfare of all those who came within the sphere of its influence.

The descent of the barbarians upon the imperial provinces of Europe completely destroyed the social and political life of the former civilization.

The Church alone remained firm and unchanged. She it was who protected the oppressed, the slaves, and the poor, suppressed superstition, and prevented feuds and bloodshed. The barbarians were so impressed by the maternal solicitude of the Church that they gradually became her devoted children and firm support.

The authority exercised by the Church was a safeguard against the tyranny of rulers and the rebellion of subjects. She inculcated in the half-savage hordes the respect for justice which eventually brought about the reign of law and order among the various parts of the now-dismembered Empire.

Besides civilizing the barbarians, the Church at this period sent forth missionaries to various and distant lands in order to bring the religion of Christ to those who dwelt in ignorance and the darkness of error.

St. Columba in Scotland, St. Augustine in England, St. Boniface in Germany, St. Patrick in Ireland, and St. Ansgar in Scandinavia not only converted these peoples, but by living with them, establishing monasteries, and training them in the arts of peace, founded a society based on Gospel principles and firm with the stability of Christian faith.

Besides monks, missionaries, and clergy, there was another class of Christians who contributed towards the social betterment of the Empire, devastated by the barbarian inroads. These were the hermits, devout persons who to escape the contagion of vice in the cities or to seek greater sanctification by a life apart, withdrew to the deserts of Egypt and Palestine, there to devote themselves to prayer and mortification for their own and the world's salvation.

St. John the Baptist led this kind of life in preparation for his mission as the herald of the Messias. In the Roman Empire St. Paul, the first hermit, lived upwards of a hundred years, and his successor, as head of a community of solitaries, was St. Anthony.

These solitary communities were a refuge for those who, disheartened by barbarian vice and cruelty, sought a place of peace and quiet where they could sanctify their souls and pray for the salvation of the world.

The Church, by the patience of the faithful, the labors of the monastic orders, the fortitude of the clergy, and the prayers and penances of the solitaries, not only survived the invasions of the barbarians but, moreover, conquered the conquerors and made them willing subjects of the Gospel.

It was, therefore, due to the Church that civilization did not perish with the Roman Empire.

SUMMARY

As the Roman Empire weakened, the barbarians, half-savages, entered in droves. Eventually they became dominant.

Rome, abandoned by the emperors at Constantinople, had no protection against rapine and injustice except in the Church. As a consequence the prelates of the Church gradually became temporal as well as spiritual rulers.

The pope became the protector of the Western Empire, and later was made head of the Italian states by Pepin, King of the Franks, in 755. This was the beginning of the temporal power of the papacy.

Gradually the Church converted the barbarians and made of them the Christian nations of Europe.

The monastic institutions were a considerable factor in the conversion of the barbarians and the preservation of civilization.

The monasteries were the universities of that period, wherein the learning of classic antiquity was transmitted to modern times.

The monks also taught the barbarians agriculture, architecture, road-building, and various trades, which transformed them from nomads into permanent dwellers.

Besides monks there were hermits, persons seeking to escape from the vice and brutality of the barbaric invasions, and who withdrew to the desert in order as solitaries to pray and do penance for themselves and the world.

The Church at this period sent missionaries to distant pagan lands, and witnessed the conversion of Scotland, Britain, Ireland, Germany, and Scandinavia.

It was thus that, by means of the patience of the faithful, the labors of the monastic orders, the fortitude of the clergy, and the prayers and penance of the solitaries, the Church saved civilization from perishing with the Roman Empire.

POINTS FOR DISCUSSION

1. Christ established His religion for the salvation of souls. The Church, however, sought mainly the material welfare of the barbarians.

2. Christ declared that His kingdom was not of this world, but the pope became the ruler of a worldly kingdom.

3. The Church, during the barbarian invasion, was so immersed in material things that she lost sight of her spiritual mission.

4. How did the Church civilize the barbarians?

5. What is the difference between a monk and a hermit, and what motive impelled men to become hermits?

6. What countries were converted to Christianity by the Roman missionaries?

7. How did the Church preserve civilization after the collapse of the Roman Empire?

8. What were the principal factors in the conversion of the barbarians to Christianity?

CHAPTER X

The Middle Ages

THE MIDDLE AGES were the period from the eleventh to the fourteenth century. The important things to be understood in connection with this period are feudalism, lay investiture, the crusades, universities, scholasticism, architecture, guilds, and the eastern and western schisms.

Feudalism originally was a system based on land tenure in which every lord judged, taxed, and commanded the class next below him. In the Middle Ages the poorer classes were not always able to pay taxes. In their extremity they appealed to their lord. The lord paid the taxes, but demanded their land in return. This land he returned to them in fief; that is, they were to be his vassals. The land of his own which a lord possessed was often that which was given him by a superlord or by the king as a reward of service, and on condition of his furnishing further service when required of him.

There were lords of all degrees, each in turn being under obligation to an overlord.

Because of the condition of the times, prelates of the Church had become temporal as well as spiritual rulers. These prelates were subjects of temporal overlords and were themselves lords of those under them. This condition of affairs resulted eventually in lay investiture; that is, the nomination and frequently the appointing of bishops by superlords and kings, in order to have them subservient to their purposes. As the purpose of these

superlords was often the accumulation of wealth
and the extension of power, it frequently happened
that unworthy persons were designated or appointed to
ecclesiastical dignities.

Eventually this led to very great abuses, as men altogether unsuitable were imposed on the Church as bishops.
The emperor not only made his own selection of bishops,
but moreover invested them with the insignia of office,
the ring and the crosier.

It was Gregory VII, known as Hildebrand, who to a
great extent remedied this abuse, being obliged in doing
so to excommunicate Henry IV in 1076.

A few years after this victory over state interference
with Church government, the papacy engaged in another
tremendous undertaking, the crusades.

Many Christians made pilgrimages to the sacred places
of Palestine. Not infrequently the Turks, in possession
of the Holy Land, abused and murdered these pilgrims
and even plundered the sacred shrines.

The purpose of the crusades was threefold: first, to
secure protection for the Christians; second, to rescue the
sacred places and guard them against profanation and
destruction; and third, to drive back the Saracens who
threatened Christendom.

The first of seven crusades was under Pope Adrian II
in 1096, preached by Peter the Hermit. The Christian
army under Godfrey de Bouillon and other princes numbered about a half-million men. These crusaders took
Jerusalem in 1099, and proclaimed Godfrey king.

Following this, six other crusades were organized for
the deliverance of the Holy Land.

The second crusade was preached by St. Bernard, and

both Louis VII of France and Conrad III of Germany led their hosts in an attempt to take Damascus, but failed of their purpose.

Saladin having conquered Jerusalem and seized the holy cross, Frederick I of Germany, Philip Augustus of France, and Richard the Lion-hearted of England combined their forces and took Acre, in the third crusade.

The remaining crusades accomplished little in the Holy Land except to give a demonstration of Christian faith and fortitude.

The crusades, although failing of their main purpose, were not without many notable results and benefits. They furnished to the world a marvelous spectacle of idealism and religious fervor; secured Europe against the power of Mohammedanism; stimulated intellectual development in geography, physical science, and Greek and Arabian literature; gave birth to the glorious institution of chivalry; promoted the spirit of unity among the nations of Europe; strengthened the influence of the papacy; gave rise to independent cities; developed citizenship and weakened feudalism; gave a new impulse to manufacture and commerce; and finally furnished an outlet for the warlike spirit of the age, which was only too ready to engage in mortal combat with fellow Christians.

From the field of battle we may now turn to that of knowledge, and consider one of the greatest glories of the Middle Ages, the universities.

In the Middle Ages Europe possessed forty-five universities. It was mainly due to the encouragement, support, and prestige of the papacy that these advanced institutions of learning were founded and flourished. Oxford and Cambridge, the glory of England today, are the heritage of the Middle Ages, as also are the most renowned universities of Europe.

In these halls of learning was taught the accumulated wisdom of the ages. The universities of Salerno, Paris, Bologna, Rome, Pavia, and Ravenna numbered their students by thousands drawn from every nation of Christendom.

A conspicuous feature of the student body as a whole was its cosmopolitan character. The exact number of students at the great universities is not altogether certain. According to the most reliable records Bologna had seven thousand students; Oxford six thousand; Paris between eight thousand and ten thousand.

The university of the Middle Ages was a potent factor for law and order; it aroused enthusiasm for learning and enforced discipline; it was the center in which the philosophy and jurisprudence of antiquity were restored and adapted to new requirements. The university is evidence, also, that the Church of the Middle Ages was the patroness of learning, that she fostered art and science, and that she was the main cultural influence of those centuries.

In connection with the universities must be mentioned scholasticism, which consisted in applying the system of scientific philosophy, especially that of Aristotle, to Christian doctrine, and developing it accordingly. Scholasticism made use of philosophy to render the teaching of Christian revelation more methodical and philosophical.

Turning back to the great thinkers of pagan antiquity, the scholastic teachers found a basis for their procedure in the methodical treatises of Aristotle.

The keenest Catholic teachers came to realize that in
the philosophy of Aristotle they had an incomparable
implement, together with the Scriptures and the works
of the fathers, in building up the complete edifice of
Christian truth.

St. Thomas Aquinas, one of the greatest thinkers of all
time, and St. Bonaventure, known as the Seraphic Doctor, brought scholastic science to the highest point it has
ever attained. The *Summa* of St. Thomas is regarded as
the most enlightened and comprehensive system of scholastic doctrine which the Church possesses, and fully entitles him to the name of Angelic Doctor which the
learned world has given him.

Passing from the study of the Christian religion to the
worship of its divine Founder, we contemplate with wonder the cathedrals which the Middle Ages erected as
temples of prayer and sacrifice.

Religion entered into the whole life of the Middle Ages,
and the majestic cathedrals of that period are an eloquent
expression of the vital importance of religion to its people. These masterpieces of ecclesiastical architecture are
the wonder of mankind even today with all the modern
marvels of construction before our eyes.

These cathedrals are witness to the faith, devotion, and
culture of the Middle Ages, of which the thirteenth
century is considered to be the greatest of all centuries.

The cathedrals were a symbol of the consecration of
external life and external things to the service of God
on the largest and most generous scale. It was by these
magnificent temples that the ages of faith also expressed
their genius for art and loveliness.

It seemed only proper to the men of those days that

the house of God should far surpass baron's castle or prince's palace. The Mass was the greatest and holiest action in which they participated, and they believed that the altar of sacrifice was deserving of the most glorious dwelling that the genius, skill, and labor of man could erect. That explains the miracles in stone which their faith and devotion raised to the God whom they worshiped.

The Middle Ages were not so absorbed in spiritual and eternal things, however, as to be unmindful of temporal and material welfare. The Middle Ages saw the institution of trade unions called guilds, which were the forerunners of the modern labor unions.

Every craft had its organization, whose members were pledged to a high standard of workmanship and mutual assistance. These guilds were under the protection of the Church, each guild having its own patron saint and its own chaplain.

The fraternity known as Freemasons had its origin in these guilds, and in the following manner.

Masons were one of the many crafts which formed guilds. When a mason found no work in one place, he went looking for it elsewhere. Coming as a stranger to another place, he had to present credentials that he was qualified for work as a mason.

His credentials were a testimonial from his guild and certain manual signs which confirmed his testimonial. When these were satisfactory he was admitted to the guild and given work. He was called a free mason because he was free and qualified to accept work.

When modern secret societies arose, they called themselves 'Freemasons,' adopted manual signs suggested by the guilds of the Middle Ages, and claimed origin from antiquity, although their existence began only in late modern times.

The guilds gave their members protection against unfair competition, guaranteed them a just wage, and insisted on proper working conditions.

These guilds are evidence that the Church of the Middle Ages was a solicitous mother for her children at a time when but for her they would have been at the mercy of powerful and grasping barons and other covetous masters.

The Middle Ages were ages of faith—not merely belief in revealed truth as it concerned the individual, but as it affected public life and action. We should not be surprised, therefore, that for everything that relates to real culture and human welfare the thirteenth has been proclaimed the greatest of all centuries. Modern times may glory in material progress and mechanical conveniences, but life is more than the body, and it is to be feared that what the present day has gained in comfort, it has lost in contentment. At all events, guided by the Church, the Middle Ages stand out as a period of splendid idealism, the inspiration of chivalry and high romance, and above all as the ages of faith.

Every substance, however, has its shadow, and a blight on the Middle Ages was the plague of schism; namely, the Greek schism in the East and the papal schism in the West.

Schism differs from heresy in that schism is a denial of authority, while heresy is a denial of doctrine.

Very often schism leads to heresy, for when persons withdraw from the jurisdiction of the infallible Church, they are without that divine guidance which Christ promised to His own Church and to no other.

In brief, the Greek schism was a refusal of the Eastern Church at Constantinople to acknowledge the supremacy of the pope.

The Greek schism had a beginning some centuries before it came to a head in the eleventh century. It was due to the jealousy of Constantinople against Rome. In the year 857 Photius, Patriarch of the Eastern Church, appealing to the pride of the people, opposed the pope and denied Roman supremacy.

This schism lasted for a few years only, but left among some prelates a feeling of antagonism against Rome.

In the year 1054 the Patriarch of Constantinople, Michael Cerularius, urged on by ambition and encouraged by some of the influential clergy and people of the Eastern Church, denied the supreme authority of the pope, and proclaimed independence of Roman jurisdiction. The schism thus begun has lasted to the present day.

As a consequence of the schism the Eastern Church has fallen under the domination of secular powers and has lost much of the vitality which characterized it when united to the see of Peter, and has moreover fallen into heresy.

The Great Western Schism arose from a dispute about the election of Pope Urban VI in 1378.

Some cardinals of the electoral conclave claimed that this election was invalid because of intimidation by the Roman people, who demanded the election of an Italian pope. These cardinals assembled again and elected a Frenchman as pope under the title of Clement VII, who made Avignon, France, his papal residence. For forty years Christendom was divided into two allegiances, one upholding the pope at Rome and the other the claimant at Avignon.

So great was the confusion that saints and theologians were to be found on either side. The situation became so grave that the Council of Constance was convoked to end it. The claimants, who at this time were three, either abdicated or were deposed, and a new pope, Martin V, was elected in 1417. This schism was responsible for serious consequences, among which was the lessening of reverence for the papacy and the encouragement of those opponents of ecclesiastical authority who a century later brought about the Protestant Reformation.

Unless the Church was truly supernatural she could not have survived the confusion, divisions, and animosities occasioned by this schism.

It may be asked whether this schism broke the continuity of papal succession. To this the answer is that one of the claimants was the legitimate successor of St. Peter, and through this legitimate pope the succession was maintained unbroken.

It is dissension that tests the strength of an organization. No merely natural institution could have withstood the long and bitter disruption which divided Christendom into two hostile camps for nearly half a century.

The Catholic church not only survived this division in the camp, but has emerged from it the most united, the most vigorous, and the most authoritative institution in the world.

The Great Western Schism brought to a close the Middle Ages. No period in the history of Christendom reflects more glory on mankind than these centuries of faith, resplendent in art, architecture, learning, chivalry, social action, missionary zeal, and sublime idealism.

The names of Thomas Aquinas, Albertus Magnus, and Bonaventure in the realm of ideas, of Roger Bacon in science, of Dante in literature, of St. Dominic and St. Francis Assisi in holiness will be household words as long as mankind admires the good, the true, and the beautiful.

SUMMARY

The Middle Ages were the period from the eleventh to the fourteenth century.

Feudalism, a feature of the Middle Ages, was due to the need of a protector by the masses.

As bishops, acting as temporal rulers, became underlords of some powerful ruler, these rulers insisted on nominating to bishoprics prelates who would serve their interests. This led to lay investiture, which caused unworthy prelates to be in office.

Pope Gregory VII remedied this abuse.

The crusades were organized to free the Holy Land from the domination and plunder of the Turks.

There were altogether seven crusades, of which only three were of great importance.

The first was preached by Peter the Hermit under Pope Urban II; the second by St. Bernard with the support of Louis VII of France; the third had as one of its heroes Richard the Lion-hearted of England.

Although the crusades failed of their main purpose, they resulted in many benefits to Europe.

The Middle Ages saw the rise of universities all over Europe, mainly under papal patronage.

At this period also scholasticism was dominant. This was a system of employing science and philosophy in the study of revealed doctrine. Its greatest exponents were Aquinas and Bonaventure.

Science had its great glory in Roger Bacon; literature its lofty poet in Dante; architecture its monuments in the majestic cathedrals, which are even today the wonder of mankind.

Guilds were associations of workmen for mutual protection and high standards of work. They originated and flourished in this period.

A blight on the Middle Ages was schism.

The Greek or Eastern Schism arose from the ambition of the patriarch of Constantinople to be independent of the pope.

The Great Western Schism was caused by what some considered an invalid papal election. This schism lasted forty years and did much harm to religion.

The Church survived these and other ordeals because she was truly a supernatural institution.

POINTS FOR DISCUSSION

1. The Church was responsible for feudalism, a form of human slavery.

2. Catholic bishops were temporal lords, and consequently parties to feudalism.

3. Lay investiture constituted worldly rulers the supreme authority of the Church.

4. The crusades were a military enterprise, and the Church had no business engaging in them.

5. During the Middle Ages the Church neglected her real work, the salvation of souls.

6. What is meant by scholasticism?

7. The Church of the Middle Ages neglected the poor for the rich.

8. The Church fell into decline during the Middle Ages.

9. The Great Western Schism broke apostolic succession, and thus ended the Catholic church as the Church of Christ.

CHAPTER XI

THE REFORMATION

THE REFORMATION OF THE SIXTEENTH CENTURY was an attempt to reform some abuses in the Catholic church by abolishing her altogether.

Christ, who guaranteed His Church infallibility, did not guarantee her members impeccability. The divine Founder of the Catholic church foretold that there would be scandals even among those in high places in His Church.

In the small circle of which He Himself was the head, there were abuses and scandals, but neither the treason of Judas nor the perjury of Peter detracted from the truth or holiness of Christ's teaching.

Christ proclaimed that He was the light of the world, and He also said of His Church: "You are the light of the world" (Matthew 5:14).

Light is a beacon which guides but does not compel. God created man a free being and He wants man to serve Him freely. Hence neither Christ nor His Church forces man to serve, but gives every motive and help to do so.

There have always been abuses of conduct in the Church and always will be, to the end of the world, because man, being free, may use his great gift of free will to serve himself rather than God, even though he incur eternal chastisement by doing so.

God has given man free will and will not destroy it by forcing it, but if man does not use his freedom as God directs, he defies Omnipotence, and will incur the eternal penalty meted out to transgressors of God's law. This is said as preliminary to the consideration of the Reformation because most of the misunderstanding which exists in regard to this matter comes from confusing doctrine with discipline or conduct.

A doctrine may be most true and holy, but it does not follow that all who believe in it will be holy. Holiness comes not merely from knowing what is right, but from the firm will to do right. Christ proclaimed that His Church would never err in doctrine. Luther declared that the Church had erred in doctrine. Here was flat contradiction.

It is accordingly a choice between Christ and Luther. If Luther was right Christ was wrong, and that would be the end of Christianity, for Christ could not be God if He had failed in His promise.

It comes to this, in brief:

The divine Founder of the Catholic church declared that she should never err in doctrine; Luther declared she had erred. It was Luther against Christ. This alone should have been sufficient to settle the matter, and doubtless would have settled it, had not human weakness and passion entered into the controversy.

The Reformation began, really, in a fit of disappointment on Luther's part because he did not receive a coveted honor. For some time ecclesiastical authorities paid little or no attention to him and his declarations. It was not until he passed from accusations against abuses to denial of doctrine that he was taken seriously.

Even then it was thought that he would yield to the reasonable presentation of the Church's claims, but having once started on an impetuous and erroneous course nothing seemed able to stop him. He was urged on, more-over, by various persons who had much to gain by a rupture with the Church. He ended by attacking the sacraments, denying the authority of the pope, and finally rejecting the Church itself.

The doctrine of indulgences was the subject of his first attack. From this he passed on to open heresy. He denied supreme teaching authority in the Church, rejected all the sacraments except baptism and the Eucharist, abolished the Sacrifice of the Mass, and at last repudiated the Church as a visible authoritative society established by Christ.

Luther proclaimed that the Bible and the Bible only was sufficient for salvation, forgetting that it was the Catholic church that gave us the Bible as the inspired word of God. The Church was in a flourishing condition long before she gave us the Bible. Moreover, Christ did not leave us a written line. Instead of a book, He gave us a Church, and said: "He that heareth you heareth Me," and "I am with you all days, even to the consummation of the world" (Luke 10:16, Matthew 28:20).

In view of this it may be asked, What accounted for the rapid spread of the Reformation? The principal reasons were the following four:

First, Luther proclaimed that faith alone without good works was sufficient for salvation. This was a doctrine very congenial to human nature, inclined as it is to evil. Luther even went so far as to declare that good works, such as fasting and mortification, were not only unnecessary but sinful. When such a doctrine was proclaimed by a religious leader, it is no wonder that it gained adherents from among those who were only too glad to find a justification for licentiousness.

Second, Luther proclaimed the doctrine of private judgment in religious matters. This doctrine constituted each person the founder of his own religion. It virtually made every man his own pope. It flattered man's pride, making him independent of every authority but himself. What was the use of a Church at all if everyone could be the author of his own religion? In the heat of passion and controversy the inconsistency of this doctrine did not deter people from accepting it.

Third, Luther denied free will in man, thus making him irresponsible for conduct. This was a most attractive doctrine, as it declared that man was not accountable for what he did. It left him at liberty to do with impunity whatever he chose. Man too often sins even with the fear of God's judgments over him. If he is told by a religious leader that he cannot help committing sin, it removes all restraint and leaves him free to gratify every inclination, no matter how base.

Fourth, Luther, in order to gain support for his cause, informed princes, lords, and persons in authority that, if he succeeded, the possessions of the Church would be turned over to them.

In hopes of being enriched by church lands and endowments, many of the nobility became firm supporters of Luther and by their aid and influence the people in large numbers embraced his doctrine.

When we contrast the austere morality of Catholicism with the licentiousness of Luther's doctrine, we are not surprised that many people were only too ready to listen to him and embrace his easy-going religion.

Here let it be said that Protestants of a later day, who inherited their religion, were not actuated by the same motives as their predecessors.

Cardinal Newman has said that Protestants, generally, are better than their religion, while Catholics are not as good, generally, as their religion.

Although Luther rejected ecclesiastical authority, he himself dogmatized with all the assurance of infallibility. People bowed down before him because he gave them what they wanted.

There is no doubt whatever that at the time of Luther's revolt the Church stood in need of reform in conduct. The Church herself felt the need of it, and great saints of the period wore praying earnestly for it. The human side of the Church was ailing and required the services of the spiritual physician.

But the remedy for an ailing patient is not to decapitate him. The reformers sought to remedy the ills of the Church by destroying her entirely. They denied that Christ established an authoritative Church to perpetuate His divine mission among mankind.

They affirmed that the Bible alone was God's message to mankind, and that each reader would be enlightened by the Holy Spirit to receive religious guidance from it. But the Bible does not baptize, administer the sacraments, or offer the Sacrifice of the Mass, all of which things Christ commanded His Church to do. It is evident that the Bible without an organized Church is not sufficient.

But the reformers were not guided by reason or logic. They wanted the Church out of the way and did all in their power to abolish it, without regard to reason or consequences.

And the consequences of the Reformation were dreadful from the very beginning. The common people, incited by Luther's licentious preaching, put it into practice in a way he little dreamed of. The peasants decided to abolish taxes and thrones; they perpetrated inhuman outrages; they destroyed churches, monasteries, and works of art; and they forced Germany into a war of class hatred between the nobles and peasants in which a hundred thousand peasants were slain.

As the reformers denied teaching authority in religion, everyone was free to make his own religion, which many proceeded to do. Strange to relate, however, although they proclaimed private judgment in religion, they persecuted those who differed from themselves. As a result of private judgment, Protestant sects multiplied to such an extent that soon there were hundreds of different and contradictory denominations, each claiming inspiration by the Holy Spirit.

The Reformation reformed nothing; rather it introduced new and worse evils in Christendom. Besides destroying religious unity among Christians, it fostered absolutism among rulers, resulting in that tyranny which eventually destroyed thrones and decapitated crowned heads.

Although the Reformation reformed nothing, it was the occasion of the Church's reforming herself.

The Council of Trent (1545) not only defined clearly and definitely the doctrines of the Church which the Protestants disputed, but also issued decrees for the correction of the abuses of conduct which had been the source of sorrow and harm to her and the faithful. It also brought about a notable Catholic revival, due in great measure to the religious orders, especially the Dominicans, Franciscans, and Jesuits.

The Catholic church, like her Founder, is human and divine; human in her members, divine in her constitution.

Because of Christ's guarantee of infallibility to His Church she cannot err in doctrine. Her members, however, except the pope speaking 'ex cathedra,' may err in doctrine; and also, from the pope down, they may err in conduct.

There will be sinners to the end of time because human nature is so very human. Christ came to save sinners and died for them. He established the sacrament of penance in order to enable those who might lose His friendship by sin to regain it.

He likened His Church to a field in which good seed was sown, but in which weeds also grew up.

At times the human element in the Church has asserted itself so strongly that unless she had been divinely sustained she would have perished long ago.

Christ called Himself the Good Shepherd who sought the sheep that strayed from the fold. His Church likewise is the shepherd of souls, sinners as well as saints.

But no matter how far afield the members of the Church may stray, she herself is always the light of the world, the guardian of faith and morals. Her doctrine can never mislead mankind with regard to belief or conduct.

The Reformation by its doctrine of private judgment has opened the floodgates of religious error upon the world. Rationalism, materialism, agnosticism, and countless other erroneous -isms rapidly followed in the wake of the Reformation.

Moreover, by its doctrine of the denial of the freedom

of the will, the Reformation has introduced animal conduct among mankind, making the law of the jungle,
which is the law of force and cunning, prevail among
many human beings. Rugged individualism, which means
every man for himself regardless of others, is one phase
of this code which declares that might is right.

Protestantism is fast disintegrating and will soon be a
social rather than a religious institution. Its preachers
now hold almost any belief from naturalism to the
borders of Catholicism.

The religion of the reformers has so changed that if its
founders came back to earth now, they could not recognize it. It began by proclaiming justification by faith only.
It has ended by declaring that faith does not matter, that
it is not what you believe that counts, but what you do.
Those who speak thus overlook the fact that what you
do depends on what you believe. The gangster believes
in violence and accordingly kills to rob. Action ordinarily
follows belief. So after all, what we believe does matter.

The Reformation doctrine has changed so radically
because it is the nature of error to change. Error in
seeking to rectify itself necessarily changes; but truth,
because it needs no rectification, is ever the same. That
is why the Catholic church has never changed its doctrine
and never will.

If the apostles came back to the world now they would
find the doctrine of the Apostles Creed the same in the
Church today as in early Christianity.

Because the Church does not change her doctrine it
does not follow that she is sterile or unprogressive. The
mathematical tables do not change, yet they are the basis
of all the calculation that enters into the construction of

our mightiest edifices. So it is with truth; although it is changeless it is, nevertheless, dynamic, and the source of all that is really good and beautiful in life.

The Reformation was in reality a challenge to revelation. Despite the fact that the reformers appealed solely to Scripture to uphold their doctrine, they really denied the most outstanding fact of the Gospels; namely, that Christ established a visible, corporate society called His Church, to which He guaranteed His divine presence to the end of time, and which He also guaranteed against religious error.

The reformers wanted to remain Christians and yet not be Catholics, so in order to discredit the Church without discrediting Christ, they said that His guarantee was not given to a visible and organized Church, but only to the Church of the spirit, which consisted of those who believed in His word. This was the real issue between the reformers and the Catholic church.

If Christ had founded a visible Church that Church could not err, and since the Catholic was the only visible Church of Christ, to accuse her of error was to denounce Christ. And so the reformers, to save themselves from condemning Christ, declared that He had not founded the Catholic church.

The issue, therefore, in brief was this: the existence of an authoritative Church versus a book-religion, the Bible, which everyone might interpret for himself. Of course there were many differences besides the above, but all were the result of individual religion against divinely authoritative religion.

Time is the test of truth, and time has been on the side of Catholicism.

The religion of the reformers is fast disappearing. Catholicism, however, is now the most vigorous, extensive, unified, and authoritative religion in the world. Truly Christ is with her as He foretold.

SUMMARY

The Reformation is the name given to an attempt to remedy some Church abuses by abolishing the Church altogether.

Christ foretold scandals in the Church. He guaranteed her infallibility, but did not guarantee her members impeccability.

Luther's method of reform was to destroy the Church.

He denied an authoritative, visible Church, and made each one his own authority.

Christ declared that His Church would never err in doctrine; Luther affirmed that she had erred. It is a choice between Christ and Luther.

Four reasons account for the rapid spread of the Reformation:

1. It declared that salvation was by faith only, giving great license to man's passions, and so forth.

2. By the doctrine of private judgment it flattered man's pride, making each one his own pope.

3. It denied freedom of the will, thus making man irresponsible for his conduct.

4. It gave to rulers the possessions of the Church, and thus secured their support.

There have always been abuses in the Church and always will be.

Among Christ's own little Church there was a traitor and a perjurer. But the sins of Judas and Peter did not detract from the truth or holiness of Christ.

The Reformation destroyed religious unity in Christendom. It also enabled rulers to exercise absolute and tyrannical power.

The Reformation began by proclaiming that faith alone mattered, and has ended by holding that belief does not matter, but conduct only.

Protestantism is fast breaking up. It has changed so much since its origin that its founders could not now recognize it.

Catholicism is the same today in doctrine as in the time of the apostles.

Error changes, truth does not.

The Reformation in brief was a personal religion opposed to an authoritative religion.

No fallible body can be the Church of the infallible Christ.

POINTS FOR DISCUSSION

1. Luther was justified in reforming the Church.

2. Luther held that the Church erred in doctrine as well as in conduct, hence it should be abolished.

3. Christ did not establish a visible Church.

4. Time is a great test of truth. Time justifies the Reformation.

5. Christ declared that they who believed would be saved; therefore faith alone is sufficient for salvation, as Luther claimed.

6. The rapid spread of the Reformation is proof of its claims.

7. Christ instituted only two sacraments, but the Catholic church has seven; hence she errs in doctrine.

8. Religion is a matter between God and the individual, hence there is no need of a Church as an intermediary.

CHAPTER XII

The Church Today

THE EXISTENCE OF THE CATHOLIC CHURCH today is a miracle. It is the only institution in the world now that existed as a corporate society in the time of Christ. No dynasty, no corporate organization, of the days of the Caesars now exists.

By a corporate society is meant an organization like the human body, consisting of various members united under a head which controls the entire body.

The Jews as a race existed even long before the Caesars, but the Jews have no supreme head, no high priest, no temple of sacrifice. From the time they rejected Christ, they have been a scattered people, without a king or a land that is ruled over by their own sovereign.

It is the same with the oriental dynasties, which, despite claims to great antiquity, have come and gone in the course of the past twenty centuries. But the papacy goes back in direct succession to the very days of Peter, and during all these centuries has exercised supreme authority over the universal Church established by her divine Founder.

This, let it be repeated, is a miracle, an achievement possible to divine power alone. It is evidence that Christ, the living Christ, is the invisible head of the Church of which His vicar is the visible head on earth.

It is a miracle because, contrary to the ordinary course of nature, the Church does not decay with years, but on the contrary grows more vigorous. This is proof that she is not merely a natural, but, as she claims to be, a supernatural institution.

The Catholic church is unique among all the institutions existing in the world today. It is the only religious organization which though worldwide is ruled by one supreme head.

The Episcopalians of the United States are not under the same jurisdiction as those of England.

Lutherans of Germany are governed by a different authority from those of America.

Baptist Church North is not of the same organization as that of the South.

And so with other religions. Buddhism, Hinduism, and other oriental religions have no corporate organization, and moreover are confined to certain territorial limits.

Although embracing all races and lands, the Catholic church is not identified with any nation or race. If it is called the Roman Catholic church it is because the seat of government has to be somewhere, and it is, and has been, at Rome.

Catholics have a right to be proud of their Church. If a Roman of old could proudly boast that he was a Roman citizen, the Catholic today may justly be proud that he is a Catholic.

For, truly, a Catholic is a member of the most glorious organization that this world has known. It is true that in some countries at certain times there is not much external glory to the Church. Because of persecution or other causes the Church is, at times, like Christ before Pilate. Pilate and his court represented the power and wealth of Jerusalem, while Christ was a nobody, apparently. But Christ now reigns, while Pilate and his courtiers are but a name.

A great temptation to Catholics in some countries, like England and the United States, is the fact that the prominent, wealthy, and influential citizens are mostly not of the Catholic faith. The respectability of Protestants thus becomes a temptation to Catholics, who may wonder how it is that these distinguished persons are wrong and their social inferiors right. But Pilate and his distinguished court were wrong, and Christ, the despised one, was right.

Christ declared that His kingdom was not of this world. But although not *of* this world, the Church is *in* the world, and from the beginning has been the glory of mankind by her achievements, her conquests, her standards of belief and conduct, her influence on civilization, her inspiration of the arts and sciences, and her heroic labors for the material welfare of man here and his eternal welfare hereafter.

Above all, the Church is glorious for the fact that, although for twenty centuries she has been assailed by the most persistent and intense attacks from without and hampered by human frailty from within, she stands today before the world as the most vigorous and effective barrier against the various forces which threaten to destroy civilization. Communism, materialism, rationalism, and all the *-isms* which have led mankind astray find in the Catholic church their strongest opponent.

Likewise the social vices that tend to undermine the family, which is the basis of the state, find their most effective restraint in the doctrine and practices of the Catholic church. Divorce, birth control, sex promiscuity, obscene plays and literature—these and other morally destructive practices and diversions would work indescribable harm to society were it not that they were held in check by Catholic standards and conduct. Not that all Catholics are examplars of their Church's standards of behavior; but despite the black sheep of the fold, the Church presents a solid front against the inroads of theories and practices dangerous to human welfare.

The Catholic church is the only church which has made no concession of doctrine to worldly demands. She alone proclaims now every article of the Apostles Creed, she alone upholds Christ's teaching on marriage, divorce, the Mass, and the divine guidance of the Holy Spirit by which the Church cannot err in doctrine.

She alone declares that a fallible church cannot be the church of the infallible Christ. She alone speaks and is heard as the voice of God. It is very remarkable that the Catholic church, which makes no concession to the world, grows constantly stronger, while the churches which make concessions are gradually decaying.

As evidence of the Church's vitality today let us here consider briefly some of the many aspects of its growth and activity.

In the United States there are some twenty million Catholics. In the United States the Church has had a more or less free field for expansion and for her activities. The result is shown in the marvelous growth of her ministry and institutions.

In the United States there are at present, besides the apostolic delegate, four cardinals, fourteen archbishops, one hundred and eighteen bishops, sixty seminaries, ninety-seven colleges and universities, thirty thousand priests, and over one hundred and twenty thousand religious brothers and nuns.

There are more Catholic institutions of higher learning in the United States than of all other denominations combined. Catholic academies and high schools abound in every part of the country, to say nothing of the thousands of parochial schools.

When we reflect that these educational institutions are supported by the voluntary contributions of those who are not blessed with much of this world's goods, and who consequently make great sacrifices for religious education, we may form some idea of the character and strength of the Church which inspires such heroic efforts on the part of her adherents.

Sacrifice is the language of love and loyalty. The sacrifices which Catholics make for religious education and for divine worship attest the love and loyalty they have for Holy Mother Church.

In Europe and some other lands the Catholic church has not always been free to exercise her ministry and influence, with the result that, in some places, for the time being, she is not in the flourishing condition in which we find her in our own country. But though she is persecuted, enslaved, and hated in those lands, she is not despised.

The very fact that she is so hated and persecuted is a tribute to her vitality and influence. People do not fight shadows nor hate what is feeble. The Catholic church is feared and hated by the enemies of religion because she is the sole church which stands in their way.

They know that if they can destroy the Catholic church they will destroy supernatural religion. They also know that if they destroy every other religion in the world, yet do not destroy the Catholic church, Christianity will prevail. That is why the Catholic church is the shock troops of Christianity.

It is the Catholic church which must bear the brunt of the assaults made by opponents of religion in those countries whose governments wish to rule regardless of justice. If the Catholic church would stand by idly and see human and divine rights outraged, she would not be the object of the hatred and violence of the enemies of law and order.

The Catholic church has never been persecuted except when, loyal to her divine Founder, she has opposed injustice or immorality.

The Church is not surprised at persecution. She does not expect better treatment than that of her divine Founder. He, the most perfect being ever in this world, was maligned, hated, and persecuted because He stood out against the injustice and immorality of His day.

It is the same with His Church, which for upholding His standards meets with His treatment by the world.

But despite hatred and persecution the Church goes on, generation after generation, doing the work of her Master, meeting with the opposition He incurred, and because He is with her, surviving it all. The Church not only survives, but continually grows.

Not content with laboring for those who are already her children, she sends her missionaries to distant lands to bring the kingdom of God to those who are in ignorance and error. There is not a corner of the world, no matter how remote or how lacking in attractive features, where a Catholic priest may not be found, living among its people, sharing their mode of life, and at the same time leading them to higher and better things. Missionary nuns are also sacrificing themselves in the same way in every part of the half-civilized or savage world.

And it is to be noted that these modern apostles serve without recompense, and most of them without the expectation of ever returning to civilization and the comforts of home and friends. The zeal and sacrifice of the Catholic missionaries of the twentieth century compare favorably with the missionary labors of the apostolic age. This is evidence of the vitality of the Catholic church after centuries of conflict with a hostile world.

A most gratifying indication of the flourishing condition of the Church today is its devotional life, not only among the clergy and in religious communities, but also among the laity.

Daily Mass and Communion, monthly First Friday devotions in honor of the Sacred Heart, frequent novenas, annual missions, and various other services which are not of obligation, but nevertheless widely attended, attest the splendid devotional life in the Church today.

Besides these devotional practices there are the various organizations whose purpose it is to foster piety and zeal in their members. Pious sodalities for men, women, and children; confraternities of the rosary and scapular; societies of St. Vincent de Paul for relief of the poor; Holy Name societies for honoring the name of Jesus—these and numerous other organizations of piety give evidence of an active spiritual life in the Church today.

A distinctive feature of the Church at present is Catholic Action. This means the co-operation of the laity with the clergy for the welfare of Church and state.

The forces of evil are strongly organized, and to meet them it is necessary to organize against them. Under the leadership of the bishops there are established in various dioceses social-study clubs, which endeavor by Christian methods to remedy the evil conditions which communists and other such groups would remedy by revolution and destruction.

Besides these social and pious organizations and activities, there are the Catholic summer schools and postgraduate schools, to enable the teaching orders of nuns and brothers and the studious laity to equip themselves for the exacting demands of the present day. The Legion of Decency keeps an eye on the press, radio, movies, and stage in order to correct misrepresentations of Catholic faith and practice.

The test of any cause is the sacrifices its adherents are willing to make for it. Judged by this test the Catholic church stands out as the strongest religious organization in the world. Both in the United States and in European and other countries, Catholics are making tremendous sacrifices for their religion.

In our own country the upkeep of the parochial schools imposes a very great burden on pastors and people, yet they generously bear it, realizing that if this generation be without religious schools, the next generation will hardly need churches.

Financial sacrifices are only one of the sacrifices that Catholics make for their religion. Socially and professionally and in ordinary business employment they often meet with unjust discrimination, but bear it in the spirit of Christian fortitude.

Abroad, especially in some countries of Europe,

Catholics are persecuted to almost the same extent as were the early Christians.

But instead of surrendering to the forces of evil they stand firmly for the faith, thus giving the world a heroic example of Christian fortitude.

A cause that is not worth suffering and fighting for is not of much worth. For twenty centuries Catholics have suffered and fought heroically for the faith. Today, on account of the forces of evil let loose on the world, Catholics are called upon to show in a special manner their loyalty and fidelity to the Church of Christ.

It is a cheering and inspiring consideration in the present warfare between the Church and the world that the head of the Catholic church, the vicar of Christ, is the most respected and most influential ruler in the world. When he speaks the world listens, whether in reverence or concern. With no power but that of the spirit, he addresses mankind as did Christ in His day, without fear or favor.

Under such a leader Catholics are prepared to fight the good fight, knowing that in God's own time they will receive the reward of fidelity.

The Church in the world today is worthy of her divine Founder. True, she has her shortcomings, being human in her members; but despite human frailty she upholds the standards of her Founder in a world that is floundering amidst error and evil. Let it be repeated, the existence of the Catholic church today is evidence that she is not merely natural but supernatural, for no merely natural institution could survive the assaults from without and the defections from within which have been her portion for twenty centuries. The past is guarantee of the future.

Christ said: "Behold I am with you all days even to the consummation of the world" (Matthew 28:20).

Only God could utter those words with effect. The fact that the Church is with us now shows that when Christ made that promise His words were uttered with effect. We know, therefore, that the Church founded by Him is divine, and that by being faithful to her, we shall be made partakers of divine glory.

One of the bitterest forces arrayed against the Catholic church today is communism, which denies the existence of a personal God, future life, human liberty, personal and property rights. It substitutes worship of the state for the worship of God. Its doctrines are opposed to both divine and human rights. Its chief center is Russia, whose people are now virtually enslaved. The strongest natural argument against communism is that in Russia, where it is applied in its fullness to every detail of life, the country is a vast prison-house. Communism and Catholicism are absolutely incompatible.

It is the bounden duty of Catholics to take a strong stand against communism. In order to get the support of any and every group, communism now pretends to be working for the sole welfare of the masses. This is a masked battery whose ultimate purpose is to destroy the very foundation of Christian society.

SUMMARY

The Catholic church has within herself the supernatural vitality to withstand assaults from without and frailty within.

Today, after twenty centuries of existence, she is the most vigorous and extensive corporative organization in the world.

She is the only institution of the days of the Caesars now existing—a proof that she is more than natural.

The tendency of everything natural is to decay with age; but the Church, because she is supernatural, grows stronger rather than weaker with the years.

In the United States today there are twenty million Catholics, one apostolic delegate, four cardinals, fourteen archbishops, one hundred and eighteen bishops, sixty seminaries, ninety-seven colleges and universities, over a hundred thousand religious brothers and nuns, and thirty thousand priests.

The Church is the most effective influence against communism, materialism, and the various social evils, such as divorce, birth control, and so forth.

An evidence of her vitality is shown in her devotional life as seen in daily Mass and Communion, First Friday devotions, sodalities, retreats, missions, and so forth.

The Church today meets with opposition as Christ did in His day. But she holds aloft His standard without compromise.

Clergy and people make great sacrifices for religious education, especially for parochial and high schools.

The main struggle of the Church now is against irreligion in various forms.

She upholds spiritual against material standards, eternal versus temporal welfare, although she does more for real human welfare than any other organization.

She is active in missionary work, her devoted priests and nuns sacrificing themselves heroically in distant and barbarous lands in order to bring the true religion to those in ignorance and error.

Christ, as He promised, is with the Church, and will be to the end of the world.

POINTS FOR DISCUSSION

1. The Church in the United States is now in decline —witness its lack of influence on public morals.

2. The Church presents an appearance of strength, but in reality is fast losing ground.

3. Most of the members of the Catholic church are

either ignorant or poorly educated. The Church has lost her hold on the intelligent classes.

4. The Church silences the clergy who champion the cause of the masses.

5. The Church emphasizes her material progress, but is blind to her spiritual decline.

6. The parochial schools are an unjustifiable burden on the faithful.

7. There is altogether too much insistence on money in many Catholic pulpits, instead of the preaching of the Gospel.

8. The Church is opposed by a large part of our population.

9. Why should Catholics be unalterably opposed to communism?

10. Communism aims at curing social evils which oppress the masses.

11. Communism in the United States aims solely at the welfare of the masses, as is clear from the fact that communism here desires to co-operate with any party which has the good of the people at heart.

CHAPTER XIII

The Existence of God

BY THE TERM 'GOD' IS MEANT an eternal, personal being, the author and ruler of the world.

There are some people who deny that there is such a being. They affirm that everything is matter, and that consequently matter is the source of everything that exists, man included. Those who assert that everything is matter are known as materialists. There are others who assert that there may or may not be a personal God, but that it is impossible to know for certain. Such persons are known as agnostics because they assert that God is not knowable. Then there are the atheists, who deny absolutely the existence of God as a personal author and ruler of the world. Deists are those who believe in God but not the God of revelation—that is, the God of Christians. An infidel is one who does not believe that Christ is God, and who consequently rejects Christianity.

Our present consideration concerns materialists, agnostics, and atheists. Deists and infidels were refuted by establishing the divinity of Christ, which was done in a previous chapter. Our purpose now is to show that there exists a personal, intelligent being, the author and ruler of the world. By the world is meant the universe; that is, all creation. The earth which we inhabit and the visible firmament which surrounds us are part of the universe. As the whole is greater than any part, and contains at least whatever excellence there is in any part, it is logical

134

to conclude that the author of the universe possesses, at least, whatever perfections this world of ours possesses or postulates. This observation is made because there are some opponents of deity who assert that, although the law and order of this, our visible world, may indicate an intelligent designer, the cause of this, our world, may not be the cause of the universe at large. Here let it be said, once for all, that if the cause of our visible world be not the first cause of all things, it ultimately came from the first cause, which, consequently, possesses eminently whatever is possessed by every other cause.

In our demonstration we shall proceed as follows. We will first show that there is an intelligent author of the world, and then that this personal being is ultimately the first cause, itself uncaused—that is, always existing, never having had a beginning, eternal.

As we look out into the world and perceive the marvelous co-ordination of its various forces, the adaptation of one part to another, and the way everything works harmoniously towards a definite end, we are forced to conclude that there is design and intelligent direction in the world. If you have ever been aboard a battleship you were, no doubt, in admiration of its construction and operation. Although it consists of thousands of parts, it is a structural unit. Every part has a special function in the smooth workings of the huge whole. The pressure of a button sets into operation various devices which do the work of a thousand men. Massive guns as well as delicate instruments respond to the slightest touch of the operator. Mighty engines drive the immense bulk through the water at astonishing speed. A turn of the wheel directs the Titan at the will of the navigator. Yet a battleship, superb as it is, is but a clumsy contrivance compared to the marvelous mechanism of the universe. A battleship, nevertheless, would be an impossibility without an intelligent designer and builder. The man of ordinary common sense would laugh at anyone who asserted that a battleship *just happened,* that its exquisite co-ordination and adaptation did not require an intelligent maker.

Again, have you ever examined the intricate works of your watch? Numerous parts are so arranged that they work together for one purpose, that of indicating the time of day. A sensible person would regard you as bereft of reason if you maintained that a watch did not have an intelligent designer and maker. The finest watch ever made, however, is a botch compared to the world clock. The world clock never loses a second and never requires winding. The Naval Observatory at Washington regulates the official time of the nation by the world clock high up in the sky. Every day, as the sun crosses the meridian at noon, the official time-piece of the nation is adjusted to the solar clock.

Is it any wonder that of old it was said that only the fool says there is no God? No one but a fool would declare that a battleship or an exquisite watch had no intelligent maker. Yet these wonderful creations are babies' toys compared to the marvelous structure of the universe.

The greatest scientific men have seen in the universe the clearest evidence of a personal God. Sir Isaac Newton speaks as follows: "The existence of a being endowed with intelligence and wisdom is a necessary inference from a study of celestial mechanics." Lamarck, founder of organic evolutionism, declares that "nature, being subject to law, cannot therefore be God. She is the wondrous product of His almighty will. Thus the will of God is everywhere expressed by the laws of nature, since these laws originate from Him" (*Système Analytique,* p. 43). Lord Kelvin in his presidential address to the British Scientific Association said: "Nature declares that there is one ever-acting creator and ruler."

Both science and common sense proclaim that the order, unity, harmony, and design of the universe demand an intelligent being as its author. This intelligent being, which reason postulates as the origin and cause of all things, we call the Creator. By unaided reason, moreover, we may know more about the Creator than that He is an intelligent being. Reason tells us that the Creator of the world is eternal; that is, that He existed always, never having had a beginning. We do not comprehend how a being could exist without having had a beginning, but reason forces us to admit such a being. For unless something had always existed, nothing would ever have existed. We see things about us and naturally infer that someone made them. The world was made by someone. Either this maker was the first cause of all things or not. If he was not, someone else made him. We can keep going back and back until finally we reach the first cause, before which no other existed. This first cause was itself uncaused; that is, it had no beginning, it existed necessarily.

As said previously, we cannot *imagine* anything that had no beginning, but we can *understand* that there must be such a being, otherwise nothing would ever have come into existence. Unless an uncaused first cause existed, there never would be anything. The fact that reason demands but cannot explain the existence of an uncaused first cause shows the limitation of the human intellect. On the one hand, reason is obliged to accept the existence of the first cause as uncaused; and on the other hand, it has to admit that such a cause is incomprehensible, since we cannot conceive how a thing never had a beginning.

But reason is obliged to admit many things which it finds incomprehensible; for example, the flight of the earth through space at enormous speed, yet always in a fixed orbit. What holds it to its course? Scientists say gravity. But what is gravity? Nobody understands what this force is, yet reason obliges us to accept some such force, call it what we may.

We should not be surprised that we do not comprehend God. We do not understand ourselves, let alone our Creator. We do not understand how the food we eat becomes our living body, nor the subtle process by which speech reveals our thoughts to others. If man is a mystery to himself, he should not be surprised that his Maker is a mystery to him. We know, therefore, from observation and reason that the world has an intelligent maker, and that this maker, if not the first cause, came eventually from a first cause which itself was uncaused. This uncaused first cause we call God, the eternal, intelligent, personal author and ruler of the world.

Besides the argument from design, there are various other proofs for the existence of God, the author and ruler of the world. Let us begin with the proof furnished by the fact that the world is under law. The world *is* under law. This is evident from the regularity manifested in the firmament, from the invariable reactions of chemical elements, from the fixed resultant of physical forces, and from the iron rule of instinct in the brute kingdom. But law supposes a lawgiver. A lawgiver must be an intelligent being. Therefore the world is under an intelligent being, whom we call God, the author and ruler of the world.

Nature, except man, is under fixed law, from the magnificence of the firmament to the tiny grain of wheat which dies in order to produce multiplied life. To control the forces of the universe demands not only power but intelligence. The lawgiver of the world is, therefore, a powerful and intelligent being who, if not the first cause, postulates eventually a powerful and intelligent first cause, God.

A further argument for the existence of an intelligent author and ruler of the world is furnished by conscience, nature's voice, which tells man to do what is right and avoid what is wrong. Man is the only being of visible creation not under fixed laws. All nature except man is governed by physical, chemical, or plant laws or by animal instinct. Man alone has free will. But although man is free, he is not without responsibility. He must freely serve his Maker or incur the consequences.

Conscience is the voice of nature directing man how to serve his Maker. Conscience supposes a judge. A judge must be an intelligent being; therefore conscience proves the existence of an intelligent being to whom mankind is subject. Conscience would be meaningless unless there was a tribunal to determine whether its mandates were observed, and to punish or reward accordingly. This tribunal is the author of conscience; namely, the lawgiver of mankind, the author of nature, God.

Since conscience is as universal as mankind, it pertains

to man's nature; that is, it is natural to man. Whatever is natural has the author of nature for its author, as is evident. Conscience accordingly proclaims the existence of an intelligent being, God.

The universal belief of mankind is another proof of the existence of God. Again we say that whatever pertains to man everywhere and at all times is natural to him and as such has the Maker of man for its author. Speech, for instance, pertains to man wherever found, and is consequently natural to him. Belief in a personal power above nature, who is associated with the life and conduct of each individual and to whom worship is due, is as universal as mankind. At one time it was thought that certain savage tribes had no religious worship. Later when missionaries came to know these tribes, and had won their confidence, it was found that they practiced deity worship, but that they concealed it from strangers because they suspected them of hostile intentions. When we say that mankind everywhere worships a personal power above, it is not to be understood that this personal power is the God of Christians. But the worship was always directed to a personal ruling power above who controlled nature and mankind. This was their idea of God. Universal belief of mankind in God is, therefore, natural to man, and has the Maker of man for its author, and is consequently true.

Finally, we come to a proof which to some people is the most convincing of all the arguments for the existence of a personal, intelligent first cause of all creation. The proof runs thus:

There is intelligence in the world now, hence it must have come from an intelligent source. Eventually this intelligent source is the first cause, hence the first cause is an intelligent being, whom we call God. There is no evasion of this argument if one is logical. It requires intelligence even to argue against intelligence. No intelligent being can deny the existence of intelligence, nor can he deny that intelligence must come from an intelligent source. Just as life must come from life, so must a spiritual faculty come from a spiritual source. Man's intellect is a spiritual faculty, by which he is able to reason, calculate, and invent. This intellectual faculty has for its ultimate cause a personal, intellectual being. And that is what is meant by the term God.

If belief in God did not imply living by God's laws, very few persons would be atheists. There may be various reasons for atheism and other systems of God denial. In some cases it may be the desire for freedom from moral restraint. In other cases it may be the existence of evil in the world, which to some minds seems incompatible with a wise and powerful Creator. A third reason assigned for atheism may be man's inability to comprehend God, leading him to reject what seems incomprehensible.

The reasons assigned for the denial of God, accordingly, may be either moral or intellectual. If a man denies God because he wants to have his own way in life and be a law to himself, rather than be submissive to the law of conscience, such a one needs our prayers, for he is on the broad road that Christ warned against. If the problem of evil deters man from belief in God, he should reflect that before passing judgment on a matter he should have all the data concerning it. Man knows only the present, and since God's plans embrace the future as well as the present, man is not in a position to judge of God's ways. Man compared to God is less than the infant at its mother's breast. A soldier in the ranks is not qualified to judge the orders and arrangements of the army, for he does not know the information and plans of the general. Yet man, who received his reason from God, would reject its giver because he cannot explain the reasons for the Creator's dispensations. Evil is a mystery, undoubtedly, but reason tells us that we may trust the author of reason.

Finally, we come to those who for various intellectual difficulties connected with physical or philosophical matters cannot reconcile belief in God with their scientific theories. These persons should realize that the author of the world is also the author of truth, and if at times theories of science or philosophy are at variance with the existence of God, it is because such theories are false. It is possible for theories of philosophy or science to mislead, but it is not possible for a philosopher or scientist to exist without a Creator who had at least as much intelligence as the wisest philosopher or scientist that ever lived. If any theory comes in conflict with the existence of God, it is absolutely certain to be false. Theories come and go. They change constantly. What is proclaimed true today is found false tomorrow.

But one thing never changes, and that is the principle that an effect cannot be greater than its cause. The intelligence displayed in the design, law, and order of the universe had an intellectual cause. That cause we call the personal, eternal Creator.

Man needs God. In the vicissitudes of life, unless we can look beyond to a being who is wise and just, and who in His own time will recompense those who serve and trust Him, life would too often be only a cruel and desperate ordeal. Knowing, however, that life is but a period of probation on which eternity depends, man can cheerfully face its vicissitudes if he realizes that a wise Creator and ruler presides over the affairs of the world, and that He will render to everyone according to his works.

SUMMARY

By the term 'God' is meant an eternal, personal being, the author and ruler of the world.

Materialists, who assert that everything is matter, deny a personal God.

Agnostics declare that God is unknowable and that we cannot say what He is.

Atheists altogether deny the existence of God.

Against these deniers of a personal God we prove from the design manifested in the universe that its author is an intelligent being.

The universe manifests design.

1. Design supposes a designer. A designer is an intelligent being; therefore the author of the universe is an intelligent being, a person.

2. The universe is under law. Law supposes a lawgiver. A lawgiver must be an intelligent being. Therefore the world is under an intelligent ruler, God.

3. Conscience supposes a legislator and judge, since it commands man to do what is right and refrain from what is wrong. A legislator and judge is an intelligent being.

4. Every race and tribe believes in some personal power above who is associated with the life and conduct of each one, and to whom worship is due. This belief in a deity, being universal, is natural to man and has the author of nature for its author, and is therefore true.

5. There is intelligence in the world now; hence its source must be intelligent. God is the source of all things, hence He is an intelligent being, a person.

The maker and designer of the world is either the first cause of all things or else comes from the first cause. We can keep going back and back until we come to a cause beyond which there is no other cause. This final cause is itself uncaused because there was nothing prior to it. That is, it always existed, never had a beginning, is eternal. This first cause is the source, eminently, of every other cause.

Hence law, order, design, and intelligence come from this first cause, which possesses every known attribute and more.

This first cause is God, a personal, intelligent being.

POINTS FOR DISCUSSION

1. There is no personal God, for the entire universe is matter only.

2. God must be an infinite being, hence unknowable by finite reason.

3. Atheists are justified in denying God altogether, since an all-wise and powerful being is incompatible with the evil in the world.

4. The apparent design in the universe is no proof of intelligence, since no intelligent designer would have his work marred by earthquakes, tornadoes, and other catastrophes of nature.

5. Conscience is no proof of God, for conscience is only the result of experience and convention.

6. Many tribes outside civilization give no evidence of conscience. This shows that conscience is the result of civilization.

7. Why does the fact that the universe is under law attest a personal God?

8. Why can not chance explain the design and laws of the universe?

CHAPTER XIV

THE IMMORTALITY OF THE SOUL

THE IMMORTALITY OF THE SOUL is a most important consideration. Indeed, it is vital to man's right understanding of life and to his conduct in life. If man's career ends with the grave, he need have no regard for anything except present consequences. But if the grave is not the end, but only the portal to a future life, man must shape his mortal career in such a way that it will not imperil his immortal destiny.

It makes all the difference in the world whether man is made for time or eternity. If man is made for this life only, he is justified in getting all he can out of it, regardless of any future considerations. Today there are various false theories, dressed up most attractively in order to persuade man that this present life is man's only existence. This false view of life is the basis of materialism, communism, determinism, and all the other *-isms* which proclaim that man is but a high-grade animal and that his end is the same as that of the brute.

The immortality of the soul is made known by supernatural and natural reasons. Supernaturally it is made known by Jesus Christ, eternal truth. "Amen, amen, I say unto you, he that believeth in Me hath everlasting life" (John 6:47). Again Christ said: "I am the resurrection and the life. He that believeth in Me, although he be dead, shall live" (John 11:25). We know, therefore, from divine revelation that man's career extends into eternity. But apart from revelation, reason, unaided, proclaims the immortality of the soul.

To begin, let us define what is meant by the immortality of the soul. It means that man's soul will never cease to exist, that it will live on forever. We know that the material part of man, his body, will decay. But besides his body, man has a soul which is not material. By faith we are assured of the resurrection of the body, even though death claims it for a while. But the soul, unlike the body, can never cease to be.

The reason why the soul can never cease to exist is that it is spiritual. A spiritual substance is by its nature indestructible because destruction comes about by disintegration, or the separation of a thing into its constituent parts. The soul has no parts, so it is by its very nature indestructible.

These statements require proof. We shall first show that destruction of a thing is effected by the separation of its parts. Take a piece of wood, for example. It remains wood, no matter how much it be reduced by cutting or shaping. In order to destroy it as wood, the various elements which compose it must be separated from each other by fire or chemicals or some such method. When a piece of wood is put in the fire, the heat breaks up its elements, some of which go off as light, some as heat, some as gases, and there is left only the ashes. The wood is no longer wood; it has ceased to exist as wood. Destruction of a thing, accordingly, is effected by the separation of the parts which compose it.

Now, we say that the soul, being spiritual, has no parts, and consequently cannot be disintegrated or destroyed. But how do we know that the soul is not material; that is, that it has no parts? For several reasons, of which the first is that the soul, whole and entire, can perfectly reflect on itself; that is, turn back completely on its whole self. Nothing that has parts, nothing that is material, can act upon itself, but only on something else. For instance, the tip of your little finger can touch various parts of your body, but it cannot touch—that is, turn back completely on—itself. One material part can touch another part, but cannot turn back—that is, touch or reflect —on itself.

The soul, however, because it is a simple substance— that is, one having no parts—can act or reflect perfectly on itself. For instance, I can put myself under my own observation, examine myself, approve or disapprove of myself, analyze myself as if I were analyzing another. By so doing, the soul—that is, the spiritual part of myself—reflects wholly on its whole self. Now, nothing that has parts, nothing that is material, can thus turn back on itself by complete reflection of the whole upon the whole. One part of a material thing can touch another part, but no material thing, as a whole, can wholly turn back on itself. We see, therefore, that the soul is spiritual, and as such is by nature indestructible.

Since the spirituality of the soul is the main reason for affirming its indestructibility, we shall give further proof that the soul is spiritual. The soul can deal with things which have no material existence, such as futurity, responsibility, liability, and so forth. Such things are known as ideas; they belong to the realm of the mind; they have no material existence.

There are other notions which have no material existence in themselves, but which are derived or abstracted from what is material. These notions are called abstract ideas. For example, honor, bravery, generosity are abstract ideas. These things have no material existence. Everything material has size, color, weight, and so forth. What size is honor? What is its color? How much does it weigh? No one ever saw honor. What does it look like? How then do we get the idea of honor? By the power of abstraction and generalizing which the soul possesses.

For instance, we see people doing noble and generous things, and note that there is a certain distinctive quality displayed in such actions. This quality, which is immaterial, we call 'honor.' It is a notion originated by the mind, a process possible to a spiritual faculty only, since it is the result of comparison, analysis, and deduction. This power of forming abstract ideas, or of *idealizing,* which the soul possesses gives another proof of its spirituality, which to some people is the most convincing of all the proofs.

A third proof of the spirituality of the soul is found in a power possessed by man which depends upon his ability to form abstract ideas. This is his power of inventing, of producing by thought and reflection something which did not exist before.

Our faith tells us that man is made to the image and likeness of God. By his power of inventing and composing, man is, in a certain sense, a creator, not as God is a creator, but nevertheless a creator. When God creates He makes something out of nothing, but when man creates he uses something pre-existing, but nevertheless produces something new, something that never existed before. Radio waves existed before Marconi invented wireless transmission. Electricity existed before Edison gave us the arc light. Radio transmission and the arc light are nevertheless creations of a sort, and show that man is indeed an image or reflection of the Creator. Hamlet is Shakespeare's dramatic, as Parsifal is Wagner's operatic, creation. When a genius gives us a poem or a musician originates a melody, it is an effect absolutely impossible to a merely material cause.

It is because man, and man alone, has a spiritual soul, that he is the only being in the world who has ever invented a machine or composed a melody. This alone is sufficient to show that there is an essential difference between man and the brute creation. This essential difference is in the nature of man's soul. No brute, no matter how high in the scale of animal intelligence, has ever devised anything artificial for maintenance or defense. Contrast this static condition with the many human inventions for safety and defense.

Man's power of invention proves that he has a spiritual soul, for mere matter is incapable of calculating, composing, adapting, and inventing. Animal instinct marvelously directs the brute in all that it does, but instinct is an iron law of nature, always acting in the same way, fixed and determined by the Author of nature. Instinct in animals is sometimes mistaken for intelligence. It is not, however, intelligence in the true sense. An animal does not reason in what it does, but acts blindly, although unerringly. Instinct is the intelligence of the Creator guiding the animal in what pertains to its nature and needs. The bird, the bee, and the beaver construct wonderful habitations, but always in the same way, and without being taught and without knowing the principles of construction. Man reasons out what he does, modifies his procedure to suit conditions, and provides means adapted to various ends. Man displays real intelligence in all that he undertakes.

Man's soul, therefore, is shown to be spiritual by its power of perfectly reflecting on itself, by its power of idealizing, and by its power of creating or inventing. And since it is spiritual, it has no parts and thus by nature is not subject to destruction, and must consequently be immortal.

Besides the above reasons for the immortality of the soul, there is another taken from the very nature of man. Man has a natural instinct or craving for perfect happiness. The Author of nature does not create anything in vain; hence this craving or instinct for perfect happiness must have an object to satisfy it. Nothing, however, in this life gives perfect happiness, and hence there must be another life which does satisfy this natural instinct. That other life must be everlasting, because happiness that does not last forever would not be perfect.

A few words of explanation are in order regarding these statements. Man has a natural desire for perfect happiness because wherever man exists this desire exists. That the Creator makes nothing in vain is evident from the fact that hunger and thirst have as objects to satisfy them food and drink. Man has always craved perfect happiness, yet never has found it, for no happiness that is not lasting will perfectly satisfy man. Happiness that may end any day or hour is not perfect. Yet the happiness of this life is always uncertain, as experience attests. In the next life, no matter how great the happiness, if it were destined to end, it would not be perfect, for the shadow of the end would always cloud it. Hence the desire or instinct in man for perfect happiness demands another and everlasting life.

There are two other arguments for a life beyond, but not necessarily for everlasting life. These arguments are based on the justice of the Creator and on the universal belief of mankind in a future life. With regard to the justice of the Creator, it is clear that unless there is a life beyond, where the good will be rewarded and the wicked punished, God often allows those who are faithful to Him to meet only adversity, while those who are disloyal to Him enjoy prosperity. In other words, if this life is all, the Creator sometimes rewards those who break His laws and chastises those who observe them. The Creator would not be a just ruler if He thus treated His subjects, so we know that there is a life beyond where He will justify His dealings with mankind. We know that the Creator is just, because whatever sense of justice we have comes from Him as its source.

Finally we come to the proof based on the universal belief of mankind in a future life. As said previously, whatever pertains to man always and everywhere, is natural to him and has for its source the Author of nature. Whatever has for its origin the Author of nature is true; hence belief in a future life is true. This demonstration does not prove that future life is everlasting, but only that there is a future life. Taken, however, in conjunction with man's instinct for perfect happiness, which implies perpetuity, it forms a substantial argument for the immortality of the soul.

Now that we know from reason as well as from faith that the soul is immortal, we can realize the full meaning of those words of Christ: "What doth it profit a man if he gain the whole world and suffer the loss of his own soul?" (Matthew 16:26). The world with all its allurements will eventually cease to exist. The soul will never cease to exist.

That is what gives it such importance for weal or woe. Hence Christ said: "What exchange shall a man give for his soul?" (Matthew 16:26). He, the Creator, could name nothing that would be the soul's equivalent. He, as it were, placed the soul in one arm of the balance and the world in the other, and declared that the soul outweighed in value the whole world.

The denial of the immortality of the soul tends to degrade man to the level of the brute. It makes him a creature of time rather than of eternity, with the result that might and cunning too often replace justice and charity as the law of life. Man is naturally selfish, and unless his inclinations for pleasure, wealth, and power be restrained by the realization that there is an eternal tribunal before which he must one day stand, it is to be feared that natural morality and virtue will, only too often, give way before the pressure of passion. Even with belief in eternity, life is a struggle against worldly allurements; but without faith in a life to come, man is liable to adopt the principle of conduct which proclaims: "Let us eat, drink, and be merry, for tomorrow we die." This is the principle of life on which communism rests, and the principle of the gangster, of the rugged individualist, and of those generally whose inability to recognize any values other than earthly ones makes them threats to the security of society and the welfare of the individual.

Here it is advisable to say a word about determinism, a false theory which proclaims that man's conduct is determined or governed by material forces, and that consequently there is no such thing as free will. Against this theory we have the fact that determinists themselves are a living refutation of determinism. For if man is not free, what is the use of reasoning with him? If his mind is determined by material forces, what is the use of trying to persuade him? If man is not free to change, to deliberate, and to decide, he is not open to conviction. We do not argue with a volcano or hurricane. Moreover, if there is no free will, there is no criminal, no injustice. An earthquake is not a criminal, neither is man if he is determined by physical forces. A determinist has no right to complain of the gangster who robs or wounds him, any more than he has to complain of the tide which overtakes him on the beach.

It is true that we shall one day die, that our earthly career shall end. But death is the gateway to immortality. The grave is not the goal, but the starting point, of man's final destiny. The Creator would be a monster of cruelty if this life were the whole of man's existence. The world is filled with people who, through no fault of their own, are victims of injustice, cruelty, poverty, disease, disgrace, and despondency. Unless there is another life where Providence will justify the inequalities and injustices of this life, the Creator and Ruler of the world would be a veritable tyrant.

We know that the Creator is merciful and just, for it is from Him that we derive our sense of mercy and justice. We know, therefore, from the observation of life, and from the nature of God, that man has not here a lasting city but that he is on his way to his home in eternity.

SUMMARY

The immortality of the soul means that it will never cease to exist.

PROOF I. The soul is spiritual. What is spiritual cannot be destroyed, for destruction comes from the separation of a thing into its parts. A spiritual substance has no parts, and hence is by nature indestructible. How do we know that the soul is spiritual? Because it can reflect perfectly on itself. Nothing material can do that. 'Reflecting on itself' means turning back completely on itself. I myself can analyze, examine, inspect, and judge myself. Nothing material can do that.

We say that destruction of a thing comes about by the separation of its parts. Wood, for example, remains wood no matter how much cut or shaped. It is destroyed as wood by fire or chemicals, by which its parts are separated and go off as light, heat, gas, and so forth, leaving ashes only.

PROOF II. The soul is spiritual because it can deal with things which have no material existence; e. g., abstract ideas, such as honor, bravery, futurity.

PROOF III. The soul by its power of idealizing invents, composes, calculates, and so forth. Man alone invents machines, composes melodies. No brute ever invented anything.

PROOF IV. Every natural appetite or craving comes from the Author of nature. Man has a natural appetite or instinct for perfect happiness. Every natural appetite has an object to satisfy it. Thirst has water, hunger has food.

Perfect happiness is not attainable in this life, hence it must be in a future life. Perfect happiness must be perpetual, therefore the life beyond is everlasting.

PROOF V. Justice demands a future life, but not necessarily an everlasting life. In this life the good often suffer and the wicked often prosper. The Creator would be unjust to reward evil-doers and allow the virtuous to suffer. Since the Creator is just, there must be another life where He justifies His dealings with man.

PROOF VI. Belief in a future life is universal, hence natural, and has God for its source and hence is true.

POINTS FOR DISCUSSION

1. The soul is material, as is evident from the fact that when the brain is injured the mind is impaired.

2. No one has ever seen the soul, hence it does not exist.

3. We know that ether exists because we can detect its waves, but we have nothing to show that the soul exists.

4. Everything in the world eventually decays and perishes. The soul is no exception.

5. Why does invention prove that the soul is spiritual?

6. Animals and insects do not have spiritual faculties, yet they adapt things to a definite purpose, for the beaver constructs its marvelous habitation, the bee its hive, and the spider its web.

7. Perhaps if we knew all about matter, we should be able to show that it is capable of doing what it is claimed that only a spiritual agent can do.

8. Just what is meant by saying that the soul is spiritual?

CHAPTER XV

THE CHURCH AND SCIENCE

IT IS SOMETIMES SAID in criticism of the Church that she is opposed to science. Those who make that assertion overlook the fact that from the very beginning of Christianity to the present day the Catholic church has been the greatest friend and supporter of science. Indeed, if it were not for the Church the treasures of science would not have been transmitted down the ages. It was the Church that encouraged, preserved, and transmitted the learning of antiquity to modern times. It was the Church that founded most of the universities which were the glory of the Middle Ages and in which were inculcated all the sciences then known to man. Oxford and Cambridge, now the pride of England, were up to the Reformation Catholic universities which, as far back as the twelfth century, numbered thousands of students. Oxford had eleven colleges and Cambridge fifteen.

Before the Reformation there were in all eighty-one universities. Prominent among them were Paris with seven thousand students; Bologna with six thousand; and Vienna, Cologne, Leipzig, Prague, and Salamanca, each with thousands of students. These universities, for the most part, owed their origin and renown to the Church's concern for the arts and sciences. The most celebrated of the universities were those founded and chartered by papal authority. The first university in the new world was the Catholic University of Mexico.

We do not need to go back to the Middle Ages, however, for evidence of the Church's abiding interest in and
encouragement of science. Only recently, in October 1936,
Pope Pius XI inaugurated the Pontifical Academy of Scientists, composed of the seventy most distinguished scientists in the world. This Academy embraces men of
every creed, the only necessary requirement being su-
perlative distinction in science. The Pope in founding this
Academy said:

"In our times in the scientific world, the tendency
toward religion is becoming ever more pronounced. Science, in fact, never finds itself in contradiction with the
truth of the Christian faith. . . . It is true that in recent
times it has been erroneously affirmed that between science and divine revelation thoro was conflict. But today
there are very few among the followers of the positive
sciences who persist in this error."

The seventy members of the Pontifical Academy were
chosen from fifteen nations, the Pope's sole purpose being
to assemble the best scientific minds of the world in
order to promote scientific research.

Other evidence of the Church's concern for knowledge
is the fact that Leo XIII opened the Vatican Library
even to scholars who were hostile to religion and who
hoped to obtain data from the library that would discredit the Church. It is a well-known fact that many
opponents of Christianity, while searching for matter to
discredit the Church, have been converted to Catholicism.
The reason for this is that the enemies of religion have
often falsified history in order to make the Church appear
in an unfavorable light. Students who investigated true
historical documents discovered that in many cases the

Church was grossly misrepresented. As a consequence, many of these scientific students of history embraced the religion which they had set out to discredit.

This recalls the statement of Count de Maistre that "English history since the Reformation has been a conspiracy against truth." The Church welcomes all the light that history and science can throw on her, but it must be the white light of truth, not the distorted light of misrepresentation.

Having shown, in a general way, that the Church is not the enemy but the friend of science, let us now take up specifically the matter of the Church and modern science. First of all let us have a clear notion of what is meant by science. At the present day when persons refer to science they mean, ordinarily, physical science; that is, science which deals with material things. Science really means knowledge. We have the science of theology, which pertains to religion, and the science of philosophy, which concerns ideas and the processes of thought. In scientific circles, however, and among people generally, the term 'science' is applied to the knowledge of things perceptible by the senses; that is, to what may be seen, weighed, or measured. It is in this sense that the term is used in the present consideration. By science, accordingly, we mean science which deals with material things.

An important point to keep in mind in this matter is the difference between fact and theory. Nearly all the misunderstanding with regard to science in its bearing on religion comes from a failure to realize the difference between fact and theory. A fact is a reality, an established verity. A theory is a working supposition, a speculation, a hypothesis. The fault with not a few scientists is that they mistake supposition for reality. They become so absorbed in a theory that, before it is corroborated by sufficient evidence, they proclaim it to be a fact, and then further affirm that it contradicts religion. Since nothing that contradicts a fact can be true, they declare that science is opposed to religion.

Here let it be said that whenever science is opposed to revelation, it is pseudo-science. Science which is really such cannot be opposed to revelation, for God is the author of both science and revelation, and God is absolute truth. A theory, as a working hypothesis, is often a very good thing, and may lead to splendid discoveries in the various fields in which its advocates work. Geologists, biologists, and astronomers have vastly increased our knowledge by research undertaken to obtain evidence substantiating their various theories.

Theorists may not always succeed in proving the truth of their assumptions, but in their endeavors to do so they may discover other very important things—things in fact more important than the object of their pursuit. It was thus that Columbus discovered America. He believed that by sailing west he would reach India. Instead of India, he discovered a new world. The danger with theories is that too often the wish is father to the thought, and as a consequence things are construed as evidence in support of a theory, not because they are in reality evidence, but because its advocates desire them to be evidence.

An example of this occurred a few years ago when some advocates of the evolution of man from the brute reported that they had found a skull which was midway between that of man and brute. This was the missing link long desired and sought after. The press of the world announced the discovery in bold headlines, and as final proof of man's descent from the brute. The skull was sent to various learned scientific bodies for inspection, and in the end it turned out to be not a skull at all, but the knee-cap of an elephant.

It is because the Church refuses to accept claims as proven which have insufficient or no evidence to support them that she is accused by some persons of being opposed to science. She is not opposed to science, but to the false claims of some scientists. In acting thus, she is following scientific procedure, which directs that evidence must support a claim. In the past half-century, scientific theory after theory which was proclaimed as substantiated was rejected by scientists themselves in the light of further investigation. And because the Church does not immediately accept these unsubstantiated claims, she is denounced by some scientists as an enemy of science.

Lest it be thought that a person cannot be a Catholic and a scientist at the same time, we mention some of the greatest scientists who were also Catholics: Pasteur, founder of bacteriology; Mendel (an abbot), discoverer of the laws of heredity; Fabre, the world's greatest naturalist; Schwann, founder of modern histology; Mueller, founder of modern physiology; Vesalius, founder of modern anatomy; Copernicus, father of modern astronomy; Laplace, renowned astronomer; Lavoisier, founder of modern chemistry; Roentgen, discoverer of X-rays; Marconi, inventor of radio transmission. Some of these Catholic scientists have given new words to our language. We speak of pasteurized milk, the Mendelian laws of heredity,

Roentgen rays, and a Marconigram. In electricity many terms are names of the Catholic scientists who were the inventors of special processes connected with its development and use. Luigi Galvani invented the galvanic battery, and galvanized iron takes its name from him; we measure the electric current by amperes after André Ampère; we speak of volts and of the voltaic battery, named after Alessandro Volta.

Possibly the two greatest contributions to science in modern times were by the Catholic scientists Pasteur and Marconi. By the discovery of the germ theory Pasteur has saved millions of lives, while Marconi by his invention of wireless communication has made the ocean and the air comparatively safe for navigation.

In view of what Catholic scientists have accomplished and are accomplishing in various scientific fields, it is hard to understand why some scientists persist in assuming and declaring that the Church is hostile to science. The best answer to that false charge is the fact that the present Pontifical Academy of Scientists has as its members the most distinguished scientists from every country of the world.

It may be objected, however, that the Church has learned the lesson that it does not pay to antagonize science, and that she is now endeavoring to repair her past attitude of opposition by a show of encouragement to science. These persons point to the condemnation of Galileo as evidence of the Church's hostility to progress and science. On examination, however, it will be found that the Galileo case furnishes splendid evidence of the Church's truly scientific attitude and procedure.

Huxley, a distinguished scientist, and not a Catholic,

has stated that in the Galileo case the Church had the better of it from the standpoint of scientific procedure. Cardinal Newman said that the opponents of the Church must be hard pressed for an instance of Church opposition to science, since they could find only one case in three centuries, and since that case, on investigation, proves to be no case at all.

Briefly, the Galileo case was as follows. Fifty years before Galileo, Copernicus, the father of modern astronomy, questioned the then-accepted theory about the solar system, which was that the sun moved across the firmament and that the earth was stationary. Copernicus was one of the greatest astronomers of all time, and his theory that the sun was virtually still while it was the earth that moved, created no little discussion and investigation.

Copernicus gave his view as a theory only, for as a true scientist he realized that he did not have sufficient evidence to substantiate it. He dedicated his monumental work to Pope Paul III, and was greatly honored by the Church. Galileo, without having sufficient evidence to corroborate his claim, asserted that it was a *fact* that the earth moved and that the sun stood still.

It may be asked, What had the Church to do with the matter? The Church at that time was the leader in the scientific and religious world. When Galileo proclaimed as a fact something that revolutionized the accepted notion of the firmament, the Church asked him to give proof for his assertion. Galileo acquiesced, and a Church commission was designated to hear and weigh his arguments. This commission was not the Church, but only a body of very learned men. Its purpose was to pronounce on a debated astronomical question. On hearing the arguments this commission decided that Galileo had not substantiated his claim. Some of the greatest scientists of the day opposed Galileo's views, notably Francis Bacon and Tycho Brahe. On the recommendation of the commission, the Church forbade Galileo to teach his then-revolutionary and unproven doctrine. As he persisted in proclaiming his doctrine, the Church, after warning him, ordered him to be confined in the residence of one of the officials of the Holy Office.

The question arises, Was not this condemnation of Galileo opposition to science? At the time of the condemnation the scientific world was divided on the matter, and since great scientists opposed Galileo, the Church, in the company of these scientists, cannot be said to be opposed to science. The condemnation of Galileo, however, has another phase, which it may be well to advert to briefly.

The Holy Office not only decided against Galileo's claims, but, moreover, declared them heretical on the ground that they contradicted Scripture. In thus declaring Galileo's views heretical, the Holy Office fell into error, but that does not affect papal infallibility, since no Church tribunal, no matter how authoritative, has the unique gift of infallibility. But does not Galileo's theory contradict Scripture, since it is stated in the Bible that at Joshua's prayer the sun stood still, implying, of course, that it was in motion? To this question the very obvious answer is that Scripture, like every work of literature, may be understood in various ways. The statements of Scripture can be taken not only literally, but also figuratively or symbolically.

It is because Scripture may be variously interpreted that the Church was divinely designated the sole authority for its interpretation. In point of fact, the Church has officially interpreted very few passages of Scripture, and until she does so interpret a passage, it is open to scholarly interpretation. The six days of creation, for instance, are interpreted by some to mean six periods or epochs. The Church has made no authoritative pronouncement in the matter. Until Galileo invented the telescope, and eventually substantiated his theory, the ordinary interpretation of the passage about the sun implied that it moved. When science demonstrated the contrary, the passage was interpreted figuratively, and that did away with apparent contradiction.

Every literary work—and the Bible is such—abounds in figurative and symbolic passages. Christ, for example, said He was the light of the world; again He said He was the good shepherd, and the vine; He called His disciples the salt of the earth, fishers of men, and so forth. The Bible used the language of the people of the day, otherwise it would not have been understood. Even now we speak of the sun's rising in the east and setting in the west. It was because of the prevailing notion of the time about the sun that Galileo's doctrine seemed to contradict Scripture, hence the concern of the Church and the error of the Holy Office. Later, when Galileo's claim was scientifically substantiated, the Church honored him and in so doing honored science.

The characteristic of a true scientist is to demand and to present evidence for a claim. This has always been the attitude of the Church, and in no instance is it better shown than in the Galileo case. Huxley spoke as a genuine scientist when he declared that in this case the Church followed the right procedure.

Then as now the Church proclaims that fact and faith cannot be opposed. Whenever science is opposed to revelation, it is pseudo-science. It is because truth is the basis of science as well as religion that the Catholic church has always been the friend and encourager of science. As the light of the world, the Church has always been, and always will be, the greatest friend and supporter of science that is truly such.

SUMMARY

The greatest friend of science throughout the ages has been the Catholic church. Most of the famous universities of Europe and the first in the New World (Mexico) were founded by the Catholic church.

Why, then, is it sometimes said that the Church is opposed to science? This false charge is due either to ignorance or hostility.

By science is meant, ordinarily, physical science, which deals with observable phenomena. In science we must distinguish between theory and fact. Some scientists confuse theory and fact, and consequently mistake speculation for scientific knowledge. A theory is often a very good thing as a working hypothesis, but when it claims to be a fact, it is not scientific procedure.

Whenever it is charged that the Church is opposed to science, it is to false science; that is, unproved assertion which is proclaimed as proven. The Church has never been opposed to science that is truly such.

Galileo is often cited as evidence that the Church is opposed to science. But when Galileo presented his claim he was opposed by some of the greatest scientists of the day, notably Francis Bacon and Tycho Brahe.

Recently Huxley, who was not a Catholic, stated that the

Church had altogether the better of the case as far as scientific procedure was concerned. The case in brief was as follows:

A learned commission of the Church ordered Galileo not to teach as certain a doctrine which was then not certain. Later his view was demonstrated to be true by further evidence, and the Church acclaimed it and honored him.

The Holy Office erred in declaring his doctrine heretical, but the Holy Office is not the infallible Church.

In demanding evidence for Galileo's claim, the Church was acting as true scientific procedure required.

Catholics have been and are among the most distinguished scientists, as the following names attest:

Pasteur, Fabre, Mendel, Marconi, Volta, Galvani, Roentgen, Laplace, Copernicus. These men made history by their scientific discoveries.

POINTS FOR DISCUSSION

1. The Catholic church is opposed to scientific progress.

2. The Church is opposed to the physical sciences.

3. The Church suppressed Galileo for teaching the truth about astronomy.

4. If the Church is not opposed to science, why is it that so many people believe she is?

5. The Church has discouraged advanced knowledge and thinking.

6. The Church has endeavored to keep higher education from the masses of the people.

7. The medieval universities were inferior institutions taught principally by narrow-minded monks.

8. Who originated inductive or experimental science?

9. The Church has discouraged physical science, the source of modern enlightenment.

CHAPTER XVI

EVOLUTION

ONE OF THE SUBJECTS most widely discussed at the present day is evolution. Evolution is a theory which seeks to explain the origin and existence of living things as they are today. It holds that present species were not always what they are now, but that they are descended from former different and extinct species.

There are two kinds of evolution:

1. Materialistic, which maintains that everything that exists is matter only, and that matter is the sole origin of everything.

2. Theistic, which holds that If evolution bo a fact, its origin or first cause must be an intelligent being.

Materialistic evolution is incompatible with science and revelation. Theistic evolution, if man is excluded, may possibly be a fact, and would not be fundamentally opposed to revelation.[1]

Evolution is a theory only, not a fact. It is an attempt to explain how things came to be what they are now. Until recently it was generally believed that living things as we see them now were the same from the beginning of the world. In the latter half of the nineteenth century Darwin broached the theory that present species of plants and animals were not directly created by God, but that they were the final result of an evolution from other

---

[1] See *Human Evolution and Science,* Le Buffe; *Evolution and Theology,* Messenger.

species existing in former geological periods. This theory implies the descent of the present from extinct species.

Evolution thus stated, with God as its author and provided it does not include the soul of man, is not opposed to revelation. The great Jesuit theologian Knabenbauer declared (1877) that "there is no objection, so far as faith is concerned, to assuming the descent of all plant and animal species from a few types." Evolution, as such, is therefore no bugbear to Christians.[1] Whence, then, comes the opposition we sometimes find between the Church and evolution? The conflict, when it does exist, comes from the kind of evolution in question. Materialistic evolution denies an intelligent first cause, and is, therefore, opposed not only to Christianity but to science as well.

Science proclaims that the order displayed in the universe demands an intelligent first cause. Moreover, the existence of personal, intelligent beings in the world postulates a personal, intelligent origin, a spiritual being, God. We reject materialistic evolution, therefore, as altogether incompatible with sound reason as well as with revelation.

It is this materialistic type of evolution, however, that is doing most of the harm which evolution is causing among mankind today. For by this false theory man is a high-grade brute, without a soul, conscience, or any responsibility to a power above. By this false theory man's career ends with the grave, and consequently he has to be concerned with this life only, and how to get out of it all he can, in every way, without regard for fu-

---

[1] *A Study of Modern Evolution,* Summers.

ture consequences. The effect of such a view of life, if one were consistent, would be to do just as one liked, to follow the behavior of the jungle, where strength and cunning prevail. Unfortunately, it is materialistic evolution which is found in many of our institutions of learning and among many of our popular but superficial writers, with the result that mankind during the past several decades has been afflicted with so many dreadful social evils.

This false theory of evolution degrades man to the level of the brute, and it is, in great measure, because of its prevalence that society is plagued with racketeers, gangsters, and other forms of what is termed 'rugged individualism,' by which everyone is out for himself regardless of the rights of others. The learned professions, business, and politics are honeycombed with corruption because of the logical consequences of materialistic evolution. This is not to say that all those who disregard honesty and virtue in private and business life are materialistic evolutionists, but that the logical results of this false theory of life have gradually inoculated society to such an extent that a low standard of morals now prevails in private and public life.

We see, accordingly, that evolution creates one of the most important problems of the present day. It makes a great difference to man whether he lives for time or eternity. We know from reason and faith that man's final home is in eternity, and with this certain knowledge we dismiss materialistic evolution.

What about theistic evolution? Since it postulates a personal Creator, and provided it does not include the soul of man, it is not, as a theory, fundamentally opposed to revelation. It is, however, a theory only, not a fact. This is the first thing to understand about evolution. In many of our colleges and universities evolution is proclaimed as a fact. As we shall see, it is not an established fact. In the first place, a fact never changes. If a thing is true, it is always true, it does not vary or change. That two plus two equals four is, was, and will be true without change, to the end of time. The doctrine of evolution is changing constantly. Darwinism is only one phase of evolution. Before him was Lamarck's theory, and after him that of De Vries, and at present there are various other theories.

Evolution having been proclaimed as a fact by some scientists because of the similarity of bone structure in different species of animals, various theories or explanations were originated to explain presumed evolution. The first thing to be noted, before considering the theories, is that evolution is declared to be a fact on account of the basic structural similarity of different species. Similarity, however, is not identity, so the fact itself of evolution rests on an unproved assertion.

The theories to explain the change of one species into another have been many. Each theory for a time was more or less accepted as final, only to be rejected on closer examination. The first theory was Darwinism, which accounted for evolution by the survival of the fittest in the struggle for existence. For a long while Darwinism reigned supreme. To doubt it stamped a person as opposed to science. Now, however, it is dead. Following Darwinism's collapse there arose the mutation theory of De Vries, by which it was claimed that nature made sudden leaps from one species to another. This theory had a meteoric rise but soon came to an end. The next theory is that which is based on comparative embryology, and which is known as the recapitulation theory or the law of biogenesis. This theory maintains that various species repeat in their own growth the history of their race, as for instance the fishlike characteristics in the different stages of the development of a frog, which are said to prove that the frog is descended from a fish. Of this theory Professor Newman says: "Attractive as it sounds, there is reason for serious doubt as to its validity." Professor Morgan of Columbia rejects it altogether and so does the distinguished biologist Carl Vogt.

Despite the fact, however, that evolution itself is based on conjecture and that the theories to explain it have one after another collapsed, it is still defended as an established fact by persons who, though labeled scientists, present no scientific evidence for their contention.

Evolution is now on the wane and soon it may be as dead as Darwinism. Meanwhile, however, it is doing great harm to society, for in its most common, or materialistic, form it proclaims that man is only a high-grade animal. This doctrine is responsible for much of the dreadful immorality which has characterized the world during the past two generations.

Many lecturers, writers, and teachers, however, speak of evolution as a fact, and consequently lead multitudes into atheism, communism, rationalism, and lawlessness. Why do we say that evolution is not a fact? Because there has not been found in the whole world scientific evidence to support the claims of evolution.

The basic claim of evolution is the natural change of one distinct species into another. Since the most impor-

tant thing about evolution is its relation to man, let us
see if there is any scientific evidence of man's descent
from another different species. Later we shall consider
the matter of change of species in plant or animal life.
With regard to man, it has been affirmed that he is descended from a brute of the higher type. Some evolutionists go so far as to give in direct line the descent of man
from the ape. In the Museum of Natural History, New
York, there are on exhibition the various stages of human evolution from the cave man down to the present
type of civilized man. Despite this graphic display of
man's descent from the ape, there is no scientific evidence
to support it. By scientific evidence, with regard to evolution, is meant that which certainly derives one distinct
species from another distinct species.

In confirmation of this, let us give the verdict of one
of the greatest modern anthropologists, Virchow (pronounced Virkoff), concerning one phase of evolution;
namely, Darwinism:

> Natural science, so long as it remains science, works only
> with really existing objects. A hypothesis may be discussed,
> but its significance can be established only by producing actual
> proofs in its favor. This, Darwinism has not succeeded in
> doing. In vain have its adherents sought for connecting links
> which should connect man with the monkey. Not a single one
> has been found.[1]

Despite this clear and definite statement from an ac-
knowledged leader of science, there are many scientists
who boldly and loudly proclaim that man is descended
from the ape and that he is nothing but a brute of higher

---

[1] Address to the Twentieth Century Congress of the German
Anthropological Association.

degree. Can we be surprised at the prevalence of animal behavior when animal ancestry is so positively proclaimed from lecture platforms, in college classrooms, and in serious as well as popular magazines? Man is only too eager to get justification for being a law to himself. Perhaps that accounts, in great measure, for the readiness with which man's ape ancestry has been accepted by so many.

Darwinism, however, is not evolution, but only a now-discredited phase of evolution. In corroboration of this, we give the verdict of William Bateson, President of the British Association of Scientists:

Darwin speaks no more with philosophic authority. We read his scheme of evolution as we would those of Lucretius or Lamarck.[1]

Modern leaders in science have gone farther than rejecting Darwinism, however, and have begun to question evolution itself. In proof we give the testimony of Professor Paul Kammerer of the University of Vienna, an eminent authority on this matter:

The theory of evolution at the present time is pointing in a new direction. Celebrated biologists like Kurt Herbst of Heidelberg, and William Bateson of the University of Cambridge, openly deride the concept of evolution in their lectures.[2]

Despite the fact that most eminent anthropologists declare that evolution is a theory only, many modern educators take for granted that it is an established scientific truth. That evolution is far from being a scientifically established truth we shall now proceed to show.

The essential postulate of evolution is a change of species. Unless a former species of plant or animal life has

---

[1] Address to the British Association, 1914.
[2] *Literary Review,* February 23, 1924.

naturally developed into a later species, evolution is not a fact. A species is a group of living beings having a common inheritable type, with no major difference among themselves, and capable of surviving and propagating indefinitely in the natural state. There is no evidence so far to show that one species has ever naturally developed from another.

Evolution is not growth. An acorn, for example, develops into the majestic oak; an infant develops into a man; a caterpillar into a butterfly; a tadpole into a frog. Growth is one thing, change from one species to another is something altogether different. Evolutionists have long been seeking the missing link which gives evidence of change of species, but have never found it. Growth is not a change from one distinct species into another different and distinct species, but the natural development from the seed or embryo of a species to the full maturity of that species. If a cat changed into a dog, that would be a change from one species into another.

Nor is it evolution when by artificial means a man develops variations in a species, as for example when by various means the size, color, and other qualities of fruit or flower are modified by artificial selection and crossing. Variations, however, do not change a species. Man, for instance, is man, whether he be white, black, or yellow, tall or short, handsome or ugly, bright or stupid, savage or civilized. Man is a rational animal, and wherever you find a rational animal—that is, a creature with a body and endowed with the gift of reason and speech—you have a man.

Confusion and error regarding evolution come about, frequently, from not understanding the state of the question or the meaning of the terms employed. Evolution means the *natural* change of one species into another. The word *natural* is important, signifying that the change, if it occur, must be effected naturally; that is, without the interference and direction of an outside intelligence. So far, science has found no evidence to show that one species has ever naturally developed into another. The so-called Cro-Magnon, Neanderthal, Piltdown, and Heidelberg man, instead of being different species, were of the essentially same species as present-day man, as is evident from the relics associated with the remains of these fossils. The tools, weapons, and art found in connection with these fossils show clearly that those persons had a knowledge of cause and effect, and that they understood the relation of means to ends. This knowledge and understanding resulted in invention, of which none but the human species is capable.

Christians hold that if evolution be a fact, it owes its origin and processes to the Creator, who in the beginning made all things. Those who oppose evolution to religion hold that evolution is its own source and origin, being a power or force of eternal matter, thus excluding the Creator. They assert that matter, being eternal, had no maker, and that God has no place in the universe. But matter is incapable of designing and producing an orderly universe. Materialistic evolution must, therefore, be altogether rejected as opposed to science as well as revelation.

Theistic evolution, as a scientific theory, is not fundamentally opposed to revelation. Whenever there is apparent opposition, it is due either to the unsupported claims of unscientific evolutionists, or to ignorance of the doctrines of revealed religion. Physical science deals only with data perceptible by the senses. We have no such data regarding the origin of things.

Hence scientists can make no legitimate pronouncement concerning the beginning of things. Sir Oliver Lodge, an evolutionist, said: "Science knows nothing about the first cause of things."[1] How, then, can some evolutionists affirm that matter is the origin of everything? If they have no data, they are not entitled to do more than speculate. But even their speculation in this case results in error because they infer that intelligence can come from non-intelligence. When scientists leave the field of observation for that of speculation they are apt to go astray.

Evolution, as a scientific theory, is at present speculation, pure and simple. It is an attempt to explain something for which there are so far no material data. Sir Oliver Lodge in his address to the British Association of Scientists said:

Science is systematized and metrical knowledge, and in regions where measurement cannot be applied, it has small scope. . . . Science depends on measurement, and things not measurable are therefore excluded or tend to be excluded from its attention.

Despite the fact that science has no data for the origin of man, or of the universe, some scientists have dogmatically proclaimed that man has descended from the brute, and that the universe came originally from matter only. How do they know the origin of man or the universe, since they have nothing in connection with the subject that science can deal with? It comes to this, that it is

[1] *Literary Review,* February 23, 1924.

a guess only, and not even a good guess, because it results in an unscientific conclusion; namely, that the effect can be greater than its cause. Theistic evolution in some aspects may or may not be a fact, but materialistic evolution is an absolute impossibility. Theistic evolution, if it be a fact, cannot include the soul of man, because that would mean the origin of spirit from matter, which is an impossibility.

Christianity can grant everything that scientific evolution has established. So far it has not even established a single case of natural change of species, to say nothing of a series of changes leading back to the origin of the world. As the case stands at present, the Church, although admitting the possibility of evolution as an explanation of existing living beings, declares that the origin of the first man and the first woman was a special act of the Creator.

We have mainly considered human evolution because it is the most important feature of the subject. Moreover, space does not permit going into plant and animal evolution. Suffice it to say that there has not yet been found any scientific evidence to justify the claim of a specific change in those domains.

Lest it be thought that modern scientists are a unit in favor of evolution, we give a few of the most distinguished who deny that evolution is an established fact. Fabre, the greatest modern naturalist; Loeb, expert biologist of the Rockefeller Institute; Professor Millikan, one of the most eminent physicists of today; John Burroughs, the great naturalist—these and other prominent scientists have denied that evolution is a proved fact. Other eminent scientists deny that the evolution of man is established, among them Alexis Carrel of the Rockefeller Institute; Professor Henderson of Harvard University; Professor Richet of the University of Paris; Dr. Dwight, eminent anatomist; and Sir Bertram Windle, F. R. S.

The Catholic church can never be opposed to what is really true. Generation after generation this Church, built on the rock of truth by the divine Builder, has withstood the assaults of every conceivable wave of error and storm of passion. True science will always be in accord with revealed religion.

A few years ago those who did not believe in evolution's claims were set down as ignorant or bigoted. Moreover, the Catholic church was regarded as not only unprogressive but retrogressive because she refused to accept the unsubstantiated claims of evolutionists. Today with regard to evolution, the most progressive scientists are on the side of the Church. As the case now stands, Catholics are enjoined not to teach that man's body is evolved from the brute.[1] The soul, of course, is absolutely outside the realm of evolution, because an effect cannot be greater than its cause. Spirit, intelligence, and free will cannot result from any but a spiritual source.

Science and revelation are thus in accord that the first cause of all things is a spiritual being, God.

SUMMARY

One of the most important questions of the present day is evolution. It seriously affects man's outlook on life, and also his conduct.

Evolution is a theory which seeks to explain the origin and existence of living beings as they are now.

---

[1] Biblical Commission on Genesis I-III.

Evolution is a theory only, not an established fact.

There are two kinds of evolution:

1. Materialistic, which maintains that everything is matter only and has eternal matter as origin.

2. Theistic, which holds that if evolution be a fact its origin is an intelligent being, God.

Materialistic evolution is at present the dominant form and the source of immense harm to the individual and society, for it proclaims that man's descent is entirely from the brute, and that his career ends with this life.

Evolution, as a theory, maintains that present species of living things were not always what they are now, but are evolved from former different and extinct species.

Growth or modification is not evolution, for neither constitutes a new species. By 'species' is meant a new and distinct kind of being, capable of indefinite reproduction in the natural state.

Evolution is a theory only, not a fact.

There is no scientific evidence so far to support it. The missing link is still missing.

Science deals only with things perceptible by the senses. There are no data of this kind to prove a change of species or the origin of the world from mere matter. Hence material evolution is only speculation, a guess, and a wrong guess because an effect cannot be greater than its cause. Order, design, and intelligence must have a spiritual origin.

Even theistic evolution is only speculation, since there are no data which prove a change of species.

Theistic evolution, excluding the soul, may possibly be a fact. So far it is not proven.

Theistic evolution is not opposed to revelation.

Some of the greatest modern scientists deny that evolution is a fact, yet it is taught as a fact in many universities, and is responsible in great measure for the dreadful state of society today.

Catholics are directed not to teach the evolution of the human body from the brute.

POINTS FOR DISCUSSION

1. Evolution must be true since so many eminent scientists teach that it is true.

2. Biologists affirm that organic evolution is positively established by biogenesis.

3. Paleontology furnishes scientific proof of organic evolution.

4. New species are constantly being developed from former species, therefore evolution is an established fact.

5. The Neanderthal skull and the Piltdown man are sufficient evidence for man's descent from the brute.

6. Just as the acorn evolves into the mighty oak, so has man developed from former species.

7. Horticulturists have developed various species of flowers from one species. This is evidence of evolution.

8. The skeleton structure of the brute and of man is similar. This is proof of the same origin for both.

9. So many colleges and universities would not teach evolution if it were not true.

10. (1) What is the difference between materialistic and theistic evolution? (2) Why is materialistic evolution absolutely false? (3) What does the Church hold about theistic evolution?

CHAPTER XVII

DANGERS TO FAITH AND MORALS

FAITH, LIKE ANY VIRTUE, may be strengthened or weakened by care or abuse. A man of the strongest constitution may become a physical wreck by failure to observe normal care with regard to diet and exercise. In like manner a person of soundest faith may lose it by lack of care and cultivation. Evil associations, self-will, and harmful books are the greatest dangers to faith and morals.

In general, it may be said that anything which leads to vicious or sinful conduct tends to weaken faith. Man is so constituted that conduct reacts on creed, causing one readily to believe whatever favors his mode of behavior. That explains the rapid spread and wide popularity of various cults and doctrines which give latitude to man's weaknesses and vicious tendencies. One of the proofs that Catholicism is divinely true is the fact that it gained its adherents without ever making concessions to human frailty.

Man naturally resents any restrictions on his conduct, and when his conduct is restricted by religious belief, he is apt to rebel against that belief and eventually reject it. This is why so many persons lose their faith when their morals are loose. Anything, accordingly, that tends to make a person immoral is a danger to faith. Evil associations are among the foremost dangers to faith. It is hard for a person to rise above the level of his environment. If

181

one's surroundings are immoral, one gradually becomes inoculated with immorality. This fact is so well known that there is now a nationwide movement to do away with city slums, which have always been the breeders of vice. There is an old but very true phrase which says: "Show me your companions and I'll tell you what you are." Even under good environment it is not always easy to live up to the faith; we can imagine, therefore, the danger of attempting to preserve and practice it amidst evil associations. It is safe to say that it is ordinarily impossible to keep the faith if evil companionship be not avoided.

A second danger to faith is self-will, the tendency to do as one pleases. Man likes to be a law to himself. Faith tells him that there is a law from above to which his will must be subject. Self-will thus finds itself in conflict with God's will, with the result that there is a tendency in man to oppose God's will and to seek justification for so doing. This often leads to believing readily specious arguments against faith. The wish being father to the thought, the self-willed man magnifies specious objections to faith and ignores the sound arguments for it. The result is, most frequently, a gradual decline and eventual loss of faith.

In the parable of the sower and the seed Christ described this condition very graphically, pointing out how the good seed was destroyed by the rank growth which choked it. Man's free will is one of his most precious attributes, but unless it be controlled by God's precepts, it becomes a bane instead of a blessing. Christ, in the only prayer He taught mankind, bade us to look up to the Creator of the world and call Him our Father. Then He told us to say to God in heaven: "Thy kingdom come,

Thy will be done." In bidding us to pray thus to our heavenly Father, Christ taught us that doing the will of God was the condition of possessing the kingdom of heaven.

God gave us our free will in order that we might serve Him voluntarily. The sinner refuses to serve his Creator, saying, by action if not by word, "Not Thy will, God, but mine be done." Wilfulness, therefore, often causes man to do his own rather than God's will, and in that state of mind it takes very little to estrange him from faith. It is good to have a firm will, but when it resists divine authority it ceases to be a virtue and becomes a vice which ordinarily leads to loss of faith. We admire the soldier of strong will whom no person or danger can deter from duty, but if his strong will be exercised against the orders of his commander, it becomes rebellion instead of bravery.

When man lets his own instead of God's will direct him, the result is, ordinarily, loss of respect for divine authority and eventually loss of faith. This helps to explain the fact that many persons who were strong in faith while leading a virtuous life, find numerous objections to religion after they have entered upon the broad path of worldliness.

Besides evil associations and wilfulness, there is the danger to faith arising from the reading of immoral or anti-religious books. There is moral as well as physical contagion. The Government establishes quarantine to keep away contagion from the people, and moreover forbids the use of the mails to books which breed disloyalty or vice. The Church is solicitous for the spiritual welfare of her children and warns them against books which may breed spiritual disease. What may be dangerous for one person may not be so for another, but whatever anyone finds to be the occasion of sin must be avoided.

There are certain things, however, which are harmful to everybody. They are like those drugs which by law are labeled *poison* so as to protect people. The Church, knowing that certain books are poison to faith and morals, labels them as dangerous by putting them on the Index of Forbidden Books. Subtle poison may be in a book which the ordinary reader may not perceive until he has become its victim. As a good mother, the Church safeguards her children against spiritual harm. In time of war the Government exercises strict censorship over what is published. The Church is always at war with the forces of evil. The Index is one of the means she employs to protect the faithful. The Index binds under pain of grievous sin, unless one is dispensed by duty or ecclesiastical authority.

It is sometimes objected against the Index that it is interference with individual liberty. But when interference is beneficial and saves the individual from disaster, it is a blessing rather than a bane. The rail which is placed alongside a narrow plank, bridging a deep chasm, interferes with the liberty of movement of the one crossing. But who would complain of an interference which saves him from falling below to destruction?

Liberty is a dreadfully abused term. It does not mean freedom from reasonable restraint. There could be no authority or government without interference with individual liberty. Liberty does not entitle a person to do as he pleases. One man's liberty is another man's obligation to respect it. If one person has the right of way it restricts the liberty of another. Interference with liberty is the law of life. Parents interfere with the liberty of children as to diet and education, and this interference is for the real welfare of the children. Granted, therefore, that the Index interferes with liberty, that is no sound objection to it, since it is a truly beneficial interference.

Another objection to the Index is that it is opposed to progress. Knowledge is power, it is objected; knowledge is the basis of progress; and to restrict knowledge by arbitrarily forbidding the reading of books which one may be interested in is to restrict and prevent progress. To this let it be said that the Index does not *arbitrarily* forbid the reading of books, but wisely, considerately, and for the true welfare of those concerned. Moreover, the knowledge which might be acquired by reading the forbidden books would retard rather than promote progress. No matter how much progress one makes, if it be in the wrong direction it does not advance but retards the person so engaged. Error, vice, and any other such thing does not promote progress but rather leads to disaster.

The Index prevents persons from loading themselves with knowledge which eventually must be either rejected or regretted. If a man works hard to gather a load of toadstools, believing them to be mushrooms, he must either discard them as useless or die if he eats them. No matter how industriously one works, he does not attain his objective if his efforts be wrongly directed. By omitting the books on the Index, no one will ever miss what truly advances progress.

The Index is compiled by a commission of experts, one of the most learned bodies of men in the world. It is drawn up with the greatest care and consideration. Only those books are listed which threaten faith or morals. Sometimes opponents of the Index say that they have read a book forbidden by it and have seen no harm in the book. Perhaps they did not, but not because the book was harmless, but because either they failed to see the evil in it or because they became inoculated without being aware of it. Some poisons work slowly and imperceptibly. Often a refreshing draught of water from a wayside brook contains the germs of typhoid. The eager, thirsty traveler did not perceive the deadly germs he was imbibing, but they were there, nevertheless, and too late he realized that he quenched his thirst at the cost of his life.

Sometimes a forbidden book is very attractively and cleverly written. Its very cleverness, however, is its greatest danger. If it were stupid or poorly written, no one would care to read it. A poisoned tablet is often sugar-coated, and a morally poisonous book is frequently gotten up most alluringly. Some people are carried away by the literary merit of a book, and wonder why such a splendid piece of literature is placed on the Index. Poison can be put up in a very attractive form, but it remains deadly nevertheless.

Christ put the soul in one arm of the scale and the world in the other, and declared that the soul outweighed in value the whole world. People take very good care of their possessions, whether they be money, jewels, or other treasures. They take no chances when there is question of the security of these valuables. Man has a jewel more precious than all the diamonds of the Orient, and no care is too great to secure its safety.

Today, more harm is done to faith and morals by immoral and erroneous literature than by almost any other

one cause. If a person knew that a rattlesnake was in a
room, he would not from curiosity try to see how close
he could approach it without becoming the victim of its
deadly fangs. It is curiosity, very frequently, that induces
people to trifle with the deadly poison of evil associations
and vicious literature. Some people, relying too much on
their strength of will, forget that they who love danger
shall perish therein. One cannot touch pitch without being
defiled.

Today there is very special need of avoiding dangerous
occasions. Never before was vice so alluringly attired.
Never before was vice so flagrant and so bold. Theaters,
magazines, amusement resorts, and even social gather-
ings seem to have discarded Christian decency, and
adopted instead pagan disregard of decorum and modesty.
In such an atmosphere Catholic young people need to be
on their guard lest, almost imperceptibly, they adopt pagan principles and fall into pagan conduct.

In tropical countries explorers fortify themselves
against fever by quinine. No matter how strong they may
be, no matter how careful they are of their diet and surroundings, the impregnated air will lay them low with
fever unless they have recourse to this drug. The atmosphere of civilization today is impregnated with pagan
germs. No precaution is too great to avoid this pagan
contagion, which is deadly to both soul and body.

The world is strewn with the mental and physical
wrecks of vicious living. But worse than the ruin of mind
and body is the loss of the soul. Christ said: "What exchange shall a man give for his soul?" (Matthew 16:26).
The modern world holds the soul very cheap. The world's
estimate, however, is not final. The world with its stand-

ards will one day be summoned before the eternal Judge. The judgment of that august tribunal establishes the value which Catholics put on the soul, and the measure of the precautions they take for its safety.

This present life is only the first stage of man's immortal career. On this stage, however, depends the eternal hereafter. It is the part of wisdom not to barter everlasting welfare for passing pleasure. Catholics are acting wisely, therefore, when they avoid whatever endangers their eternal inheritance.

SUMMARY

Faith like any virtue may be strengthened or weakened by care or abuse. The man of strongest constitution may become a physical wreck by failure to observe normal care with regard to diet and exercise. So may a man of soundest faith lose it by lack of care and cultivation.

Evil associations, bad books, and self-will are the greatest dangers to faith and morals. There is moral as well as physical contagion.

The Government establishes quarantine to keep away contagion, and forbids the use of the mails to books which breed disloyalty and vice.

The Church is solicitous for the spiritual welfare of her children. She warns against vicious amusements, persons, books, and places. What may be dangerous for one person may not be so for another.

Whatever anyone finds to be the occasion of sin must be avoided.

There are certain things, however, which are harmful to everybody. They are like those drugs which, by law, are labeled poison, so as to protect people.

The Church is as solicitous for her subjects as the state is for hers, even more so. Knowing that certain books are poison to faith and morals, she so labels them in the Index of Forbidden Books.

Subtle poison may be in a book which the reader may not perceive until he has become its victim.

In time of war the Government exercises strict censorship over what is published. The Church is always at war with the forces of evil.

The Index is one of the means she employs to protect the faithful. The Index binds under pain of mortal sin unless one is dispensed by duty or ecclesiastical authority.

Eternal welfare depends on this present life. No sacrifice is too great for everlasting happiness.

POINTS FOR DISCUSSION

1. If a person has real faith, there is no danger of losing it.

2. Faith that is based on divine truth should make a person immune to assaults against it.

3. The Index of Forbidden Books is a hindrance to progress.

4. The Index interferes with intellectual research.

5. The Index is interference with human liberty.

6. Each one should judge for himself what to read or do.

7. One who knows his faith is sufficiently informed to direct himself.

8. One would have to get off the earth to avoid dangerous occasions, since vicious persons and places are everywhere.

9. Soldiers are supposed to meet the enemy, not run away. Christians are soldiers of Christ.

CHAPTER XVIII

CONFESSION

CHRIST'S CHURCH, LIKE HIMSELF, is both divine and human. She is divine in her constitution and doctrine, human in her members. The Church is infallible, but her members are not impeccable. Everyone, from the pope down to the lowliest of the faithful, may fall into sin. Christ, knowing the frailty of human nature, instituted the sacrament of penance to restore to His friendship those who might lose it by sin. Christ said: "They that are well have no need of a physician, but they that are sick" (Mark 2:17).

In the confessional Christ is the physician of the soul. When absolution is given by the priest it is confirmed by God. The priest is the delegate of God; the wire, as it were, between the penitent and God. Confession is a wonderful comfort to the sinner. Many persons go from bad to worse because they have started on the wrong path. Confession gives a new start and a new heart. Confession, however, is not only for those who are in serious sin, but for everyone who tries to advance in holiness. Confession is a preventive as well as a remission of sin. It is not only a preventive, but also a means of sanctification, since it confers a special sanctifying grace. Some very holy persons go to confession daily, for, as was said previously, confession, although necessary for mortal sin only, is advisable for all those who aim at a holier life.

It is safe to say that no one who perseveres in frequent

confession is in danger of losing his soul. It is advisable to have a regular confessor who will give wise advice and direction in the affairs of conscience and life. Confession duly practiced is one of the best helps for right living and eternal welfare.

Unless confession was divinely instituted it never could have obtained acceptance among mankind. No human power or authority could establish such a practice. Christ first demonstrated that He was God and, that He had power to forgive sins, and then He delegated this power to the ministers of His Church.

On a certain occasion, when Christ was surrounded by a multitude, including some of the leaders of the Jews, He was interrupted in His discourse by the arrival of a cripple, carried on a bed, and placed directly before Him. The assemblage was immediately on edge, expecting to witness a miraculous cure. Now, Christ knew that in the crowd before Him there were scribes and Pharisees intent on finding something in His speech or action to criticize or condemn. The Jewish authorities were opposed to Christ because He would not be their king and free them from the Roman yoke, and make them a dominant power on earth. When He declared His kingdom was not of this world, they rejected Him. But despite their rejection the people believed in Him and followed Him in great multitudes. The leaders realized that, unless they destroyed Him, they would lose their power over the people. Accordingly, they sought on every occasion to find some accusation against Him either before the Roman or the Jewish tribunal.

On this occasion Christ decided to manifest in a most unmistakable manner that He was truly God and King of kings, even if His kingdom was not of this world. Among the Jews it was a matter of unquestionable belief that God alone could forgive sins. They did not believe that even Moses, whom they so greatly revered, had this power. As the cripple lay before Him silently pleading to be cured, Jesus, to the astonishment of the multitude and of the cripple, instead of healing him said: "Thy sins are forgiven thee." Immediately the scribes and Pharisees said in their hearts: "He blasphemeth; only God can forgive sins."

Christ, who read their thoughts as we read a book, turning towards them said: "Why do you think evil in your hearts? Whether is easier, to say, Thy sins are forgiven thee, or to say, Arise and walk? But that you may know that the Son of Man hath power on earth to forgive sin (then said He to the man sick of the palsy), Arise, take up thy bed and go into thy house. And he arose and went into his house" (Matthew 9:4-7).

On this occasion Jesus presented evidence that He had the power to forgive sin. Anyone could say to another, "Thy sins are forgiven thee," but only God could directly say to a cripple, "Arise and walk." The visible healing of the man's body, by a word only, was evidence of the invisible healing of the soul by a word only. Christ, therefore, had the power of forgiving sin. This power He delegated to the ministers of His religion, saying to them: "As the Father hath sent Me, I also send you. . . . Whose sins you shall forgive, they are forgiven them" (John 20:21-23). By these words Christ delegated to His representatives the exercise of His own power of forgiving sins.

It will help us to understand this power of delegated

authority if we consider that something similar occurs daily in modern affairs. There is in law what is known as the 'power of attorney.' If a man of great wealth becomes ill or goes abroad, he designates a person to represent him financially. This person so delegated might not have any money of his own. If he went to a bank and in his own name presented a demand for a thousand dollars, he would be ejected or arrested. But if he has the power of attorney, he could present a demand for a million dollars and it would be honored. This great power is conferred merely by a word or a line, legally attested.

Christ gave the power of attorney to His Church with regard to the forgiveness of sins, saying: "Whose sins you shall forgive they are forgiven them." We know, accordingly, on divine authority, that when the priest in the confessional pronounces forgiveness it is ratified in heaven. On leaving the confessional the penitent has the same certainty of forgiveness as if Christ Himself in person said to him: "Thy sins are forgiven thee."

It is sometimes objected to confession that there is no need of going to confession to a priest, since one may go directly to God for forgiveness. To this it is answered that God has already replied to that objection by the very fact that He instituted the sacrament of penance. Christ would not have established confession if it were not His will to dispense pardon in that way. If a monarch decrees that his subjects should transact affairs with him through designated officials, that would be the ordinary way of conducting such affairs.

Confession is the ordinary way that God has decreed for obtaining pardon for transgressions against Him. We say 'the ordinary way' because under extraordinary cir-

cumstances the sinner may go direct to God for pardon.
In cases of fire, shipwreck, or sudden accident, when confession is not possible, a person by making an act of perfect contrition for his sins will be forgiven directly by
God, but if he survives the danger, he must afterwards
go to confession, because the act of contrition made in
time of danger implied doing God's will when possible,
and once the danger is over, confession is possible. A
person who falls into serious sin should make an act of
perfect contrition at once, as this, with the intention of
confessing later, remits the sin.

The main reason for confession is that it is God's ordinance. There are, however, several reasons besides
God's ordinance for this manner of regaining His friendship after it has been lost by sin. Confession causes a
man to take inventory of his soul's state. Business men,
no matter how careful and systematic, take inventory of
stock at stated times in order to see just how they stand.
By confession the penitent examines the state of his soul
in order to see how he stands with God. This examination
of conscience may disclose a spiritual condition which
warns him that unless he change his ways he may find
himself on the broad road which ends in destruction.

A person may gradually get accustomed to a sinful
manner of living without realizing that he is in the grip
of a dangerous enemy of salvation. Preparation for confession affords the sinner a spiritual mirror in which he
may see his soul in all its deformity, and this sight should
arouse him to a determination to mend his ways before
it is too late. Scripture warns us that many fall away
from virtue because they do not reflect on their evil
course. Confession causes a man to reflect seriously on

the state of his soul, and this alone would be a reason for the institution of this sacrament.

Another reason for confession is that it affords the penitent a means of repairing the offense to God which sin has caused. Every mortal sin is, in effect, an act of pride. When a person commits a sin he violates one of God's ordinances. God, as it were, stands before the sinner and says: "You shall not do this evil; if you do you shall not enter into eternal life." The sinner defies God and says by action: "Not Thy will but mine be done." The sinner thus opposes his will to that of God, challenges his Maker, and in pride does as he pleases regardless of divine authority.

Confession affords a means of atoning for this arrogance and pride. By kneeling down before a fellow man and disclosing the hidden sins of his soul to him, the penitent performs an act of humility, which is in direct contrast to the pride manifested in his defiance of God's ordinance. It requires no little humility at times to reveal to the confessor the vile state of one's soul. But this very humility is partial atonement for the arrogance of sin, and also acts as a preventive against sin thereafter.

A third reason for the institution of confession is that it affords a practical means of exercising the virtue of faith. Every time the penitent goes to confession he declares by act, if not by word, that Christ is God. The penitent in going to confession does so because he believes that He who instituted this sacrament is what He declared Himself to be, the Son of God. He believes on the word of Christ that when absolution is pronounced it is ratified in heaven. Confession, accordingly, keeps alive active faith, and with faith active a person is fortified against the evils and sinful allurements of the world.

It is thus seen that confession, although a divine institution, is not a merely arbitrary ordinance, but a sacrament admirably adapted to the needs and welfare of mankind. Many people outside the Catholic church ardently long for the guidance and comfort which the sacrament of penance gives. Catholics too often fail to appreciate the marvelous benefits of their religion. Persons outside the Church may go through life without a thought of doing penance for their sins. Yet every sin must be atoned for either here or hereafter.

The Catholic is assigned a penance when he receives absolution. Besides this sacramental penance there are various seasons and practices of penance in the Church. For it should be understood that the penance given in confession may or may not satisfy for the sins confessed. In the early ages of the Church the penances given were very severe, sometimes lasting for weeks, months, or years. The purpose was to offer satisfaction in this life for the chastisement still due to sin after the guilt was remitted.

The consequences of sin are twofold, eternal and temporal. By sin a person incurs the guilt of offending God, and loses God's friendship and his right to the inheritance of eternal happiness. Absolution remits this guilt and loss. The second consequence of sin is chastisement, either here or hereafter, for violating God's ordinances. This chastisement must be satisfied by penance here or atonement in purgatory. The penance which the priest gives in confession is imposed in the hope that with the proper disposition of the penitent it will satisfy for the temporal chastisement due for the sins confessed. The penance imposed may not, however, adequately satisfy for the chastisement due the sins; hence it is customary for penitents voluntarily to do various works of satisfaction for their sins, although absolved. The Church by her seasons and practices of penance reminds the faithful of the need of doing penance outside that imposed in the confessional.

Indulgences are one of the means of satisfying for sins. An indulgence means a milder form of satisfying for sin. The Church acts towards the faithful as an indulgent mother to her children. By the power granted her by her divine Founder she applies the merits of Christ and the saints to the penitent who is properly disposed, and changes the severe penances which were formerly imposed to a mild one by which piety is fostered and faith exercised. That is the reason it is called an indulgence.

Formerly penances were given for forty days or seven years or for life. When an indulgence is granted now, it means that by fulfilling the conditions prescribed, satisfaction is offered for sin equivalent to that which in the early ages was satisfied for by those severe penances. That is the reason why Catholics eagerly avail themselves of this treasure house of satisfaction for the chastisement due to their sins.

Frequent confession not only fosters piety, but also enables one to acquire an abundance of merit from the sacramental grace which flows from this holy institution. This is why saints as well as sinners have recourse to confession, the saints in order to advance in holiness, the sinners in order to retrieve the past and to enter upon the sure road which leads to everlasting happiness. No merely human institution could devise and perpetuate the practice of confession. It is visible proof that Catholicism is indeed the religion of Christ, the eternal Son of the living God.

SUMMARY

Christ's Church, like Himself, is both divine and human. She is divine in her constitution, human in her members.

The Church is infallible, but her members are not impeccable.

Christ established the sacrament of penance to restore to His friendship those who should lose it by sin.

No one, no matter how low he has fallen, need remain down unless he wills.

Christ said: "They that are well have no need of a physician, but they that are sick." In the confessional Christ is the physician of the soul.

The priest is as it were the wire between the penitent and God. When the penitent receives absolution, it is God who forgives.

Many go from bad to worse because they have started on the wrong path. Confession gives a new start and new heart.

Confession is not only for the sinner but for all who aim at holiness, since it is not only a remission but also a preventive of sin.

Many pious people go to confession weekly; and some go every day in order to advance in sanctity.

Confession is necessary for mortal sin only, but is advisable for venial sins, and besides it confers sanctifying grace.

In case of danger of death one may go directly to God for forgiveness. By an act of contrition, with the intention of going to confession if possible, one is assured of God's merciful pardon.

It is safe to say that no one who perseveres in frequent confession is in danger of losing his soul.

It is advisable to have a regular confessor if possible, for such a one is able to give wise advice in the affairs of conscience and also in the various problems of life.

Confession duly and frequently practiced is one of the best helps for right living and eternal welfare.

POINTS FOR DISCUSSION

1. Only God can forgive sin.

2. There is no need of confessing to a priest, since we may confess directly to God.

3. There should be no medium between God and man. Confession to a priest constitutes such a medium.

4. Man can forgive an offense to himself, but not to God.

5. Confession is an encouragement to sin.

6. A bad priest may use confession to the detriment of the penitent.

7. An indulgence is not necessary, since absolution entirely remits sin.

8. The Church commercializes indulgences.

9. Confession was invented by priests in order to increase their hold on the people.

CHAPTER XIX

Holy Communion

Association with good and refined persons ordinarily makes one good and refined. By Holy Communion we associate with the most perfect being in the world, who is also the source of all holiness. By Holy Communion we not only abide with Jesus, but also receive from Him help to live in the way most pleasing to Him. The more we live as He wishes, the surer shall we be to share His eternal companionship and bliss.

The two greatest wonders of creation are the incarnation and the Eucharist. By the incarnation the eternal Son of God united Himself with humanity. By the Eucharist the Son of God made man unites Himself with the human individual. Once we realize the fact that the Son of God assumed human nature and became man, we should not be surprised that in His goodness He devised a means of intimate association with each one of us. The Eucharist is the divine invention of love by which Christ effects this holy union.

During the three years of His public life Christ instructed His apostles in the mysteries of His kingdom on earth, the Church. But it was especially during the forty days between the resurrection and the ascension that He outlined the constitution and essential rites and ceremonies of His religion. It was during this period of intimate intercourse with His apostles that He explained to them the full significance of what He meant at the

Last Supper, when, after instituting the Eucharist, He
said to them: "Do this for a commemoration of Me"
(Luke 22:19). By saying to them "Do this" He signified
the very act which He had just performed, by which He
changed bread and wine into His body and blood, His
living self. By those words, "Do this," He ordained them
the first priests of His Church.

At the Last Supper Christ said the first Mass, ordained
the first priests, and gave Holy Communion for the first
time. We say He said the first Mass because it was then
that He offered Himself as a victim for our redemption,
saying: "This is My body which is given for you." The
body which He then gave in an unbloody manner for our
salvation He gave the next day in a bloody manner on the
cross as the victim of atonement. In the Mass Christ renews in an unbloody manner the sacrifice which He made
of Himself on Calvary. The celebrant of the Mass is only
the minister or agent by whom the sacrifice is offered,
Christ Himself being both the sacrifice offered and the
one making the offering. Attendance at Mass is the same,
in effect, as standing at the foot of the cross with Mary
and John and Magdalene. Christ offered Himself once
in a bloody manner, but He renews the offering in an
unbloody manner every time the holy Sacrifice of the
Mass is celebrated.

When Christ said to the apostles: "Do this for a commemoration of Me," He ordained them priests to do what
He had just done; namely, to change bread into His body.
And from that day to this, wherever Mass is celebrated,
the officiating priest acting in the name and by the
power of Christ effects the very same change that He
accomplished at the first Mass which He Himself cele-

brated in the presence of the apostles on the eve of the crucifixion.

The Last Supper witnessed not only the first Mass and the first ordination to the priesthood, but also the first Holy Communion. "Whilst they were at supper, Jesus took bread and blessed and broke, and gave to His disciples, and said: Take ye and eat. This is My body" (Matthew 26:26). Thus was fulfilled the promise He made previously when He said: "I am the living bread which came down from heaven. If any man eat of this bread he shall live forever; and the bread that I will give is My flesh, for the life of the world" (John 6:51-52).

By means of the Eucharist Christ gives Himself to us, communicating His body and blood to the faithful. Some of those who heard Christ say that He was to give them His flesh and blood were shocked, saying: "How can He give us His flesh and blood?" Christ did not explain how, but repeated even more emphatically what He had said.

There are many things which we do not understand, but which nevertheless we accept as facts. A mother, for example, nursing her babe, gives her flesh and blood to the infant at her breast by means of the milk which she imparts to her child. By a process unknown to the mother, part of her own self becomes milk, and when she communicates it to the child at her breast, it in turn becomes the flesh and blood of the child. By means of milk, therefore, the mother gives her flesh and blood to her babe. By means of the Eucharist Christ gives Himself to the faithful.

Mysteries are all around us. We do not know how the grass and water, which the cattle eat and drink in the pasture, become the hide, hair, bone, nerve, muscle, brain,

and heart of these creatures. Nor do we know how it is
that when we eat the flesh of these cattle, it becomes
part of our living selves.

St. Augustine declared that he would not believe that
Christianity was a divine religion if it did not contain
mysteries. Every other religion teaches only what the
mind of man can invent, but Christianity teaches what
never could emanate from the intellect of man. The Trinity, incarnation, and Eucharist are mysteries which the
Creator alone could originate, and they stamp the religion
of Christ as truly supernatural and consequently divinely
true. Christ never explained His doctrine, but only proclaimed it. He did not propose His teaching for debate,
but imposed it for acceptance. He spoke as God and demanded to be believed on His word only.

The Eucharist is both a sacrament and a sacrifice. As
a sacrament, it is the body of Christ given to the faithful
in Holy Communion, preserved in the tabernacle of the
altar, and publicly adored at the service of Benediction of
the Blessed Sacrament. As a sacrifice the Eucharist is
the body and blood of Christ, Christ Himself, offered
anew at the consecration of the Mass. The act by which
the bread becomes the body of Christ is called *transubstantiation*. It is so named because it signifies a change
of the substance of bread into Christ's body. This change
is unique in creation and is termed 'the mystery of faith.'

In order to have some faint idea of what this change
is, we must know what is meant by substance. In every
material thing there are two elements, the internal and
external. The internal element is not perceptible by the
senses; the external is perceptible. An example will help
to make this clear. A diamond looks very much like a

piece of glass. As a matter of fact an imitation diamond can be so cleverly made that only an expert can distinguish the piece of glass from the diamond. What makes the diamond a diamond and not glass? Something internal and not discernible by the senses. This internal something which constitutes the diamond to be what it is, we call substance, while the external qualities, such as size, color, shape, and so forth, we call accidents.

Ordinarily, when the substance of a thing—that is, its internal element—changes, there is a corresponding external change, showing the thing to be different from what it was before. For instance, when a piece of coal burns out, it ceases to be coal and becomes a cinder, something entirely different in appearance, weight, color, and so forth.

Now, the mystery of transubstantiation is that while the substance of bread no longer exists, the external appearance, or accidents, of bread remain, not changing as ordinarily happens when a substance changes. In the Eucharist we have no discernible evidence of a substantial change. We have instead the word of Christ. That is why it is termed the mystery of faith. Our reason for believing the change is not the testimony of our senses, but the word of God. If at the consecration the external elements of the bread visibly changed, there would be no mystery of faith, and no act of faith.

We believe in the Eucharist on the same authority we believe in the Trinity. Our religion is called 'our holy faith' for the very reason that it is based on faith in Christ, who can neither deceive nor be deceived. Catholicism is a supernatural religion. Its origin, doctrine, and existence cannot be accounted for by any natural explanation. The Eucharist is the heart of Catholicism, for it is the Eucharist that constitutes the Mass a sacrifice. The priest is ordained to celebrate Mass; the altar is built and the Church erected in order to have a temple for the sacrifice of the Mass and the 'worship of the Eucharistic God. The Eucharist being such an essential element of Catholicism, Christ took pains to prepare His followers for its acceptance on His word only. At the marriage feast of Cana He changed water into wine by His will only, speaking no word. On the occasion when He fed the thousands of men and women with a few loaves and fishes, it was done by creative power possible to God alone.

By these and other acts possible to the Creator alone, Christ showed that He was what He claimed to be, the eternal Son of God. As such He is truth itself, and His word alone suffices for our belief, for God can neither deceive nor be deceived. It may be objected that it is unreasonable to believe what is contrary to the testimony of the senses. To this it is answered that substance is outside the range of the senses, for the senses can deal only with what falls under their observation. We can observe only the effect of a change of substance; that is, the external modification which results. In everything except the Eucharist an external change follows the substantial change. As said before, we believe the substantial change on Christ's word only, since there is no external evidence of a change of substance.

The Eucharist is the sacrament of love, showing God's love for us, and also affording us the means of showing our love for Him. By the Eucharist Christ remains with us in the tabernacle of the altar, dwells within us in Holy

Communion, accompanies us on our last journey, as Viaticum, and in the Mass offers Himself as a sacrifice for our eternal salvation.

The Eucharist in its various aspects is a miracle of love. Nothing but love can explain the depths of humility implied in this sacrament. The Son of God, having as it were emptied Himself of His glory by the mysteries of the incarnation and the Eucharist, turns to us saying: "Child, behold what My love for you has prompted Me to do! In return give Me your love." And just as the Eucharist shows Christ's love for us, so does it also afford us the means of showing our love for Him.

First of all, if we truly love Christ, we shall frequently receive Him in Holy Communion. Love shows itself by desire to be with the beloved. Those who love seek occasions of being together. By Holy Communion we are intimately united with Christ. If our soul be properly prepared for His visit, it not only shows our love for our divine guest, but also receives from His visit sanctifying grace, which makes us more and more dear to Him each time He comes. The Gospel declares that "as many as received Him, He gave them power to be made the sons of God" (John 1:12). We receive Jesus in various ways, whether it be by believing in His word, living by His precepts, or in any other manner; but by Holy Communion we receive Him in the most intimate and real sense. By Holy Communion we begin even in this life that participation in divinity which will result hereafter in our becoming members of the divine family.

Jesus in speaking of Holy Communion said: "He that eateth My flesh, and drinketh My blood, abideth in Me, and I in him; . . . He hath everlasting life, and I will raise him up in the last day" (John 6:57, 55). The nature of Holy Communion is such that it tends in various ways to assure salvation.

Apart from the fact that in receiving Christ we receive the author and source of sanctifying grace, the preparation for Holy Communion is a most efficacious means of sanctification. The worthy reception of Holy Communion implies making our soul an acceptable place for the divine guest. For this reason if there should be anything in the soul seriously displeasing to God, it must be removed.

In proportion as we receive Holy Communion more worthily, the more careful shall we be to have the soul more worthy of its divine guest. It is true that we can never be really worthy to receive Christ, but He comes to us not because of our worthiness, but because of His goodness. The greatest saint is not really worthy to receive Christ; but when we do our part to prepare for His coming, He delights to be with the children of men. Nothing helps us to be pleasing to Him so much as frequently opening the door of our heart to welcome Him in. Each visit He makes adds to the beauty of our soul and makes it more and more a place of delight for His dwelling.

Tradition has it that the chalice used by our Divine Lord at the Last Supper, and which held for the first time His redeeming blood, was given by Christ Himself to Joseph of Arimathea. This devoted follower of Christ was cast into prison for confessing Christ and was left there to die of neglect and starvation. Christ appeared to him and gave him the sacred vessel, by which he was miraculously sustained for forty-two years, until liberated under the Emperor Vespasian. Joseph after his liberation brought the vessel to Britain, where he died, and the chalice vanished. Then resulted the quest of the Holy Grail, as the chalice was called, and the various legends concerning Percival and other knights which have been immortalized in literature and the drama.

Each one of us who receives Holy Communion possesses the Holy Grail without being forced to go in quest of it. The recipient of Holy Communion is himself the Holy Grail, the living chalice of the blood of the Redeemer. "To as many as receive Him He gives the power to become the sons of God." Frequent Holy Communion is the best assurance of blissful union with Christ in heaven.

SUMMARY

Association with good and refined persons ordinarily makes one good and refined. By Holy Communion we associate with the most perfect being in the world, who is also the source of all holiness.

By Holy Communion we not only abide with Jesus, but also receive from Him help to live in the way most pleasing to Him.

The two greatest wonders of creation are the incarnation and the Eucharist.

By the incarnation the Son of God united Himself to humanity. By the Eucharist the Son of God made man unites Himself to the individual human being.

By the consecration at Mass the substance of bread and wine becomes Jesus Christ. This change is termed transubstantiation.

Every material thing is constituted of internal and external elements. The internal elements, not perceptible by the senses, are called substance; the external elements, perceptible by the senses, are called accidents.

To illustrate: A diamond externally has the appearance of a piece of glass, but it is, notwithstanding, something essentially different. The element which makes the diamond what it is—the internal something—is termed substance.

When a substance changes there is a corresponding change of the accidents. In the Eucharist, however, when the substance of bread becomes Christ, there is no external change to show it.

We believe the substantial change on the word of Christ.

The Eucharist is the sacrament of love, showing Christ's love for us, and affording us the means of showing our love for Him.

Frequent reception of Holy Communion is the best means of assuring our eternal companionship with Christ in His heavenly kingdom.

POINTS FOR DISCUSSION

1. The doctrine of the Eucharist contradicts the testimony of the senses, and is therefore not true.

2. There is no change whatever after the consecration of the host, therefore there is no change of substance.

3. The senses report correctly about other things, hence about the Eucharist also.

4. Every change of substance is followed by external changes, but there are no external changes after the consecration.

5. Many of those who receive Holy Communion are no better for it, a proof that it is not the body of Christ.

6. No one is worthy to receive the body and blood of Christ.

7. Many people receive Holy Communion without fully realizing what they are doing.

8. Little or no benefit comes from Holy Communion unless one fully realizes its significance.

9. Frequent reception of Holy Communion leads to routine. Once a year is often enough to receive.

CHAPTER XX

PRAYER

PRAYER IS VERBAL OR MENTAL CONVERSE with God or the saints. By prayer a man associates with the supernatural world, interests supernatural beings in his welfare, and receives supernatural aid in his journey to his eternal destiny. Man's final destiny is eternity—either a happy eternity with God or an accursed eternity apart from God, according as he has been faithful or disloyal to the Lord of time and eternity during the period of probation called life.

Prayer is necessary in order to attain our supernatural destiny. Whatever is merely natural, man may accomplish by natural means, but since man's destiny is supernatural, he needs supernatural aid to attain it. Just as man naturally cannot fly through the air, but must devise artificial means such as an airplane in order to do so, in like manner without help from above, he cannot rise above his natural element. Prayer obtains for man the aid which is necessary in order to rise from the natural to the supernatural state. By prayer we are put in communication with another world, whose dwellers have it in their power to aid us to attain the blissful existence which is theirs forever.

It will help us to realize the existence of this supernatural world if we reflect that there is another world alongside and within our own, and of which we should never know the existence except for the radio. In a room, as silent as death, there is a world of activity not perceptible by man's unaided senses. Turn on the radio, and the activity of the ether waves fills the room with the harmony of a symphony concert, the voice of an orator, the cry for help from a shipwreck, the description of an athletic contest, or the report of the news of the world. All this activity of the air would never have been known if radio transmission had not been discovered.

The radio world is a reality, even though we do not perceive it by our unaided senses. Perhaps if we had a device for vision, such as we have for hearing, we could see, as well as hear, another world.

For all we know, heaven is a condition of existence rather than a place. If we were granted the power of seeing the supernatural world, we might behold very near us the saints and angels and our beloved ones who have gone before us.

In the Apostles Creed we affirm our belief in the communion of saints. This means the bond of union between ourselves and those who are now God's friends in the eternal realm. We know that they can hear our prayers and that they desire to aid us to be sharers with them of the glory and bliss of the heavenly kingdom. We are continually getting nearer and nearer to the unseen world. Already television enables us to see persons and events at a distance. Until recently it would have been deemed impossible for a person in New York to see and speak to a person in London. If this can be done by human ingenuity, imagine what may be done by divine power. If in this material world such marvels exist, what must be the potentiality of the spiritual world, limited by neither time nor space!

We do not need to conjecture, however, for we know, on the word of God Himself, that communication between earth and heaven, between man and the blessed dwellers of the world beyond, is a reality. Christ Himself, by word and example, taught us to converse with the world beyond. He bade us to look up to heaven to the Creator of the world and address Him as our Father, and to pray to Him for what we need in our journey to the blessed abode where He awaits us.

Most people who fail to attain eternal happiness neglect to keep before them the blessed goal to which life should be the path. Prayer helps us to keep constantly in mind the glorious end for which we were created, and if we do our part, enables us to reach it. If a traveler forgets about his destination he will not, ordinarily, arrive at it. The road from time to eternity is crowded with allurements which tend to make us forget our destination unless we keep in mind that we have not here a lasting city. Prayer reminds us that we are not made for time but for eternity, and by keeping this truth before us saves us from taking the alluring by-paths which lead to destruction.

Prayer, moreover, obtains for us aid to do what is naturally beyond our capability. All the power and genius in the world cannot enable man to do a single supernatural act. Human genius may accomplish wonders, but it cannot do anything in a realm above its own. The term 'supernatural' means that which is above the natural. By its very meaning, accordingly, supernatural acts are not possible to us unless supernatural aid is given. Prayer obtains this supernatural assistance and enables us to do what will eventually result in our being made partakers of the divine nature. Man, by the favor of God, has the potentiality of becoming a child of God by adoption into the heavenly family.

An example may help us to understand this transformation, although no example in the natural or material world exactly parallels what is supernatural.

A caterpillar is a vile worm of earth, crawling on the ground, and subsisting on the soil. By the power with which the Creator has endowed it, this vile worm is destined to become a beautiful winged creature of the air. In the course of time the caterpillar buries itself in a tomb of its own making. After a certain period, it bursts its tomb and flies forth from the cocoon a resplendent thing of the air, a butterfly. This transition, although natural, is due nevertheless to the Author of nature, who imparted to the lowly worm its capability of developing into its final glorious form.

In a somewhat similar manner, but not due to man's nature, the Creator in His goodness has endowed man with the power of being made a partaker of the divine nature. This glorious supernatural state is a favor of the Creator conferred on man, His masterpiece of visible creation, and requires the co-operation of man for its final realization. Christ said: "If thou wilt enter into life, keep the commandments" (Matthew 19:17). He addressed these words to those who already possessed natural life, and was accordingly referring to supernatural life.

It is to be noticed that He said *"if* thou wilt enter," showing thereby that there is a condition attached to our final destiny; namely, the keeping of the commandments.

Heavenly life, besides being a favor of God, is also a reward for fidelity in His service during the period of probation called life. Probation implies a test, a trial. If we were not tempted there would be no discernment of the faithful from the unfaithful. It is because of this that Christ bade us pray lest we enter into temptation—that is, lest we yield to it.

Prayer has for its object, however, not only to obtain strength to overcome temptation, but also to give to God the worship which the creature owes to the Creator. By prayer we show our submission to a power above, for in pleading for divine assistance we acknowledge our dependence on a superior being. Also by prayer we honor God by thanking Him for His benefits, especially for the glorious destiny to which He has in His goodness elevated us. By prayer, moreover, we plead for pardon of our sins. One of the petitions of the Lord's Prayer is: "Forgive us our trespasses." No one but Him whom we have offended can forgive those offenses. Prayer obtains for us the proper dispositions for receiving in the confessional the divine mercy there dispensed by God's ministers.

Christ declared: "Without Me you can do nothing." He did not refer to acts which we do by our natural power, but to those supernatural acts which without His grace are impossible. Hence the necessity of prayer, without which those who have reached the age of reason cannot be saved. Prayer also reminds us that beyond the cross there is the crown; that the faithful soldier of Christ is assured of final victory, no matter how severe the warfare. Prayer is for mortals wings by which they can ascend from earth to heaven.

By prayer, moreover, the vicissitudes of life, its sufferings and failures, may become stepping-stones to the abode of everlasting happiness. Prayer enables man to transmute the hardships of life into gold for the kingdom of heaven, for suffering may be either a dead weight or a passport to everlasting welfare. It all depends on how we regard it. A burden may be a joy rather than a load, provided it be the source of happiness.

Consider for a moment the heavy burden a miner carries as he traverses difficult and unknown territory in quest of gold. The load he walks under is a grievous burden in itself, but since it is the means by which he will get the gold out of the earth he carries it cheerfully. The prospect of riches makes the burden easy to bear. Now suppose that, after several years, the miner has acquired a goodly amount of gold and is carrying it homeward. The burden may be heavy, every step he takes may make its weight cut into his flesh—but will he lighten the burden? Will he discard some of the gold in order to proceed more comfortably? Not at all. He rejoices as he goes along, bending under the burden, because he looks ahead and contemplates the years of enjoyment it will give him when he reaches home.

In like manner the hardships of life may become by prayer the passport to everlasting enjoyment in our home beyond. Suffering, borne in the spirit of Christian hope, is gold for the kingdom of heaven. Prayer, moreover, begets Christian hope and Christian fortitude, and in so doing takes the weight out of the burdens of life. Prayer, by reminding us of our last end, and that God is our Father, not only helps us to bear cheerfully and courageously the vicissitudes of life, but, moreover, gives us strength against the various temptations which assail every mortal. Prayer is the Christian's armor in the warfare of life. A soldier cannot go into battle without arms, nor can a Christian face the enemies of salvation without prayer. Prayer is the necessary armor of all those who would overcome the forces and wiles and allurements of a sinful world.

The best prayer is the Mass, which by its very nature gives God the highest worship and obtains for man the most abundant graces for salvation. Frequent attendance at Mass not only honors God, but also sanctifies the worshiper. A Catholic should be faithful to his morning and evening prayers, which are a daily reminder that, although he must live *in* this world, he must not live *for* it.

The rosary is a devotion which endears us to the holy Mother of God and assures us of her powerful assistance now and at the hour of our death. Visits to the Blessed Sacrament are another pious practice most pleasing to our Lord and most conducive to a devout life. God is everywhere, but He is especially present in the tabernacle of the altar. The church is a place consecrated to prayer, and because of its surroundings most suitable for recollection and mental converse with God and the saints. These visits, moreover, entail a sacrifice of time and leisure, and consequently afford a practical means of manifesting gratitude to God for His many benefits.

When we pray we should do so with confidence, knowing that God is our Father, and that He has our true welfare at heart. Sometimes we may think that our prayers are not heard because they are not answered as we desire. But often a refusal is a real grant. A parent frequently refuses the request of the child he loves because to grant the request would be to his disadvantage. If a child earnestly entreated his father to let him play instead of going to school, the father in granting that request would be cursed by the child later in life when his lack of education became a serious handicap. Our Father in heaven has in view not only our temporal, but also and especially, our eternal welfare, and hears our petitions accordingly.

Moreover, we must remember that prayer is a petition, not a command. One of the essential conditions of prayer is resignation to God's will. We should, accordingly, bear in mind when praying those words of the Lord's Prayer: "Thy will be done on earth as it is in heaven." God's will is for our salvation, and every prayer we make should implicitly contain that proviso. It is impossible for a person to continue faithful to prayer and lose his soul. On the other hand, by neglect of prayer many a man has strayed from the narrow path of salvation to the broad path that leads to eternal misery. By prayer, finally, man acknowledges the dominion of God over mankind. If God be our sovereign here, He will be our reward exceedingly great hereafter.

SUMMARY

Prayer is mental or verbal converse with God or with the saints.

By prayer man associates with the supernatural world and interests supernatural beings in his eternal welfare.

Man's final destiny is eternity, which will be happy or miserable according as he has been faithful or not to God during the period of probation called life. No one can reach a destination unless he tends towards it.

By prayer our final end is kept before us, and aid is given in order to reach it.

It is not easy to keep in the way to salvation. Aid from above is necessary, and this aid is obtained by prayer.

We pray:

1. To honor God, the author of our being and of the blessed destiny which may be ours if we do our part.

2. To remind us that we have not here a lasting city but seek one which is to come.

3. To obtain strength against the obstacles to our eternal salvation.

4. To obtain pardon for our sins.

Prayer enables us to make suffering and affliction wings to everlasting joy; it converts the burdens of life into gold for the kingdom of heaven.

If a person be faithful to prayer he is not in danger of losing his soul.

The best prayer is the Mass, which offers to God what is most acceptable to Him.

Morning and evening prayers are a sacred duty of religion. Neglect of daily prayers has caused many to leave the path of salvation for the broad road that leads to destruction.

The rosary beads should be possessed and frequently recited, daily if possible. This devotion not only honors the Mother of God, but obtains her powerful assistance now and at the hour of death.

Prayer, briefly, is the armor of the Christian against the assaults of the enemies of salvation. As a soldier cannot face the enemy without arms, so a Christian cannot face the enemies of the soul without prayer.

God is our Father, so we must pray with confidence, trusting Him to grant what is best for us in time and eternity.

POINTS FOR DISCUSSION

1. God knows our thoughts and needs, so there is no need of praying to Him.

2. God knows our dependence on Him, so there is no need of showing it by prayer.

3. We do not need help from above, for we have by nature all that is necessary to attain our end.

4. God does not hear our prayers, otherwise they would always be answered, for He is our heavenly Father.

5. We often pray for spiritual favors for ourselves and others, but even such prayers do not always bear fruit.

6. Some people are always praying, but their lives show no improvement.

7. The Mass is a prayer of infinite worth and efficacy; hence when we offer to God the Mass at which we assist, we should obtain our petitions.

8. The rosary is a monotonous repetition of prayers without attention.

9. Daily prayer is not necessary.

CHAPTER XXI

MARRIAGE

MARRIAGE IS THE LAWFUL UNION of one man with one woman for mutual comfort and to propagate the human race. God Himself is the author of marriage. "What . . . God hath joined together let not man put asunder" (Mark 10:9). Christ elevated marriage to the dignity of a sacrament, a grace-giving institution to enable husband and wife to live in the way conducive to temporal and eternal welfare.

Marriage is one of the most important things in the life of man. No care is too great in taking this important step. Before a man pays serious attention to a woman, he should know whether he can lawfully marry her and whether she gives promise of being the proper companion for life. Too often a man becomes attached to a woman before he knows she is not eligible for Christian matrimony, and then finds it almost impossible to break away from the attachment. Women, because they can suffer more, should be even more careful to avoid a false step.

Marriage has serious consequences to the individual, the family, and the state. Church and state will both be better in proportion as marriage is what God intends it to be. The Catholic church is the voice of God in the world, and marriage as she upholds it is the ordinance of God Himself. The importance of marriage may be realized from the fact that Pope Pius XI has issued an encyclical on it. As this document touches on the vital points of this subject, we shall briefly consider its leading topics. We shall first enumerate them in the order of sequence.

1. The Divine Institution of Marriage
2. The Indissolubility of Marriage
3. Conjugal Fidelity
4. Sacramental Grace
5. Companionate Marriage
6. Birth Control
7. The Emancipation of Women
8. Incompatibility
9. Mixed Marriages
10. Divorce
11. Reverence for God's Law

1. THE DIVINE INSTITUTION OF MARRIAGE. The first thing to observe about marriage is that it is not a human but a divine institution (Mark 10:9). Whenever man and woman are truly united in matrimony, the pact is ratified in heaven. God joins them together, and He will not permit any human power to declare them separated. God created man for His own external glory. After He had made Adam and Eve to His own image, He said: "Increase and multiply, and fill the earth" (Genesis 1:28). It is most reasonable that God should exercise a specially close supervision over the union of man and woman in marriage, since marriage is His own institution and the means He has chosen for securing the continuance of the human race. For knowledge about God's laws concerning matrimony we must turn to the statements of Christ and to the declarations of His Church, which is His living voice upon earth with divine authority to make laws for the spiritual welfare of the human race.

2. THE INDISSOLUBILITY OF MARRIAGE. A marriage validly contracted and consummated cannot be dissolved by

any human authority. Even the Church cannot dissolve such a marriage; for while the Church has authority to make laws, it cannot make laws opposed to the express will of God. "What . . . God hath joined together let not man put asunder" (Mark 10:9).

Even if God had not declared the indissolubility of the marriage bond, nature itself proclaims that it should be permanent. The ordinary consequence of marriage is children, and the proper care of children requires the home and its maintenance. When a home is broken by divorce, the children have at best only half a home—either father or mother is missing. The mother's care is especially necessary. Hence the mother cannot ordinarily discharge her home duties properly and at the same time provide for its needs by earning a wage.

If illness or death remove either father or mother, the case is indeed sad, but as it is the disposition of Providence it relieves parents of responsibility for the consequences. If, however, the bond be severed by human wilfulness, the responsibility rests with those who caused its severance. God has solemnly declared that the bond holds until death breaks it; and if man presumes to sever what God declares He has joined, it is a defiance of the eternal Lawgiver. The Pauline privilege, which permits a Christian convert to leave a pagan husband or wife who refuses to live at peace, is a divine dispensation granted to enable the Christian convert safely to practice the Christian religion.

Marriage is a contract. A contract to be valid must be made in accordance with lawful requirements. If a marriage be contracted against the requirements of ecclesiastical law, it is not valid. There are certain impediments to marriage which render it null and void. Such are called *invalidating* impediments. Other impediments, called *impeding,* render a marriage illicit; that is, unlawful but not null and void. An example of an impeding impediment is that which forbids a marriage to be solemnized at certain seasons specified by the Church.

An annulment is an ecclesiastical declaration that a reputed marriage was no marriage at all. If a marriage is declared annulled, it leaves both parties free to marry. Sometimes we hear of two Catholics who were married in the Church by a Catholic priest, and who later separated and were married to others by a priest. Whenever you hear of such a case, you will know that for a very substantial reason the first marriage was not valid, and a decree of annulment left man and woman free to marry. A valid and consummated marriage, however, has never been dissolved by the Church, except in the case of the Pauline privilege, an exception divinely authorized in order to save the faith of the Christian.

3. CONJUGAL FIDELITY. Conjugal fidelity demands the complete unity of marriage, so that neither husband nor wife is free to consort with anyone else. Husband and wife, moreover, in their mutual relations must be mindful of the law of God and of nature.

4. SACRAMENTAL GRACE. Sacramental grace is the result of the elevation of marriage to the dignity of a grace-giving institution. The apostle signified that Christian marriage was a holy state when he said: "Husbands, love your wives as Christ also loved the Church" (Ephesians 5:25). The love of husband and wife is not based on the passing lust of the moment, nor does it consist in endearing sentiments only, but in the deep attachment

of the heart expressed in kindness, consideration, and mutual sacrifice.

5. COMPANIONATE MARRIAGE. Companionate marriage, or as it is sometimes called 'trial marriage,' is only a euphemistic way of characterizing what in plain language is adultery or fornication. Such sinful unions offer all the indulgence of matrimony and its rights, without, however, the indissoluble bond, and without offspring, unless later the parties change their union into matrimony in the full sense of the law.

6. BIRTH CONTROL. Birth control or contraception is the avoidance by unnatural or artificial means of what is termed the 'disagreeable burden of offspring.' If parents wish to limit the family by virtuous continence, it is within their rights, but contraception is effected by nullifying a natural function.

Raising a family may be a burden, but it is of the nature of the marriage contract, and must be borne with Christian fortitude. No reason, however grave, may be put forward by which anything intrinsically against nature may become conformable to nature and morally good. Every state of life has its burdens, which must be accepted as inherent in each particular state. Taxes are a burden, sometimes an intolerable burden, but that does not exempt citizens from paying them. If we have to make sacrifices and bear burdens for our country, we certainly should not evade the burdens which nature and God's laws impose. Those, therefore, who in exercising the conjugal act deliberately frustrate its natural power and purpose, sin against nature, and commit a deed which is shameful and intrinsically wrong.

7. THE EMANCIPATION OF WOMEN. The emancipation

of women from the burdensome duties of wife and mother and from domestic concerns is now loudly proclaimed. This emancipation would really deprive woman of her greatest glory. If woman descends from the throne to which she has been raised in the home by means of the Gospel, she will eventually be reduced to her former pagan state of subjection, and will lose the respected position she now occupies. Man and woman both have their place in life, but man's place is not woman's nor is woman's man's. Equality does not mean denaturalization. In some things a man is superior to woman, in others woman is superior to man. The so-called emancipation of woman, instead of liberating, lowers her.

8. INCOMPATIBILITY. Incompatibility is a modern social disease. One of the reasons frequently given to justify divorce is incompatibility, by which is meant the impossibility of living agreeably with a person. Incompatibility is a disease easily contracted if either husband or wife desires to form a new union. In the old days husband and wife, knowing that marriage was permanent, made themselves agreeable to each other, or if they had their disagreements, bore them as best they could.

Every state of life has its incompatibilities, but they do not justify one in violating solemn obligations. If a soldier enlists in the army, he may find that his superior officers and his duties are disagreeable, but that will not permit him to resign. Almost every man or woman employed in a big store finds many persons and things incompatible, but they keep on working nevertheless, for they know that if they left their place they might not find another; and even if they did, it would have the same or greater incompatibilities. If in the army and business people have to submit to disagreeable conditions for the sake of a salary, certainly parents should do so for the sake of the family. But, all comparisons aside, people who marry are not free to violate the vow they made to remain husband and wife until death separates them.

9. MIXED MARRIAGES. Mixed marriages are tolerated by the Church, but greatly discouraged. A mixed marriage is one between a Catholic and a non-Catholic. Sometimes such unions prove to be satisfactory, but usually they do not. Experience shows that legions of Catholics have lost the faith on account of mixed marriages. Often the non-Catholic does not live up to the promises regarding children. Even if the promises are kept, the children gradually drift from religious practices when they observe that either parent neglects or ignores them. Those who contract a mixed marriage should be sure to comply strictly with all the requirements for such a union. Dispensations must be obtained, written promises given, and the Catholic ceremony alone employed.

10. DIVORCE. Divorce is rapidly making a mockery of the most sacred institution of society and the state. A few years ago divorce was a social crime. Decent people refused to associate with those who were divorced. Now, however, divorce is almost fashionable in certain ranks of society. Men and women marry and get divorced two, three, and four times, and find that such a proceeding affects their social standing not in the least.

Marriage in certain social groups has degenerated almost to the pagan standard. These people, knowing they can break the bond almost at will, marry with less concern than they use in buying an automobile or a house. It has actually come to such a pass that marriage is matter for vicious joking in literature and on the stage. And yet St. Thomas More laid his head on the executioner's block rather than approve the divorce of Henry VIII.

Divorce is a symptom of a disease which is attacking religion as well as society. It is a denial that Christ established an authoritative Church which He empowered to speak in His name. The only church in the world today which upholds absolutely Christ's teaching on divorce is the Catholic church. The only church which holds now the teaching on divorce which prevailed in Christendom for the sixteen centuries before the Reformation is the Catholic church.

There was no such thing as divorce in Christendom before Luther and Henry VIII. If the Church was right during all those centuries, those who differ with her now differ with the Christian doctrine on divorce which came directly from Christ Himself. Not until the sixteenth century was any cause looked upon as sufficient to justify divorce with the right to marry another. Marriage may have its difficulties and burdens, but the way to settle them is not to desert the state to which one is bound by solemn vow. If conditions become really incompatible, separation is permissible, but not with the right to marry another. Very often such a separation opens the eyes of both parties and leads to a reconciliation and a permanent peaceful union.

Every law that is made for general welfare bears hard on some individuals. Quarantine safeguards the health of a nation, but may cause very serious inconvenience to the persons detained. Traffic laws interfere at times with individual urgency, but nevertheless save thousands of lives. And so it is with every law pertaining to general welfare. If we abolished a law for its abuses or inconvenience, there is not a law on the statute books that would stand.

Divorce eventually undermines the family, which is the basis of society and of the state. The Roman Empire owed its decline and fall to the weakening of the family. That is why governments as well as religion are alarmed at the canker of divorce which is eating into and destroying society. Divorce not only undermines society; it also embitters children against either father or mother. Children usually side with either father or mother, and the one whom they take sides against becomes ordinarily an object of hatred to them. This not only embitters their life, but not infrequently mars their career.

It is true that at times the indissolubility of the marriage bond works great hardship, as when either husband or wife becomes incurably invalided or hopelessly insane. But the evil of divorce works such havoc that if it once gets slight headway it becomes a contagious disease of society, as we see to our dismay at present among the social groups it has infected.

Divorce is now sweeping over higher society like a tidal wave. Its only real barrier is the Catholic church, which alone of all religions makes no compromise on this doctrine of Christ. It is to be noticed that in proportion as divorce makes headway, religion itself declines. This is one reason why we see among the various denominations so many empty churches and such little interest in religion. It is real religion alone that can stem the evil flood of divorce. By real religion is meant that which has for its founder Jesus Christ, the eternal Son of God. Christ is truth itself. He is the way, the truth, and the life, and the light of the world. It is the truth that sets men free. Error may give latitude to man's waywardness, but it is the latitude that ends in degradation and moral slavery.

11. REVERENCE FOR GOD'S LAW. Reverence for God and His holy law may entail certain restrictions, but they are the restrictions which save from disaster here and hereafter. The faithful Catholic enjoys the liberty of the sons of God, the liberty that rejoices in knowing that service here means reigning with God hereafter. Compliance with God's ordinances gives that peace which the world cannot give nor take away.

In proportion as we truly reverence God and His holy law we shall find it easy to make any and every sacrifice which His service entails. God speaks to us by His Church. In faithfully following her guidance we are on the sure road to the kingdom He has prepared for those who serve and love Him.

After all, what does it profit a man to gain the whole world if he lose his soul? The faithful Catholic has the assurance of God Himself that they who in this life observe His commandments will be made His companions in the eternal kingdom. That assurance gives strength and fortitude to fight the good fight whose issue is everlasting victory.

SUMMARY

Marriage is the lawful union of one man with one woman for mutual comfort and to perpetuate the human race.

God Himself is the author of marriage. "What God hath joined together let not man put asunder" (Mark 10:9).

Christ elevated marriage to the dignity of a sacrament, a

grace-giving institution to enable husband and wife to live for temporal and eternal welfare.

Marriage is one of the most important things in the life of man.

Before a man pays serious attention to a woman he should know whether he can lawfully marry her and whether she promises to be the proper companion for life. Too often a man becomes attached to a woman before he knows she is not eligible for Christian marriage, and then finds it almost impossible to break away from the attachment. Women must exercise even greater care.

Marriage has serious consequences to the individual, the family, and the state. Church and state will be better in proportion as marriage is what God intends it to be.

It is because of the importance of marriage to mankind that Pius XI recently issued the encyclical *Casti Connubii* on the subject. The following gives its main topics:

1. The Divine Institution of Marriage
2. The Indissolubility of Marriage
     Impediments
     Annulment
3. Conjugal Fidelity
4. Sacramental Grace
5. Companionate Marriage
6. Birth Control
7. The Emancipation of Women
8. Incompatibility
9. Mixed Marriages
10. Divorce
11. Reverence for God's Law

Every Catholic should be well informed on each of these points, as they form the subject matter of conversation, lectures, books, and so forth.

Christ is the light of the world. His Church is also the light of the world.[1]

---

[1] For the development of this subject see the encyclical *Casti Connubii*.

POINTS FOR DISCUSSION

1. (1) What is marriage? (2) What is the difference between divorce and annulment? (3) What are the conditions for a valid marriage?

2. Marriage is natural to man, and is therefore a human, not a divine, institution.

3. Marriage is a contract, and should be dissolvable by the contracting parties.

4. If either party to a marriage becomes insane or a prisoner for life, it is unjust to hold the other party to the contract.

5. If one party to a marriage violates its obligations, the other party is free to do the same.

6. Since marriage entails such serious consequences, companionate marriage should be allowed.

7. Birth control is often necessary for the maintenance of the family.

8. Birth control is forbidden by the Church in order to increase membership.

9. Birth control should be a matter for the individuals concerned to decide.

10. Incompatibility should justify divorce.

11. The Church's marriage laws are tyrannical.

CHAPTER XXII

Vocation

EVERYONE IS BEST SUITED for some one definite place in life. Most people are not in a position to choose their place, since as a rule circumstances determine it. Others can choose in a general way but not definitely.

Vocation means a calling. People are called in various ways to a career. If a person finds his right career, work will be congenial rather than burdensome. We see, therefore, the importance of knowing one's right place in life and, as far as possible, securing it. How may we know our vocation? In the same way as we know anything else: by observation, reflection, consultation, and prayer. There are two main divisions of vocations, civic and ecclesiastical. Civic vocations embrace the various professions, trades, and businesses which constitute a worldly career. Ecclesiastical vocations include the various activities which pertain to service in the kingdom of God on earth. They comprise the religious orders, the priesthood, and the missionary life. After a person has decided broadly on either of these two general states of life, the next step is to select the particular employment or profession for which he is best suited.

We shall first consider the civic career. Ordinarily a person has a liking or preference for some particular line of activity. But a preference, although an indication, is not sufficient to decide a career. Circumstances must be taken into consideration. A particular career might strongly appeal to a person, and yet not be attainable without imposing hardship or privation on those who look to him for support. Parents are often willing to make very great sacrifices to advance the prospects of their children, but it not infrequently happens that the home needs the active support of children, and then duty to parents comes first.

Again, a person might be attracted to a career or profession which requires years of study and preparation, but unless he can see his way clear to attain the goal he should not undertake the endeavor. This is said not to discourage ambition in the young, but to save them from embarking on a venture without mature consideration. Obstacles often serve as a spur to success, provided the person has a strong will and the necessary intellectual qualifications. Every career in life has its stage and its back-stage. Before a man decides on a career he should try to find out, not only its apparent advantages, but also its inherent difficulties and disadvantages. Many careers have a superficial attraction which vanishes on closer inspection. A doctor, lawyer, or merchant is usually on dress parade to the ordinary observer. But behind the dress parade there are the routine and service which characterize every condition of life.

If a person is adapted to the career he has chosen, he will find its work a pleasure rather than a task. For this reason no care is too great in choosing one's state of life. It is always advisable to consult with members of the calling one has in view in order to learn more intimately about it. Also, parents should be consulted, even if eventually their guidance be not followed. Parents, with their experience of life and their knowledge of their offspring,

may readily see that a proposed career would be altogether unsuitable. There are certain persons, however,
who despite all opposition decide for themselves, and occasionally this very self-reliance and determination is an
indication of a real vocation and an assurance of a
successful career.

Prayer should be an important factor in making one's
decision as to one's proper place in life. The assistance
of the Holy Spirit is assured to those who in the sincerity
of their heart seek divine guidance in the problems of
life. All that has been said concerning vocation in a civic
career applies also to a vocation to the ecclesiastical
state. The ecclesiastical vocation embraces not only the
sanctuary but also the school, the lecture platform, the
written word, and the missionary labors of the apostolate
in distant lands. A vocation to such a state of life is a
privilege and an honor.

As in the civic state there are those who are not content with doing only what they are obliged to do, but as
patriotic citizens do all they can for the country's welfare, so in the Church there are those generous souls who
are not satisfied with keeping the commandments, but
also aim at promoting the welfare of God's kingdom on
earth by consecrating their lives to service and sacrifice
for the salvation of souls. These consecrated persons are
the chivalry of Christianity, the patriots and heroes of
the Church. A call to this generous service is a vocation
to the priestly or religious life, and is a special favor and
grace of God. Christ said to His apostles: "You have not
chosen Me, but I have chosen you" (John 15:16).

The apostles were the first persons in Christendom to
consecrate their lives to the ecclesiastical vocation, and

our Divine Lord distinctly declared that their vocation was due to a special call on His part. But although a religious vocation is a special favor of God, it is a favor which He freely grants to those who show good will in His service. And how is a young man to know that he has a vocation to the ecclesiastical state?

A true religious vocation manifests itself primarily by a strong desire to do something special for God. Christians may be compared to a vast army passing in review before their commander, Christ. As they pass, some are sweetly but powerfully attracted by His gentle character and the knowledge of His great suffering and sacrifices for them. They know that He has extended an invitation for special service to those who desire to serve Him with distinction. They know that He manifested His love for them by service and sacrifice, and that the best way to show their love for Him in return is by service and sacrifice. They also know that in His kingdom there is a large body of the faithful who limit their duty to the observance of the commandments, content with His declaration: "If thou wilt enter into life, keep the commandments." Besides this declaration, they recall that He said: "If thou wilt be perfect, come, follow Me." This invitation to the higher life is a call to the ecclesiastical state, extended to all those generous souls who wish to be distinguished in His service.

Christ, as it were, stands before the great army of Christians and says: "I, the eternal Son of God, have become one of you, in order to lead you to everlasting happiness. In order to attain eternal blessedness it is necessary to overcome the enemies of salvation. For this purpose I have entered upon a campaign against the

world, the flesh, and Satan. I guarantee victory to everyone who perseveres in this campaign. Everyone who
fights under My standard of the Ten Commandments will
enter into eternal life. This guarantee is to everyone
under the banner of the Cross.

"Moreover, in this campaign I need a special body of
generous volunteers who will co-operate with Me regardless of the special hardships and dangers that My service
may require of them. I want no one to volunteer who is
not prepared for devoted service and unlimited sacrifice.
I state plainly that this special service to which I invite
volunteers will be replete with dangers and hardships, but
I will ask no one to endure what I Myself will not endure.
I ask these volunteers to follow Me, to share My lot, to
be close to Me in this campaign, to be, as it were, My
bodyguard. Everyone in the army will be victorious if
he perseveres to the end. Volunteers for this special
service, however, must enroll not merely for ordinary
service and victory, but for arduous duties which call for
devotion to the cause, and generous love of Me.

"I promise no recompense while the campaign is on,
except the assurance of My appreciation and love, and
the peace which the world cannot give nor take away.
Those of you who volunteer to share with Me the special
hardships and sacrifices of this warfare, will be distinguished in My service and will share abundantly in the
eternal triumph."

This appeal of Christ has met a most generous response
in every generation from His day to our own. Christ,
furthermore, issued the following special appeal to those
who would be very close to Him: "If thou wilt be perfect,
go sell what thou hast and give to the poor, and thou

shalt have treasure in heaven; and come follow Me" (Matthew 19:21). The legions of monks, hermits, priests, religious, and others consecrated to service and sacrifice in the kingdom of God on earth are evidence that Christ's words have struck a responsive chord in countless hearts.

The special service to which these devoted souls have consecrated themselves embraces several distinct classes. There is first the priesthood, the members of which labor as other Christs to promote the extension of the kingdom of God and the salvation of souls. Then there are the various religious orders, such as Dominicans, Franciscans, Benedictines, and Jesuits, whose members take the vows of poverty, chastity, and obedience, thus renouncing much for Christ, who renounced so much for them. Besides, there are the numerous religious congregations of men and women, who also take the three vows, and dedicate themselves to service in schools, hospitals, missions, and other activities for the benefit and promotion of religion and for ministering to the wants of the helpless and afflicted.

Such a vocation, as is evident, demands more than ordinary generosity and courage. It calls for real heroism in many cases. But it is because it is heroic that it is so distinguished in God's sight. A cheap gift indicates but little love, but a gift which costs dearly is proof of much love. The religious vocation is one of the greatest sacrifices man can make. It means the renunciation of what is dearest to the human heart. It is the very greatness of the sacrifice that so enhances a religious vocation.

But sacrifice is easy when inspired by love. Most religious vocations are the result of a strong personal love of Christ engendered by the great love He has shown for us. Love is the best and highest motive for consecration to Christ in the religious state. Other motives may be less exalted, but nevertheless sufficiently effective.

In general, it may be said that the sufficient indication of a vocation to the ecclesiastical state is a special desire to please God by doing for Him more than is obligatory. If this desire be based on the love of God, it will sustain the religious in all the difficulties and obstacles which the religious vocation entails. The obstacles with regard to a religious vocation not infrequently arise even before the final step is taken to embrace the religious state. Sometimes the obstacles come from parents, who in their misguided solicitude for their children try to divert them from a career which calls for the great renunciation which a vocation entails. Such parents forget that patriots make heroic renunciation for country, and that God's kingdom must also have its heroes.

Again, obstacles come from attachments to pleasure, friends, and, in general, the allurements of the world. But the very thing which makes a religious vocation so acceptable to God is that these attractions are renounced for His sake. Finally, obstacles arise from human weaknesses and inclinations, which sometimes cause a person to hesitate to undertake a life which demands the subordination of these various tendencies. It is true that the religious state demands self-mastery in a high degree, but it is this mortification of self which makes the religious a close follower of Christ, who from the cradle to the cross endured so much for us. It was because He renounced everything for us that He was entitled to say: "If any man will come after Me, let him deny himself, and take up his cross and follow Me" (Matthew 16:24).

It is because the close following of Christ in the religious state places one near Christ that it is such a distinction to be a religious. Moreover, the intimate association gives assurance that those who are close to Christ in this life will be close to Him in eternal glory.

A religious vocation is a delicate plant which requires care and cultivation to bring it to maturity. Prayer, pious practices, self-denial, and the frequentation of the sacraments are the means of fostering a vocation. Also, it will help greatly to have a regular confessor who by his intimate knowledge will be able to cultivate a true vocation and also discourage one that is not real. A priest rejoices to see a person called to the religious state, but unless the vocation be genuine, he is the last one in the world to promote it.

We should always bear in mind that consecration to God's special service is no guarantee of immunity from the various trials which are part of man's mortal career. Religion does not remove the cross, but gives strength to carry it cheerfully until in the end it is replaced by the crown of everlasting joy.

SUMMARY

Everyone is best suited for some one definite place in life. Most people cannot choose their place except in a general way.

Vocation means a calling. People are called in various ways to a career.

If a person finds his right career, work will be a pleasure rather than a task.

We may know our vocation by observation, reflection, consultation, and prayer.

There are two main divisions of vocations: civic and ecclesiastical. The civic embraces the various professions and businesses which constitute a worldly career. The ecclesiastical embraces the various activities which pertain to service in the kingdom of God on earth. It comprises the priesthood and the various religious orders of men and women.

After one has decided broadly on either of these two general vocations, the next step is to select the particular service for which one is best suited.

As in the state there are those who are not content with doing only what they are obliged to do, but as patriotic citizens do all they can for the country's welfare, so in the Church there are those generous souls who are not satisfied with keeping the commandments, but aim, moreover, at promoting the welfare of God's kingdom by consecrating their lives to service and sacrifice for the salvation of souls. These consecrated persons are the chivalry of Christianity.

Such a vocation is a favor of God, but readily granted to those of good will. A strong personal love of God and a desire to do more than is of obligation are signs of a religious vocation.

Vocation is a delicate plant needing care and cultivation. Piety, prayer, and a regular confessor are special helps.

POINTS FOR DISCUSSION

1. Name the two main divisions of vocation.

2. Give examples of some special profession or business of each general division of vocation.

3. How may one know one's vocation?

4. What are the indications of an ecclesiastical vocation?

5. Does a vocation depend altogether on one's self?

6. How do citizens show extraordinary devotion to the state?

7. How may Catholics show extraordinary devotion to the Church?

8. What class of persons in the Church are her heroes and patriots?

9. What are the chief motives for consecrating one's life exclusively to the service of the Church?

10. What is the vocation of all mankind?

11. How does God recompense those who are faithful to their state of life?

12. Good people can do more good in a secular than in an ecclesiastical career.

13. One's main duty is to one's family.

CHAPTER XXIII

Home and Parish Duties; Catholic Action

RELIGION IS NOT THEORETICAL BUT PRACTICAL. Knowing what is right is not doing right. Doing God's will is the main purpose of life. Man is inclined to do his own will instead of God's. Religion directs our will and conduct by God's will. The practice of religion should begin and be prominent in the home. Some people limit their kindness and consideration to outsiders, disregarding meanwhile those in the home, to whom they especially owe kindness and courtesy. There is a phrase which aptly describes such persons: "house devils, street angels." These persons keep all their good manners for strangers, reserving their rudeness for members of their own family.

In the home a young person should, in the first place, honor his parents by due respect and obedience. Parents are to be honored even if at times they seem not to deserve it. There would be little merit in honoring honorable parents only. No important step should be taken without consulting father or mother, even if on some matters it be not advisable to agree with them. Very great pain is caused parents by a child who ignores them in deciding serious issues. Nowadays, especially, it is incumbent on youth to be mindful of the Fourth Commandment, which bids us to honor father and mother. The spirit of independence and license which now prevails has led many young men not only to ignore but to defy their parents. It is common of late to hear a young man say that he must lead his own life without dictation from anyone. Such a policy not only grieves parents, but leads, ordinarily, to detrimental if not tragic consequences.

The youth who ignores his own father or mother must not expect different conduct from his own children later on. But apart from temporal consequences, disregard of parents is a direct offense against God, who has solemnly commanded children to honor their father and mother. Besides showing due respect to parents, a young man should aid in supporting the home if he be able to do so and the home requires his help. If he must sacrifice some comforts or pleasures in order to give assistance to the family, he should cheerfully do so, remembering that his parents made many sacrifices for him when he was entirely dependent on them. Besides the duty of sharing the burden of home maintenance with his parents, a young man has also obligations to the rest of the family. He should be chivalrous toward his sisters, and a good example to his brothers. Consideration for the feelings and position of others should characterize the conduct of a young man in the home. The daughter in the family has duties parallel to those of the son.

It may be said, in brief, that the key to home happiness and welfare is consideration for others. Nearly all domestic disturbances and unhappiness come from neglecting to put oneself in the place of others and to consider how a contemplated action will affect them. Ordinarily, selfish people are very unhappy. Having regard only for themselves and their own advantage, selfish people gradually become isolated, even in the family, and thus miss the genuine sympathy and co-operation which smooth the rough paths that everyone must at times traverse.

Besides home duties there are parish activities which should engage the interest and co-operation of Catholic young people. Such activities are outside one's obligatory religious duties, such as attendance at Mass and fidelity to the sacraments. It is taken for granted that a Catholic youth will attend to his necessary religious duties. But besides the duties which bind under penalty of sin, there are activities which everyone should engage in who has the welfare of religion at heart.

Pope Pius XI calls these activities 'Catholic Action,' meaning by the term the co-operation of the laity with the clergy in promoting the welfare of Church and state by showing forth Catholic principles and practices. For it is a certainty that in proportion as Catholic principles of conduct prevail, the state as well as the Church will be benefited. Catholic Action embraces various phases, such as engaging in parish activities, joining pious societies, promoting recreational and educational projects, and in various other ways supporting and encouraging whatever advances the welfare and piety of the parish. Such Catholic Action is as old as the Church. In his letter on Catholic Action Pius XI said among other things: "Catholic Action is not a new thing, since St. Paul in his epistle to the Philippians says he is mindful of his fellow laborers, and asks aid for those women who have labored with him in the Gospel" (Philippians 4:3).

Especially in our time is Catholic Action necessary, by which the laity comes to the aid of the clergy in order that under the direction of the bishops the faithful may uphold Catholic principles and practices, and by so doing not only diffuse and defend the faith, but also make sure for themselves eternal salvation in the world to come.

Catholic Action is nothing other than the participation of the laity in the apostolate of the hierarchy.

Catholic Action consists not merely in the pursuit of personal Christian perfection—which is, however, before all others its first and greatest end—but also in social activity legitimately constituted, and as a result aided and encouraged by the authority of the bishops. Such social action tends to extend the reign of Christ and to procure for society the greatest good for all citizens.

Catholic Action should keep itself outside of and above all political parties, aiming primarily at the diffusion, the defense, and the practice of Christian faith and doctrine in individual, family, and civil life. For this reason Catholic Action should affect every man in his private and public life, providing him with the best basis of thought for private and public matters, which is essential to any sort of participation in the apostolate of the hierarchy.

Catholic Action embraces every work or association that can be particularly directed towards the formation of youth and the progress of Christian piety. Catholic Action will make citizens better fitted for public office and will thus advance the welfare of the state as well as the Church by forming honest and able officials. Catholic Action commands its followers to respect legitimate authority and to be obedient to the laws, and to maintain and defend public decency and integrity, the purity of domestic life, the mutual peace of social classes—in a word, everything that contributes to make human society peaceful and safe.

It is very important to realize that Catholic Action is not political, that it is not aligned with any civil group or party. Members of any legitimate party may engage in Catholic Action by following the guidance of the hierarchy whenever it becomes necessary to uphold the principles and practices of Christianity.

From this brief résumé it is clear that Catholic Action is an appropriate means by which the Church may confer on the state all sorts of benefits, and bring the public, regardless of creed, to see that the Catholic church is the true friend of law and order and the promoter of the real welfare of the state. And now let us consider specifically how Catholic young people can engage in this activity for the peace and welfare of Church and state.

First of all, they should be well informed on their religion with regard both to doctrine and history. The end of Catholic Action is the diffusion, defense, and practice of the faith. In order to aid in the diffusion of the faith, it is necessary to know its doctrines and be able to impart the knowledge of them to inquirers or objectors. In this way a Catholic layman may really engage in the apostolate of the Gospel. Many people are opposed to the faith because of distorted notions of it. Once they are set right, they ordinarily look more favorably on the Church, and frequently examine further into her doctrine and history, which results often in their embracing the faith.

Besides the apostolate of doctrine, the Catholic layman may and should be an apostle of integrity, showing by his conduct that a Catholic stands for what is most honorable in public and private life. Too often it has happened that Catholics in public life have been a libel on Catholicism. Unfortunately, the bad example of a nominal Catholic often gives an adverse impression of the faith which it is almost impossible to eradicate. Catholic Action which does not embrace a life of integrity is a misnomer, and regardless of other activities, will never accomplish its object of diffusing, defending, and extending Catholic principles and practices.

Besides the lay apostolate of diffusing, defending, and practicing the faith, there are the various religious and social movements which are organized for the promotion of piety, charity, and social welfare. In almost every parish there are pious sodalities and confraternities, and also societies such as those of St. Vincent de Paul to aid the poor and of the Holy Name to reverence the sacred name of our Divine Lord. These pious or philanthropic organizations exhibit Catholic principles and practices to the world, and confer special spiritual benefits on the individual members. Frederick Ozanam, founder of the St. Vincent de Paul Society, declared that nothing helped more for personal holiness and the good of religion than activities for the spiritual and temporal welfare of others. His own career in behalf of the poor and unfortunate is proof of the truth of his assertion.

A St. Vincent de Paul Society is now in almost every parish in the world, offering the Catholic layman the opportunity of doing something worth while for God, the Church, and mankind. In almost every parish there is ordinarily some activity which may engage a layman desirous of co-operating in the apostolate of diffusing, defending, and extending the kingdom of God on earth.

The Church is the bride of Christ, espoused on Calvary. We call her our Holy Mother the Church because she rears the children of men to become the children of God. From the cradle to the cross, Christ had the faithful children of the Church in mind in all His privations and sufferings of body and mind. He proved His love for us

by action as well as by word—rather, *more* by action
than by word. Whatever we do for His Church we do for
Him. Sometimes it may have occurred to us that we
should like to have lived in Christ's day and to have been
able to do Him a kindly service. Without any romancing,
we may now do for Him what we should like to have
done when He was on earth. For He declared solemnly
that He was always to be with His Church. "Behold I
am with you all days, even to the consummation of the
world" (Matthew 28:20).

In reality, therefore, whatever we do for the Church,
the spouse of Christ, we are doing for Him. It is a privilege and honor to be allowed to do a service for a worldly
monarch. By engaging in activities which promote the
welfare of the Church, we are doing a service to the King
of Kings—not that He really needs us or our help, but
that He deigns to honor us by accepting our co-operation.

It is for our own interest and eternal welfare that God
permits us to do Him a service. That is why the saints
and missionaries rejoiced to labor and suffer in order to
bring Christ into the lives of those who knew Him not,
or who, knowing Him, loved Him not. We do not, however, have to be saints or missionaries in order to show
our devotion to Christ. In the home and in our own parish
we have the opportunity of manifesting our interest in
what concerns Him.

He has said that whatever we do unto the least of His
brethren He takes as done to Himself. Right in the home,
accordingly, we have numerous occasions of doing a
kindly service to Christ. If we keep in mind that father
and mother, brother and sister are representatives of
Christ, it will not be hard to be kind and considerate to

those with whom we live. Likewise in the parish, if we reflect that those whom we aid spiritually or socially are the living representatives of Christ, it will make service and sacrifice a pleasure.

Non-Catholics have often wondered at the peacefulness of nuns in hospitals and other places where they behold them untiringly ministering to the afflicted. Sometimes these holy nuns meet with ingratitude and insult, but they labor on cheerfully just the same. The reason is that they are working for God, and that as a result disagreeable work and hard work matters not. What matters is that they are doing something acceptable for One whom they love.

Fulfilling one's duty in the home and parish and engaging in the activities of the lay apostolate may demand service and sacrifice, but these are the things that count with God. Sacrifice is the language of love. It was by sacrifice that Christ showed His love for us. It is by sacrifice in the home and parish and in the lay apostolate that we can show our love for Christ. God will not be outdone in generosity and love. When life's day ends and we enter the home which God has prepared for those who love Him, we shall rejoice exceedingly that during the brief period of mortal life we devoted some of our time and efforts to the service of the King of time and eternity.

SUMMARY

Religion is not theoretic but practical. Knowing what is right is not doing right.

Doing God's will is the main purpose of life. Man is inclined, however, to do his own instead of God's will.

In the home young persons should honor their parents by

due respect and obedience. Parents should be honored even if at times they seem not to deserve it. There would be little merit in honoring honorable parents only.

No important step should be taken without consulting parents, even if in some matters it be not advisable to agree with them.

A young man should share in the maintenance of the home if it needs his support and he is able to give it. He should be chivalrous toward his sisters and a good example to his brothers. Young women have duties parallel to those of young men.

Selfishness is the curse of domestic welfare. Consideration for the feelings and position of others should always be shown.

Besides home duties there are those of the parish. Young people should engage in parish activities by joining pious societies, recreational and entertainment groups, and in other ways help to promote the welfare and piety of the parishioners.

Catholic Action means the co-operation of the laity with the clergy in promoting the diffusion, defense, and practice of Catholic principles and practices. This calls for a life of integrity, and a good talking knowledge of the doctrines and practices of Catholicism.

If the priest calls for volunteers for engaging in activities which promote the knowledge and practice of Catholicism, young men and women should respond generously.

Catholic Action is not aligned with any political party. Its aim is religious and social.

It not only benefits others, but very especially helps to sanctify those engaged in it.

In almost every parish there is some society or organization which may interest young persons who are desirous of religious or social activity.

What is done for the Church is done for Christ Himself, who said He would be with her to the end of the world.

Catholic Action may call for service and sacrifice, but it gives substantial evidence of one's love of God.

POINTS FOR DISCUSSION

1. Religion is out of place in modern life.

2. Man's main concern is for family welfare.

3. Only good parents should be obeyed.

4. Parents of today are not qualified to decide their children's careers in life.

5. Youths who earn their own living are not obliged to help support the family.

6. A person fulfills his parish duty by attending to his own spiritual concerns.

7. Define Catholic Action.

8. Catholic Action should be left to the clergy.

9. Specify some ways by which the laity can engage in Catholic Action.

10. Why is it that whatever is done for the Church is done for Christ Himself?

11. How does Catholic Action show one's love for Christ?

CHAPTER XXIV

BUSINESS AND POLITICS

RELIGION HAS AN IMPORTANT PLACE in business and politics. The real test of religion is, in great measure, concerned with these activities. In business and politics self-interest often usurps the place of justice and charity. It requires genuine virtue to walk uprightly in business and politics as they are today. But anyone may be virtuous if not tempted. Temptation *shows* the criminal, does not *make* him. If there were no trials calling for the exercise of faith and virtue, there would be no distinction between the good and bad.

Wrong is wrong always. Deliberately to do what is dishonest or unjust is wrong in business and politics as well as in any other matter. Success is not everything in life. A good conscience and business honor are worth all they may cost. If a Catholic does not set an example of integrity in business and politics, whom may we expect to do so? The avoidance of dishonesty is not, however, enough for a Catholic, who should, besides, be an example of rectitude in whatever career he finds himself.

It is on account of the flagrant injustice in business and politics that Pope Pius XI issued the encyclical *Quadragesimo Anno*. Its purpose is to remedy social evils by putting into practice the Christian virtues of justice and charity. The main social evil at present is the greed and injustice of the powerful few who control wealth and the sources of production. They aim at:

1. Economic control
2. Control of the state
3. State supremacy among nations

This policy tends to give a lion's share of the profits of industry to the powerful few, leaving the masses without even a lamb's share of the fruits of production, so that in many cases they receive a non-living wage. The result is that our own country is top-heavy with millionaires while the masses are underprovided for.

The United States has the largest number of millionaires of any country in the world, and also the longest bread-line. This means that there is something radically wrong with the distribution of the products of industry. Men who invest their money in production and take many and great risks are entitled to a large share of the profits, but not so large a share as to leave the workers insufficient for the proper maintenance of themselves and their families. Workers do not complain because capitalists receive a large share of industry's profits, but because their share is altogether out of proportion to their deserts.

Capital is unproductive without the workers. Labor is as necessary as money for manufacturing, and should consequently receive a living wage as its share of production. A business that does not provide a living wage for the workers, as well as a fair return for the capitalist, is, by the very fact, in default. But what we behold is capitalists amassing millions while the workers have barely enough to keep alive. In many factory towns the mill-owners live like kings while the workers are housed in homes little better than cattle sheds.

It is this unjust inequality that the encyclical protests against. It is this inequitable distribution of the results of production that has caused the worldwide uprising of labor that we witness today. Pius XI foresees that unless capital remedies present abuses, violent measures will be resorted to by the desperate masses; hence he pleads the cause of social justice in order to prevent social disaster. For unless capital of its own accord sees to it that workers get a living wage, labor will take things into its own hands with destructive results to all concerned.

The measures which the Pope proposes for a remedy of the inequalities and injustices which now exist between capital and labor are *social justice* and *Christian charity*. The points which the encyclical stresses are:

1. A realization of man's nature and needs
2. The responsibility of man to a power above
3. The organization of the workers
4. Labor's respect for the rights of capital
5. Labor's regard for its obligations as well as its rights
6. The mutual need of capital and labor for co-operation
7. A spiritual instead of a materialistic conception of life

1. A REALIZATION OF MAN'S NATURE AND NEEDS. With regard to the first point, it should be borne in mind that man is not a tool which can be taken up or laid aside at will. Nor is he an animal which can roam at will, caring only for its own maintenance. Man is a social being with others depending upon him, and ordinarily not free to migrate from place to place. Society is composed of families, and most families are supported by workers, and if the workers are not properly employed society itself suffers.

A *living wage* for the worker is, accordingly, a strict requirement of social justice, and when workers have not a living wage, there results eventually a social upheaval.

By a living wage is meant a salary on which a man can maintain his family in decent condition. As it is at present, when workers have illness or death in the family, they frequently have to go in debt in order to meet the emergency.

Maintenance means not only food and shelter, but providing for the ordinary contingencies of life. Man's nature and needs, accordingly, postulate a living wage, and unless it be given him, it will only be a question of time when he will turn against the social order which denies it to him.

2. THE RESPONSIBILITY OF MAN TO A POWER ABOVE. The second point proposed for social justice is that capital, and labor also, realize that man is accountable to God for the use made of the possessions and opportunities of life. Unfortunately, too many people have been misled by the false doctrine that man is only a high-grade animal. This has resulted in what is termed *rugged individualism,* or "each man for himself and the devil take the hindmost." This is the law of the jungle, not of civilized man. It prevails, however, to a large extent, among the powerful ones of the mercantile world.

The workers, however, are gradually organizing for protection, and unless their just demands are granted, the greed of the powerful and rugged individuals of capitalism may act as a boomerang for their destruction and for the overturning of the present social system. It is safe to say that, if the world had listened to the warning of Leo XIII on this matter forty years ago, we should not now be witnessing the awful state of affairs prevailing in many parts of the world. Rugged individualism may suit animals, but it is destructive of human society.

3. THE ORGANIZATION OF THE WORKERS. The Pope, realizing the helplessness of the worker as an individual to obtain redress of his grievances, advises the workers to combine for protection and to secure a proper living wage. In advocating labor unions the Pope is not assailing capital, but defending labor. Capital needs no protector, but does need a restraining hand if it is not to overreach itself and bring about its own destruction. Labor united is a force which can stand up for its rights. Capital will consume itself and perish unless it have the aid of labor. Capital needs labor as much as, under present conditions, labor needs capital.

In former times the individual worker was independent; all he needed was his kit of tools. Now, however, factories and machinery have taken the place of the tool bag, and the worker is at the mercy of the factory owner. But the factory is at the mercy of the workers if they unite. Hence it is that the Pope advocates labor unions in order that capital may be induced to listen to the just demands of labor.

4. LABOR'S RESPECT FOR THE RIGHTS OF CAPITAL. The Pope is not unmindful of the fact that labor, when in the saddle, has at times been as arbitrary as capital. Hence he counsels the workers that capital has rights as well as labor, and that if social justice is to prevail, the rights of the owner must be respected. Private property and ownership of productive agencies are as sacred as the toil of the mechanic. Any infringement of right, no matter by whom, upsets justice and will never truly remedy wrongs.

5. LABOR'S REGARD FOR ITS OBLIGATIONS AS WELL AS ITS RIGHTS. The Pope, accordingly, warns workers that if

they are to bring about social justice they must bear in mind that they have obligations as well as rights. Too often it happens that labor is so insistent on obtaining its rights that it altogether overlooks its obligations. The obligations of workers to employers are just as sacred as those of employers to workers. This phase of the relationship between owner and worker is frequently ignored by the worker. The encyclical frankly tells labor that if it is to expect justice it must render justice.

6. THE MUTUAL NEED OF CAPITAL AND LABOR FOR CO-OPERATION. This leads to the crux of the whole matter; namely, that capital and labor are, or should be, partners, not competitors. Money is useless unless it can be put to work. Also, under present conditions, a worker is useless unless he can get a job, and he cannot get a job unless the store or factory or some industry employ him.

Store, factory, and all forms of commercial enterprises require capital for their commencement and continuance. The worker, whose capital is his toil, is thus at the mercy of the money power. On the other hand, the largest factory and the finest machinery are so much dead weight unless put in operation by the skill and toil of the worker. This is made evident when a strike is on. For this reason the strike is the main weapon of labor against capital. It is true that capital can find investment in government bonds and other securities, but bonds depreciate and lose their value unless manufacturing goes on. Since, therefore, capital needs labor and labor needs capital, the sensible thing to do, the Pope declares, is for capital and labor to join hands.

7. A SPIRITUAL INSTEAD OF A MATERIALISTIC CONCEPTION OF LIFE. Rationalism and evolution have misled man-

kind into rejecting God and deifying self. Man is falsely informed that he is his own master, a law to himself; that the only restriction on his conduct is detection, the fear of being found out. Clever persons can evade detection, and accordingly as rugged individuals, whose code is that might is right, they have succeeded in attaining wealth and power to the detriment of the less rugged masses.

If man believes he is only a high-grade brute, of course he will employ the tactics of the jungle, where force and cunning prevail. Man is naturally selfish, only too prone to profit by the weakness of his fellow men, and if he be told that he has no soul, that there is no future life, no Power above to whom he is accountable, that conscience is only a myth, it is not surprising that social injustice prevails.

Rationalism, Darwinism, and other false -*isms* explain to a great extent the greed of the powerful few who have brought about the present industrial crisis between the masses and their employers. The remedy advocated by the Pope is the realization of the truth regarding man and his destiny.

Man is a rational being, whose career only begins in this life, and whose eternal welfare hereafter depends on doing God's will here. God's will is expressed in the commandments. Christ said: "If thou wilt enter into life, keep the commandments." God's law proclaims that man is a subject of the Creator and that right, not might, is the law of life. It is the realizing and living by the law of God which will restrain the otherwise rugged individual from overreaching his fellow men. Knowledge of God's law will not necessarily make a man just, but at least it will be a beacon saving him and society from the rocks of social shipwreck. The more the powerful few guide their course by the Light of the World, by Christ, eternal truth, the more will social justice prevail, and the more peaceful and prosperous will mankind be, both masters and masses.

Christ said of Himself: "I am the light of the world" (John 8:12). He also said of His Church: "You are the light of the world" (Matthew 5:14). The Church, the vicar of Christ, warns the world that unless it guides its course by the light of social justice and Christian charity, it will meet with the fate always awaiting those who turn their back on truth. It is because the Church is the light of the world that her divine Founder destined her for all nations and ages.

There yet remain lands and people upon whom this light does not shine. We who have been blessed with the divine guidance of Catholicism should be concerned for those who still sit in darkness and error. From the beginning of Christianity missionaries have gone forth to carry the Gospel message to the various nations. It is due to the missionary spirit of the Church that we ourselves have received the faith.

Out of gratitude as well as duty we should do our part in order that others may be benefited as we ourselves have been. All cannot be missionaries, but all can aid the missions by prayer and sacrifice. The missionaries sacrifice the comforts of civilization and their very life in order to extend the kingdom of Christ. We should be ready and willing to make sacrifices for the same holy cause. By depriving ourselves of little comforts and pleasures, we may be able to send to missionary lands contributions to help our priests and nuns who are there devoting their lives for the conversion of those people. We who remain at home and have the blessings of the true religion should be willing to do our part to carry out the purpose of Christ to have His Church benefit all lands and peoples.

The martyrs and missionaries have given all they possessed, including life, for the confession and propagation of the faith. Christian charity as well as social justice should urge us to co-operate, in every way possible, with our distant brethren who are laboring in barbarous lands for the spiritual and temporal welfare of those neglected people. Whatever we do for the least of Christ's brethren, He regards as done to Himself. The missionaries are His chosen friends who have consecrated their lives to labor for and with Him. Whatever we do to aid their apostolate we are doing for the cause He has dearest at heart. God will not be outdone in generosity. If we show a generous spirit towards His kingdom on earth, we may be sure of a generous welcome in His kingdom of heaven.

Life is a period of probation granted to man, in order to qualify him for everlasting companionship with God and the blessed in the home He has prepared for those who have served and loved Him. In the business and conduct of life we may by social justice and Christian charity give God proof of our service and love, and thus be assured of a happy eternity.

SUMMARY

Religion has an important place in business and politics, in which very often selfishness usurps the place of justice and charity.

It requires genuine virtue to be honest in business and politics as they are today.

Temptation, however, does not make the criminal, but shows him. If there were no temptations to dishonesty or other vices, there would be little or no discrimination between good and bad people.

Deliberately to do what is dishonest in business or politics is wrong, no matter what the temptation.

The avoidance of dishonesty, however, is not enough for a Catholic, who should be an example of honor in business and politics.

It is to assure honesty and justice in man's dealings with man that Pius XI issued the encyclical *Quadragesimo Anno,* which is directed against the powerful few who by their greed cause injustice to the masses.

The remedies which the Pope proposes for the injustice and inequalities which now exist between capital and labor are the following:

1. A realization of man's nature and needs
2. The responsibility of man to a power above
3. The organization of the workers
4. Labor's respect for the rights of capital
5. Labor's regard for its obligations as well as its rights
6. The mutual need of capital and labor for co-operation
7. A spiritual instead of a materialistic conception of life

Rationalism and evolution and other false *-isms* have misled mankind into rejecting God and deifying self.

If man believes he is only a high-grade brute, he will employ the tactics of the jungle, where force and cunning prevail.

Man, however, is a rational being, whose career only begins in this life and whose eternal welfare hereafter depends on doing God's will here.

The Catholic church is the voice of God in the world.

It is because she guides mortals to a blessed immortality that we should be interested in her and make sacrifices for the propagation of the faith.

Missionaries sacrifice their comfort and life to extend God's kingdom on earth. Those at home should aid them by contributing according to their means.[1]

POINTS FOR DISCUSSION

1. It is impossible to be honest and succeed in business?

2. Dishonest competition must be met with the same policy.

3. A business man must accommodate himself to the conditions of competition.

4. One is not supposed to be conscientious in politics.

5. It is all right to receive graft in politics.

6. In business or politics it is fair to meet sharp practice with the same methods.

7. Religion has nothing to do with politics.

8. Business lies are not wrong.

9. Labor is justified in opposing capital.

10. Labor unions are justified in having recourse to violence.

11. Capital is the enemy of labor.

12. Why is it wrong for a worker to idle on a job, or to give careless service?

13. Why is it wrong for an employer to take advantage of a worker's poverty to lower his wages or discharge him?

14. The Church is the friend of capital and favors the rich.

15. There is more need of missionary work at home than far off.

16. It is enough to support parish activities without contributing to missionaries.

---

[1] For the development of *Quadragesimo Anno* see the encyclical.

APPENDIX

SELECTIONS FROM THREE ENCYCLICAL LETTERS[1]

THE CHRISTIAN EDUCATION OF YOUTH
Encyclical Letter *Divini Illius Magistri* of His Holiness
Pope Pius XI

REPRESENTATIVE ON EARTH of that divine Master who while embracing in the immensity of His love all mankind, even unworthy sinners, showed nevertheless a special tenderness and affection for children, and expressed Himself in those singularly touching words: "Suffer the little children to come unto Me," we also on every occasion have endeavored to show the predilection wholly paternal which we bear towards them, particularly by our assiduous care and timely instructions with reference to the Christian education of youth. Such insistence is called for in these our times, when, alas, there is so great and deplorable an absence of clear and sound principles, even regarding problems the most fundamental.

Indeed, never has there been so much discussion about education as nowadays; never have exponents of new pedagogical theories been so numerous, or so many methods and means devised, proposed, and debated, not merely to facilitate education, but to create a new system infallibly efficacious, and capable of preparing the present generations for that earthly happiness which they so ardently desire.

The reason is that men, created by God to His image and likeness and destined for Him who is infinite perfection, realize today more than ever amid the most exuberant material progress, the insufficiency of earthly goods to produce true happiness either for the individual or for the nations. And hence they feel more keenly in themselves the impulse towards a perfection that is higher, which impulse is implanted in their rational nature by the Creator Himself. This perfection they seek to acquire by means of education. But many of them pretend to draw education out of human nature itself and evolve it by its own unaided powers. Such easily fall into error, because, instead of fixing their gaze on God, first principle and last end of the whole universe, they fall back upon themselves, becoming attached exclusively to passing things of earth.

---

[1] For permission to use these selections from the encyclicals we are indebted to the America Press.

It is therefore as important to make no mistake in education, as it is to make no mistake in the pursuit of the last end, with which the whole work of education is intimately and necessarily connected. In fact, since education consists essentially in preparing man for what he must be and for what he must do here below, in order to attain the sublime end for which he was created, it is clear that there can be no true education which is not wholly directed to man's last end, and that in the present order of Providence, since God has revealed Himself to us in the person of His only begotten Son, who alone is "the way, the truth, and the life," there can be no ideally perfect education which is not Christian education.

Education is essentially a social and not a mere individual activity. Now there are three necessary societies, distinct from one another and yet harmoniously combined by God, into which man is born: two, namely the family and civil society, belong to the natural order; the third, the Church, to the supernatural order.

In the first place comes the family, instituted directly by God for its peculiar purpose, the generation and formation of offspring; for this reason it has priority of nature and therefore of rights over civil society. Nevertheless, the family is an imperfect society, since it has not in itself all the means for its own complete development; whereas civil society is a perfect society, having in itself all the means for its peculiar end, which is the temporal wellbeing of the community; and so, in this respect, that is, in view of the common good, it has pre-eminence over the family, which finds its own suitable temporal perfection precisely in civil society.

The third society, into which man is born when through baptism he receives the divine life of grace, is the Church, a society of the supernatural order and of universal extent; a perfect society because it has in itself all the means required for its own end, which is the eternal salvation of mankind; hence it is supreme in its own domain.

Consequently education, which is concerned with man as a whole, individually and socially, in the order of nature and in the order of grace, necessarily belongs to all these three societies, in due proportion, corresponding, according to the disposition of Divine Providence, to the co-ordination of their respective ends.

And first of all education belongs pre-eminently to the Church by reason of a double title in the supernatural order, conferred exclusively upon her by God Himself, and absolutely superior therefore to any other title in the natural order.

The first title is founded upon the express mission and supreme authority to teach given her by her divine Founder: "All power is given to Me in heaven and in earth. Going therefore teach ye all nations." The second title is the supernatural motherhood in virtue of which the Church generates, nurtures, and educates souls in the divine life of grace with her sacraments and her doctrine. With good reason then does St. Augustine maintain: "He has not God for father who refuses to have the Church as mother."

Hence it is that in this proper object of her mission, that is, "in faith and morals, God Himself has made the Church sharer in the divine teaching office and, by a special privilege, granted her immunity from error. Hence she is the mistress of men, supreme and absolutely sure, and she has inherent in herself an inviolable right to freedom in teaching." By necessary consequence the Church is independent of any sort of earthly power as well in the origin as in the exercise of her mission as educator. And this must be so, because the Church as a perfect society has an independent right to the means conducive to its end, and because every form of instruction, no less than every human action, has a necessary connection with man's last end, and therefore cannot be withdrawn from the dictates of the divine law, of which the Church is infallible guardian, interpreter, and teacher.

The extent of the Church's mission in the field of education is such as to embrace every nation, without exception, according to the command of Christ: "Teach ye all nations"; and there is no power on earth that may lawfully oppose her or stand in her way. In the first place, it extends over all the faithful, of whom she has anxious care as a tender mother. For these she has throughout the centuries created and conducted an immense number of schools and institutions in every branch of learning. All this the Church has been able to do because her mission to educate extends equally to those outside the fold, seeing that all men are called to enter the kingdom of God and reach eternal salvation. Just as today when her missions scatter schools by the thousands in districts and countries not yet Christian, from the banks of the Ganges to the Yellow River and the great islands and archipelagoes of the Pacific Ocean, from the Dark Continent to the Land of Fire and to frozen Alaska, so in every age the Church by her missionaries has educated to Christian life and to civilization the various peoples which now constitute the Christian nations of the civilized world.

Hence it is evident that both by right and in fact the mission to educate belongs pre-eminently to the Church, and that no one free from prejudice can have a reasonable motive for opposing or impeding the Church in this her work, of which the world today enjoys the precious advantages.

This is the more true because the rights of the family and of the state, even the rights of individuals regarding a just liberty in the pursuit of science, of methods of science, and all sorts of profane culture, not only are not opposed to this pre-eminence of the Church, but are in complete harmony with it. The fundamental

reason for this harmony is that the supernatural order, to which
the Church owes her rights, not only does not in the least destroy
the natural order, to which pertain the other rights mentioned, but
elevates the natural and perfects it, each affording mutual aid to
the other, and completing it in a manner proportioned to its respective nature and dignity.

This becomes clearer when we consider more closely and in detail the mission of education proper to the family and to the state.

In the first place the Church's mission of education is in wonderful agreement with that of the family, for both proceed from
God, and in a remarkably similar manner. God directly communicates to the family, in the natural order, fecundity, which is the
principle of life, and hence also the principle of education to life,
together with authority, the principle of order.

The family therefore holds directly from the Creator the mission
and hence the right to educate the offspring, a right inalienable
because inseparably joined to the strict obligation, a right anterior
to any right whatever of civil society and of the state, and therefore inviolable on the part of any power on earth.

That this right is inviolable St. Thomas proves as follows:

> The child is naturally something of the father . . . so by natu-
> ral right the child, before reaching the use of reason, is under the
> father's care. Hence it would be contrary to natural justice if the
> child, before the use of reason, were removed from the care of its
> parents, or if any disposition were made concerning him against
> the will of the parents.

It must be borne in mind also that the obligation of the family
to bring up children, includes not only religious and moral education, but physical and civic education as well, principally in so far
as it touches upon religion and morality.

This incontestable right of the family has at various times been
recognized by nations anxious to respect the natural law in their
civil enactments. Thus, to give one recent example, the Supreme
Court of the United States of North America, in a decision on an
important controversy, declared that it is not in the competence
of the state to fix any uniform standard of education by forcing
children to receive instruction exclusively in public schools, and it
bases its decision on the natural law: the child is not the mere
creature of the state; those who nurture him and direct his destiny have the right coupled with the high duty, to educate him
and prepare him for the fulfillment of his obligations.

History bears witness how, particularly in modern times, the
state has violated and does violate rights conferred by God on
the family. At the same time it shows magnificently how the
Church has ever protected and defended these rights, a fact proved

by the special confidence which parents have in Catholic schools. The Church is indeed conscious of her divine mission to all mankind, and of the obligation which all men have to practice the one true religion; and therefore she never tires of defending her right, and of reminding parents of their duty, to have all Catholic-born children baptized and brought up as Christians. On the other hand so jealous is she of the family's inviolable natural right to educate the children, that she never consents, save under peculiar circumstances and with special cautions, to baptize the children of infidels or provide for their education against the will of the parents, till such time as the children can choose for themselves and freely embrace the faith.

From such priority of rights on the part of the Church and of the family in the field of education, most important advantages, as we have seen, accrue to the whole of society. Moreover, in accordance with the divinely established order of things, no damage can follow from it to the true and just rights of the state in regard to the education of its citizens.

These rights have been conferred upon civil society by the Author of nature Himself, not by title of fatherhood, as in the case of the Church and of the family, but in virtue of the authority which it possesses to promote the common temporal welfare, which is precisely the purpose of its existence. Consequently education cannot pertain to civil society in the same way in which it pertains to the Church and to the family, but in a different way corresponding to its own particular end and object.

Now this end and object, the common welfare in the temporal order, consists in that peace and security in which families and individual citizens have the free exercise of their rights, and at the same time enjoy the greatest spiritual and temporal prosperity possible in this life, by the mutual union and co-ordination of the work of all. The function therefore of the civil authority residing in the state is twofold, to protect and to foster, but by no means to absorb the family and the individual, or to substitute itself for them.

Accordingly in the matter of education, it is the right, or to speak more correctly, it is the duty of the state to protect in its legislation the prior rights, already described, of the family as regards the Christian education of its offspring, and consequently also to respect the supernatural rights of the Church in this same realm of Christian education. It also belongs to the state to protect the rights of the child itself when the parents are found wanting either physically or morally in this respect, whether by default, incapacity, or misconduct, since, as has been shown, their right to educate is not an absolute and despotic one, but dependent on the natural and divine law, and therefore subject alike to the authority and jurisdiction of the Church and to the vigilance and administrative care of the state in view of the common good.

It pertains to the state, in view of the common good, to promote in various ways the education and instruction of youth. It should begin by encouraging and assisting, of its own accord, the initiative and activity of the Church and the family. It should moreover supplement their work whenever this falls short of what is necessary, even by means of its own schools and institutions. Over and above this, the state can exact, and take measures to secure, that all its citizens have the necessary knowledge of their civic and political duties, and a certain degree of physical, intellectual, and moral culture, which, considering the conditions of our times, is really necessary for the common good.

However, it is clear that in all these ways of promoting education and instruction the state should respect the inherent rights of the Church and of the family concerning Christian education, and moreover have regard for distributive justice. Accordingly, unjust and unlawful is any monopoly, educational or scholastic, which, physically or morally, forces families to make use of government schools contrary to the dictates of their Christian conscience or contrary even to their legitimate preferences.

The state may reserve to itself the establishment and direction of schools intended to prepare for certain civic duties and especially for military service, provided it be careful not to injure the rights of the Church or of the family in what pertains to them. It is well to repeat this warning here; for in these days there is spreading a spirit of nationalism which is false and exaggerated, as well as dangerous to true peace and prosperity. Under its influence various excesses are committed in giving a military turn to the so-called physical training of boys (sometimes even of girls, contrary to the very instincts of human nature); or again in usurping unreasonably on Sunday the time which should be devoted to religious duties and to family life at home.

In general also it belongs to civil society and the state to provide what may be called civic education, not only for its youth, but for all ages and classes. This consists in the practice of presenting publicly to groups of individuals information having an intellectual, imaginative, and emotional appeal, calculated to draw their wills to what is upright and honest, and to urge its practice by a sort of moral compulsion, positively by disseminating such knowledge, and negatively by suppressing what is opposed to it.

The education of youth is precisely one of those matters that belong both to the Church and to the state, though in different ways. "Therefore between the two powers there must reign a well-ordained harmony. Not without reason may this mutual agreement be compared to the union of body and soul in man. Its nature and extent can only be determined by considering, as we have said, the nature of each of the two powers, and in particular the excellence and nobility of the respective ends. To one is committed directly and specifically the charge of what is helpful in worldly matters; while the other is to concern itself with the things that pertain to heaven and eternity. Everything therefore in human affairs that is in any way sacred, or has reference to the salvation of souls and the worship of God, whether by its nature or by its end, is subject to the jurisdiction and discipline of the Church. Whatever else is comprised in the civil and political order, rightly comes under the authority of the state; for Christ commanded us to give to Caesar the things that are Caesar's, and to God the things that are God's" (Leo XIII, Encyclical Letter *Immortale Dei*, November 1, 1885).

Whoever refuses to admit these principles, and hence to apply them to education, must necessarily deny that Christ has founded His Church for the eternal salvation of mankind, and maintain instead that civil society and the state are not subject to God and to His law, natural and divine. Such a doctrine is manifestly impious, contrary to right reason, and, especially in this matter of education, extremely harmful to the proper training of youth, and disastrous as well for civil society as for the well-being of all mankind.

It must never be forgotten that the subject of Christian education is man whole and entire, soul united to body in unity of nature, with all his faculties natural and supernatural, such as right reason and revelation show him to be; man, therefore, fallen from his original estate, but redeemed by Christ and restored to the supernatural condition of adopted son of God, though without the preternatural privileges of bodily immortality or perfect control of appetite. There remain, therefore, in human nature the effects of original sin, the chief of which are weakness of will and disorderly inclinations. Disorderly inclinations, then, must be corrected, good tendencies encouraged and regulated from tender childhood, and above all the mind must be enlightened and the will strengthened by supernatural truth and by the means of grace, without which it is impossible to control evil impulses.

Hence every form of pedagogic naturalism which in any way excludes or overlooks supernatural Christian formation in the teaching of youth, is false. Every method of education founded, wholly or in part, on the denial or forgetfulness of original sin and of grace, and relying on the sole powers of human nature, is unsound. Such, generally speaking, are those modern systems bearing various names which appeal to a pretended self-government and unrestrained freedom on the part of the child, and which diminish or even suppress the teacher's authority and action, attributing to the child an exclusive primacy of initiative, and an activity independent of any higher law, natural or divine, in the work of his education.

If any of these terms are used, less properly, to denote the necessity of a gradually more active co-operation on the part of the pupil in his own education; if the intention is to banish from education despotism and violence, which, by the way, just punishment is not, this would be correct, but in no way new. But alas! it is clear from the obvious meaning of the words and from experience, that what is intended by not a few is the withdrawal of education from every sort of dependence on the divine law. So today we see, strange sight indeed, educators and philosophers who spend their lives in searching for a universal moral code of education, as if there existed no Decalogue, no Gospel law, no law even of nature stamped by God on the heart of man, promulgated by right reason, and codified in positive revelation by God Himself in the Ten Commandments. Such men are miserably deluded in their claim to emancipate, as they say, the child, while in reality they are making him the slave of his own blind pride and of his disorderly affections, which, as a logical consequence of this false system, come to be justified as legitimate demands of a so-called autonomous nature.

Another very grave danger is that naturalism which nowadays invades the field of education in that most delicate matter of purity of morals. Far too common is the error of those who with dangerous assurance and under an ugly term propagate a so-called sex-education, falsely imagining they can forearm youths against the dangers of sensuality by means purely natural, such as a foolhardy initiation and precautionary instruction for all indiscriminately, even in public; and, worse still, by exposing them at an early age to the occasions, in order to accustom them, so it is argued, and as it were to harden them against such dangers. Such persons grievously err in refusing to recognize the inborn weakness of human nature, and the law of which the Apostle speaks, fighting against the law of the mind; and also in ignoring the experience of facts, from which it is clear that, particularly in young people, evil practices are the effect not so much of ignorance of intellect as of weakness of a will exposed to dangerous occasions, and unsupported by the means of grace.

False also and harmful to Christian education is the so-called method of coeducation. This too, by many of its supporters, is founded upon naturalism and the denial of original sin; but by all, upon a deplorable confusion of ideas that mistakes a leveling promiscuity and equality for the legitimate association of the sexes. There is not in nature itself, which fashions the two quite different in organism, in temperament, in abilities, anything to suggest that there can be or ought to be promiscuity, and much less equality, in the training of the two sexes. These principles, with due regard to time and place, must in accordance with Christian prudence be applied to all schools, particularly in the most delicate and decisive period of formation, that, namely, of adolescence; and in gymnastic exercises and deportment, special care must be had of Christian modesty in young women and girls, which is so gravely impaired by any kind of exhibition in public.

In order to obtain perfect education, it is of the utmost importance to see that all those conditions which surround the child during the period of his formation, in other words that the combination of circumstances which we call environment, correspond exactly to the end proposed.

The first natural and necessary element in this environment is the family. Accordingly that education, as a rule, will be more effective and lasting which is received in a well-ordered and well-disciplined Christian family; and more efficacious in proportion to the clear and constant good example set, first by the parents, and then by the other members of the household. We wish to call your attention in a special manner to the present-day lamentable decline in family education. The offices and professions of a transitory and earthly life, which are certainly of far less importance, are prepared for by long and careful study; whereas for the fundamental duty and obligation of educating their children, many parents have little or no preparation, immersed as they are in temporal cares. The declining influence of domestic environment is further weakened by another tendency, prevalent almost everywhere today, which, under one pretext or another, for economic reasons or for reasons of industry, trade, or politics, causes children to be more and more frequently sent away from home even in their tenderest years. And there is a country where the children are actually being torn from the bosom of the family, to be formed (or, to speak more accurately, to be deformed and depraved) in godless schools and associations, to irreligion and hatred, according to the theories of those who teach common ownership of all things; and thus is renewed in a real and more terrible manner the slaughter of the Innocents.

To meet the weakness of man's fallen nature, God in His goodness has provided the abundant helps of His grace and the countless means with which He has endowed the great family of Christ, the Church. The Church, therefore, is the educational environment most intimately and harmoniously associated with the Christian family. This educational environment of the Church embraces the sacraments, divinely efficacious means of grace, the sacred ritual, so wonderfully instructive, and the material fabric of her churches, whose liturgy and art have an immense educational value; but it also includes the great number and variety of schools, associations, and institutions of all kinds, established for the training of youth in Christian piety, together with literature and the sciences, not omitting recreation and physical culture.

Since, however, the younger generation must be trained in the arts and sciences for the advantage and prosperity of civil society, and since the family of itself is unequal to this task, it was necessary to create that social institution, the school. But let it be borne in mind that this institution owes its existence to the initiative of the family and of the Church, long before it was undertaken by the state. Hence, considered in its historical origin, the school is by its very nature an institution subsidiary and complementary to the family and to the Church. It follows logically and necessarily that it must not be in opposition to, but in positive accord with those other two elements, and form with them a perfect moral union, constituting one sanctuary of education, as it were, with the family and the Church. Otherwise it is doomed to fail of its purpose, and to become instead an agent of destruction.

From this it follows that the so-called 'neutral' or 'lay' school, from which religion is excluded, is contrary to the fundamental principles of education. Such a school moreover cannot exist in practice; it is bound to become irreligious. The frequenting of non-Catholic schools, whether neutral or mixed, those namely which are open to Catholics and non-Catholics alike, is forbidden for Catholic children, and can be at most tolerated, on the approval of the ordinary alone, under determined circumstances of place and time and with special precautions.

Neither can Catholics admit that other type of mixed school in which the students are provided with separate religious instruction, but receive other lessons in common with non-Catholic pupils from non-Catholic teachers. For the mere fact that a school gives some religious instruction (often extremely stinted), does not bring it into accord with the rights of the Church and of the Christian family, or make it a fit place for Catholic students. To be this, it is necessary that all the teaching and the whole organization of the school, and its teachers, syllabus, and textbooks in every branch, be regulated by the Christian spirit, under the direction and maternal supervision of the Church, so that religion may be in very truth the foundation and crown of the youth's entire training; and this in every grade of school, not only the elementary, but the intermediate and the higher institutions of learning as well.

And let no one say that in a nation where there are different religious beliefs, it is impossible to provide for public instruction otherwise than by neutral or mixed schools. In such a case it becomes the duty of the state, indeed it is the easier and more reasonable method of procedure, to leave free scope to the initiative of the Church and the family, while giving them such assistance as justice demands. That this can be done to the full satisfaction of families and to the advantage of education and of public peace and tranquillity, is clear from the actual experience of some countries comprising different religious denominations. In other countries of mixed creeds things are otherwise, and a heavy burden weighs upon Catholics, who under the guidance of their bishops and with the indefatigable co-operation of the clergy support Catholic schools for their children entirely at their own expense. If such education is not aided from public funds, as distributive justice requires, certainly it may not be opposed by any civil authority ready to recognize the rights of the family and the irreducible claims of legitimate liberty.

Let it be loudly proclaimed and well understood and recognized by all, that Catholics, no matter what their nationality, in agitating for Catholic schools for their children are not mixing in party politics, but are engaged in a religious enterprise demanded by conscience. They do not intend to separate their children either from the body of the nation or its spirit, but to educate them in a perfect manner, most conducive to the prosperity of the nation. Indeed, a good Catholic, precisely because of his Catholic principles, makes the better citizen, attached to his country, and loyally submissive to constituted civil authority in every legitimate form of government.

Perfect schools are the result not so much of good methods as of good teachers, teachers who are thoroughly prepared and well-grounded in the matter they have to teach; who possess the intellectual and moral qualifications required by their important office; who cherish a pure and holy love for the youths confided to them, because they love Jesus Christ and His Church, of which these are the children of predilection; and who have therefore sincerely at heart the true good of family and country. Indeed it fills our soul with consolation and gratitude towards the Divine Goodness to see, side by side with religious men and women engaged in teaching, such a large number of excellent lay teachers, who for their greater spiritual advancement are often grouped in special sodalities and associations, which are worthy of praise and encouragement as most excellent and powerful auxiliaries of Catholic Action.

It is no less necessary to direct and watch the education of the adolescent, "soft as wax to be moulded into vice," in whatever other environment he may happen to be, removing occasions of evil and providing occasions for good in his recreations and social intercourse; for "evil communications corrupt good manners."

More than ever nowadays an extended and careful vigilance is necessary, inasmuch as the dangers of moral and religious shipwreck are greater for inexperienced youth. Especially is this true of impious and immoral books, often diabolically circulated at low prices; of the cinema, which multiplies every kind of exhibition; and now also of the radio, which facilitates every kind of reading. These most powerful means of publicity, which can be of great utility for instruction and education, are only too often used as an incentive to evil passions and greed for gain.

This necessary vigilance does not demand that young people be removed from the society in which they must live and save their souls; but that today more than ever they should be forewarned and forearmed as Christians against the seductions and the errors of the world, which, as Holy Writ admonishes us, is all "concupiscence of the flesh, and the concupiscence of the eyes, and the pride of life" (I John 2:16).

The proper and immediate end of Christian education is to cooperate with divine grace in forming the true and perfect Christian. For precisely this reason Christian education takes in the whole aggregate of human life, physical and spiritual, intellectual and moral, individual, domestic, and social, not with a view of reducing it in any way, but in order to elevate, regulate, and perfect it, in accordance with the example and teaching of Christ. Hence the true Christian, product of Christian education, is the supernatural man who thinks, judges, and acts constantly and consistently in accordance with right reason illumined by the supernatural light of the example and teaching of Christ; in other words, to use the current term, the true and finished man of character.

The whole history of Christianity and its institutions is nothing else but the history of true civilization and progress up to the present day. It stands out conspicuously in the lives of the numerous saints, whom the Church and she alone produces, in whom is perfectly realized the purpose of Christian education, and who have in every way ennobled and benefited human society. Indeed, the saints have ever been, are, and ever will be the greatest benefactors of society, and perfect models for every class and profession, for every state and condition of life.

Such are the fruits of Christian education. Now all this array of priceless educational treasures which we have barely touched upon is so truly a property of the Church as to form her very substance, since she is the mystical body of Christ, the immaculate spouse of Christ, and consequently a most admirable mother and an incomparable and perfect teacher. Let us then, venerable brethren, raise our hands and our hearts in supplication to heaven, to the Shepherd and Bishop of our souls, to the divine King who gives laws to rulers, that in His almighty power He may cause these splendid fruits of Christian education to be gathered in ever greater abundance in the whole world, for the lasting benefit of individuals and of nations.

As a pledge of these heavenly favors, with paternal affection we impart to you, venerable brethren, to your clergy and your people, the apostolic benediction.

Given at Rome, at St. Peter's, the thirty-first day of December, in the year 1929, the eighth of our pontificate.

PIUS PP. XI.

ON THE RECONSTRUCTION OF THE SOCIAL ORDER
Encyclical Letter *Quadragesimo Anno* of His Holiness Pope Pius XI

FORTY YEARS HAVE ELAPSED since the incomparable encyclical of Leo XIII of happy memory, *Rerum Novarum,* first saw the light. The whole Catholic world gratefully recalls the event, and prepares to celebrate it with befitting solemnity. And now that the solemn commemoration of the fortieth anniversary of *Rerum Novarum* is being enthusiastically celebrated in every country, we deem it opportune first, to recall the great benefits which this encyclical has brought to the Catholic church and to the world at large; secondly, to vindicate the social and economic doctrine of so great a master against certain doubts which have arisen, and to develop more fully some of its points; finally, after arraigning modern economics and examining the nature of socialism, to expose the root of the present disorder, and to point out the only salutary cure, a reform of Christian morals. Such are the three topics to the treatment of which the present letter is dedicated.

Beginning, then, with the topic we have mentioned first, we cannot refrain from paying to Almighty God the tribute of our earnest gratitude for the benefits which have come from the encyclical of Leo XIII. We may summarize them conveniently under three heads, corresponding to the three forms of intervention for which our predecessor pleaded in order to bring about his great work of reconstruction.

In the first place, Leo himself clearly stated what could be expected from the Church. "The Church insists, on the authority of the Gospel, upon those teachings whereby the conflict can be brought to an end, or rendered, at least, far less bitter. The Church uses her efforts not only to enlighten the mind, but to direct by her precepts the life and conduct of each and all. The Church improves and betters the condition of the workingman by means of numerous organizations." This mighty power for good the Church did not suffer to remain unprofitably stored away, but drew upon it freely in the cause of a peace that was so universally desired. Time and again the social and economic doctrine of the encyclical

Rerum Novarum was proclaimed and emphasized in spoken and written word by Leo XIII himself and by his successors. Many learned priests and laymen earnestly devoted themselves to the problem of elaborating social and economic science in accordance with the conditions of our age, for the chief purpose of adapting to modern needs the unchanging and unchangeable doctrine of the Church.

Under the guidance and in the light of Leo's encyclical was thus evolved a truly Christian social science. The doctrine of *Rerum Novarum* began little by little to penetrate among those also who, being outside Catholic unity, do not recognize the authority of the Church; and thus Catholic principles of sociology gradually became part of the intellectual heritage of the whole human race. Moreover, when after the Great War the rulers of the leading nations wished to restore peace by an entire reform of social conditions, and among other measures drew up principles to regulate the just rights of labor, many of their conclusions agreed so perfectly with the principles and warnings of Leo XIII as to seem expressly deduced from them.

With regard to the civil power, Leo XIII fearlessly proclaimed the doctrine that the civil power is more than the mere guardian of law and order, and that it must strive with all zeal "to make sure that the laws and institutions, the general character and administration of the commonwealth, should be such as of themselves to realize public well-being and private prosperity." We do not, of course, deny that even before the encyclical of Leo some rulers had provided for the more urgent needs of the working classes, and had checked the more flagrant acts of injustice perpetrated against them. But after the apostolic voice had sounded from the Chair of Peter throughout the world, the leaders of the nations became at last more fully conscious of their obligations, and set to work seriously to promote a broader social policy.

As a result of these steady and tireless efforts there has arisen a new branch of jurisprudence unknown to earlier times, whose aim is the energetic defense of those sacred rights of the workingman which proceed from his dignity as a man and as a Christian. These laws concern the soul, the health, the strength, the housing, workshops, wages, dangerous employments, in a word, all that concerns the wage-earners, with particular regard to women and children. Even though these regulations do not agree always and in every detail with the recommendations of Pope Leo, it is none the less certain that much which they contain is strongly suggestive of *Rerum Novarum,* to which in large measure must be attributed the improved condition of the workingmen.

"In the last place," the wise Pontiff pointed out, "employers and workmen may of themselves effect much in the matter we are treating, by means of such organizations as afford opportune aid to those who are in distress, and which draw the two classes more closely together." Among these he attributed prime importance to societies consisting either of workmen alone or of workingmen and employers together. The lesson was well timed. For at that period rulers of not a few nations regarded such unions of workingmen with disfavor, if not with open hostility. There were even Catholics who viewed with suspicion the efforts of the laboring classes to form such unions, as if they reflected the spirit of socialistic or revolutionary agitators.

Eager to carry out to the full the program of Leo XIII, the clergy and many of the laity devoted themselves everywhere with admirable zeal to the creation of such unions, which in turn became instrumental in building up a body of truly Christian workingmen. These happily combined the successful plying of their trade with deep religious convictions; they learned to defend their temporal rights and interests energetically and efficiently, retaining at the same time a due respect for justice and a sincere desire to collaborate with other classes. Thus they prepared the way for a Christian renewal of the whole social life. These counsels of Leo XIII were reduced to practice differently in different places. In some countries one and the same association included within its scope all the ends and purposes proposed by him. In others, according as circumstances seemed to counsel or demand, a division of function developed, and various associations were founded. Of these some undertook the protection of the rights and legitimate interests of their members in the hiring of their labor; others had as their object the provision of mutual help in economic matters; while others, still, were exclusively concerned with religion and pursuits of a similar kind. The latter method was chiefly used wherever the laws of the country, or peculiar economic conditions, or the lamentable dissension of minds and hearts so prevalent in modern society, or the necessity of uniting forces to combat the growing ranks of revolutionaries, made it impossible for Catholics to form Catholic unions. Under such circumstances, they seem to have no choice but to enroll themselves in neutral trade unions. Side by side with these trade unions there must always be associations which aim at giving their members a thorough religious and moral training, that these in turn may impart to the labor unions to which they belong the upright spirit which should direct their entire conduct. Thus will these unions exert a beneficent influence far beyond the ranks of their own members.

In the course of these years, however, doubts have arisen concerning the correct interpretation of certain passages of the encyclical or their inferences, and the new needs of our age and the changed conditions of society have rendered necessary a more precise application and amplification of Leo's doctrine. We, therefore, gladly seize this opportunity of answering their doubts, so far as in us lies, and of satisfying the demands of the present day.

Descending now to details, we commence with ownership, or the right of property. You are aware how strenuously our predecessor of happy memory defended the right of property against the teachings of the socialists of his time, showing that the abolition of private ownership would prove to be not beneficial, but grievously harmful to the working classes. Yet, since there are some who falsely and unjustly accuse the Supreme Pontiff and the Church as upholding, both then and now, the wealthier classes against the proletariat, we have thought it well to defend from calumny the Leonine doctrine in this matter, which is also the Catholic doctrine, and to safeguard it against false interpretations. First, let it be made clear beyond all doubt that neither Leo XIII, nor those theologians who have taught under the guidance and direction of the Church, have ever denied or called in question the twofold aspect of ownership, which is individual or social accordingly as it regards individuals or concerns the common good. Their unanimous contention has always been that the right to own private property has been given to man by nature or rather by the Creator Himself, not only in order that individuals may be able to provide for their own needs and those of their families, but also that by means of it the goods which the Creator has destined for the human race may truly serve this purpose.

It follows from the twofold character of ownership, which we have termed individual and social, that men must take into account in this matter not only their own advantage but also the common good. To define in detail these duties, when the need occurs and when the natural law does not do so, is the function of the government. Provided that the natural and divine law be observed, the public authority, in view of the common good, may specify more accurately what is licit and what is illicit for property owners in the use of their possessions.

It is plain, however, that the state may not discharge this duty in an arbitrary manner. Man's natural right of possessing and transmitting property by inheritance must be kept intact and cannot be taken away by the state from man. For the domestic household is antecedent, as well in idea as in fact, to the gathering of men into a community.

However, when civil authority adjusts ownership to meet the needs of the public good it acts not as an enemy, but as the friend of private owners; for thus it effectively prevents the possession of private property, intended by nature's Author in His wisdom for the sustaining of human life, from creating intolerable burdens and so rushing to its own destruction. It does not therefore abolish, but protects private ownership, and, far from weakening the right of private property, it gives it new strength.

At the same time a man's superfluous income is not left entirely to his own discretion. We speak of that portion of his income which he does not need in order to live as becomes his station. On the contrary, the grave obligations of charity, beneficence, and liberality which rest upon the wealthy are constantly insisted upon in telling words by Holy Scripture and the Fathers of the Church.

However, the investment of superfluous income in searching favorable opportunities for employment, provided the labor employed produces results which are really useful, is to be considered, according to the teaching of the Angelic Doctor, an act of real liberality particularly appropriate to the needs of our time.

Wealth, therefore, which is constantly being augmented by social and economic progress, must be so distributed amongst the various individuals and classes of society that the common good of all be thereby promoted. In other words, the good of the whole community must be safeguarded. By these principles of social justice one class is forbidden to exclude the other from a share in the profits. This sacred law is violated by an irresponsible wealthy class who, in the excess of their good fortune, deem it a just state of things that they should receive everything and the laborer nothing; it is violated also by a propertyless wage-earning class who demand for themselves all the fruits of production, as being the work of their hands. Each class, then, must receive its due share, and the distribution of created goods must be brought into conformity with the demands of the common good and social justice, for every sincere observer is conscious that the vast differences between the few who hold excessive wealth and the many who live in destitution constitute a grave evil in modern society.

These ideas were not merely suggested, but stated in frank and open terms by our predecessor. We emphasize them with renewed insistence in this present encyclical; for unless serious attempts be made, with all energy and without delay, to put them into practice, let nobody persuade himself that the peace and tranquillity of human society can be effectively defended against the forces of revolution!

This program cannot, however, be realized unless the propertyless wage-earner be placed in such circumstances that by skill and thrift he can acquire a certain moderate ownership. But how can he ever save money, except from his wages and by living sparingly, who has nothing but his labor by which to obtain food and the necessities of life? Let us turn, therefore, to the question of wages, which Leo XIII held to be "of great importance," stating and explaining where necessary its principles and precepts.

And first of all, those who hold that the wage contract is essentially unjust, and that in its place must be introduced the contract of partnership, are certainly in error. In the present state of human society, however, we deem it advisable that the wage contract should, when possible, be modified somewhat by a contract of partnership, as is already being tried in various ways to the no small gain both of the wage-earners and of the employers. In this way wage-earners are made sharers in some sort in the ownership, or the management, or the profits.

In the first place, the wage paid to the workingman must be sufficient for the support of himself and of his family. It is right indeed that the rest of the family contribute according to their power towards the common maintenance, as in the rural home or in the families of many artisans and small shopkeepers. But it is wrong to abuse the tender years of children or the weakness of woman. Mothers will above all devote their work to the home and the things connected with it. Intolerable, and to be opposed with all our strength, is the abuse whereby mothers of families, because of the insufficiency of the father's salary, are forced to engage in gainful occupations outside the domestic walls to the neglect of their own proper cares and duties, particularly the education of their children.

Every effort must therefore be made that fathers of families receive a wage sufficient to meet adequately ordinary domestic needs. If in the present state of society this is not always feasible, social justice demands that reforms be introduced without delay which will guarantee every adult workingman just such a wage. In this connection we might utter a word of praise for various systems devised and attempted in practice, by which an increased wage is paid in view of increased family burdens, and a special provision is made for special needs.

The condition of any particular business and of its owner must also come into question in settling the scale of wages; for it is unjust to demand wages so high that an employer cannot pay them without ruin, and without consequent distress amongst the working people themselves.

The exigencies of the common good finally must be regulated with a view to the economic welfare of the whole people. We have already shown how conducive it is to the common good that wage-earners of all kinds be enabled by economizing that portion of their wages which remains after necessary expenses have been met, to attain to the possession of a certain modest fortune. Another point, however, of no less importance must not be overlooked, in these days especially, namely, that opportunities for work be provided for those who are willing and able to work. This depends in large measure upon the scale of wages, which multiplies opportunities for work as long as it remains within proper limits, and reduces them if allowed to pass these limits. All are aware that a scale of wages too low, no less than a scale excessively high, causes unemployment. Now unemployment, particularly if widespread and of long duration, as we have been forced to experience it during our pontificate, is a dreadful scourge; it causes misery and temptation to the laborer, ruins the prosperity of nations, and endangers public order, peace, and tranquillity the world over. To lower or raise wages unduly, with a view to private profit and with no consideration for the common good, is contrary to social justice which demands that by union of effort and good will such a scale of wages be set up, if possible, as to offer to the greatest number opportunities of employment and of securing for themselves suitable means of livelihood.

A happy beginning has here been made. But in order that what has been well begun may be rendered stable, that what has not yet been accomplished may now be achieved, and that still richer and brighter blessings may descend upon mankind, two things are particularly necessary: the reform of the social order and the correction of morals.

When we speak of the reform of the social order it is principally the state we have in mind. Now this is the primary duty of the state and of all good citizens: to abolish conflict between classes with divergent interests, and thus foster and promote harmony between the various ranks of society.

The aim of social legislation must therefore be the re-establishment of vocational groups. Society today still remains in a strained and therefore unstable and uncertain state, being founded on classes with contradictory interests and hence opposed to each other, and consequently prone to enmity and strife. Labor is not a mere chattel, since the human dignity of the workingman must be recognized in it, and consequently it cannot be bought and sold like any piece of merchandise. None the less the demand and supply of labor divides men on the labor market into two classes, as into two camps, and the bargaining between these parties transforms this labor market into an arena where the two armies are engaged in combat. To this grave disorder which is leading society to ruin a remedy must evidently be applied as speedily as possible. But there cannot be question of any perfect cure, except this opposition be done away with, and well-ordered members of the social body come into being anew, vocational groups namely, binding men together not according to the position they occupy in the labor market, but according to the diverse functions which they exercise in society.

Still another aim must be kept in view. Just as the unity of human society cannot be built upon class warfare, so the proper ordering of economic affairs cannot be left to free competition alone. From this source have proceeded in the past all the errors of the 'individualistic' school. This school, ignorant or forgetful of the social and moral aspects of economic matters, teaches that the state should refrain in theory and practice from interfering therein, because these possess in free competition and open markets a principle of self-direction better able to control them than any created intellect. Free competition, however, though within certain limits just and productive of good results, cannot be the ruling principle of the economic world. This has been abundantly proved by the consequences that have followed from the free rein given to these dangerous individualistic ideals. It is therefore very necessary that economic affairs be once more subjected to and governed by a true and effective guiding principle. To that end all the institutions of public and social life must be imbued with the spirit of justice, and this justice must above all be truly operative. It must build up a juridical and social order able to pervade all economic activity. Social charity should be, as it were, the soul of this order and the duty of the state will be to protect and defend it effectively.

Further, it would be well if the various nations in common counsel and endeavor strove to promote a healthy economic co-operation by prudent pacts and institutions, since in economic matters they are largely dependent one upon the other and need one another's help.

However, all that we have taught about reconstructing and perfecting the social order will be of no avail without a reform of manners. At one period there existed a social order which, though by no means perfect in every respect, corresponded nevertheless in a certain measure to right reason according to the needs and conditions of the times. That this order has long since perished is not due to the fact that it was incapable of development and adaptation to changing needs and circumstances, but rather to the wrongdoing of men. Men were hardened in excessive self-love and refused to extend that order, as was their duty, to the increasing numbers of the people; or else, deceived by the attractions of false liberty and other errors, they grew impatient of every restraint and endeavored to throw off all authority.

It remains for us then to turn our attention to the actual condition of the economic order and to its bitterest adversary and accuser. We mean socialism. On these we shall pronounce a frank and just sentence, shall examine more closely the root of the present grave evils, and shall indicate the first and most necessary remedy, which lies in a reform of morals.

In the first place, then, it is patent that in our days not alone is wealth accumulated, but immense power and despotic economic domination is concentrated in the hands of a few, and that those few are frequently not the owners, but only the trustees and directors of invested funds, who administer them at their good pleasure. This power becomes particularly irresistible when exercised by those who, because they hold and control money, are able also to govern credit and determine its allotment, for that reason supplying, so to speak, the life-blood to the entire economic body, and grasping, as it were, in their hands the very soul of production, so that no one dare breathe against their will.

Since the days of Leo XIII socialism, too, the great enemy with which his battles were waged, has undergone profound changes. One section of socialism has degenerated into communism. Communism teaches and pursues a twofold aim: merciless class warfare and complete abolition of private ownership; and this it does, not in secret and by hidden methods, but openly, frankly, and by every means, even the most violent. To obtain these ends communists shrink from nothing and fear nothing; and when they have attained power it is unbelievable, indeed it seems portentous, how cruel and inhuman they show themselves to be. Evidence for this is the ghastly destruction and ruin with which they have laid waste immense tracts of eastern Europe and Asia, while their antagonism and open hostility to Holy Church and to God Himself are, alas, but too well known and proved by their deeds.

The other section, which has retained the name of socialism, is much less radical in its views. Not only does it condemn recourse to physical force; it even mitigates and moderates to some extent class warfare and the abolition of private property. It does not reject them entirely. It would seem as if socialism were afraid of its own principles and of the conclusion drawn therefrom by the communists, and in consequence were drifting towards the truth which Christian tradition has always held in respect; for it cannot be denied that its programs often strikingly approach the just demands of Christian social reformers.

But what if, in questions of class war and private ownership, socialism were to become so mitigated and amended that nothing reprehensible could any longer be found in it? Would it by that very fact have laid aside its character of hostility to the Christian religion? This is a question which holds many minds in suspense; and many are the Catholics who, realizing clearly that Christian principles can never be either sacrificed or minimized, seem to be raising their eyes towards the Holy See and earnestly beseeching us to decide whether or not this form of socialism has retracted so far its false doctrines that it can now be accepted without the loss of any Christian principle, and be baptized into the Church. In our fatherly solicitude we desire to satisfy these petitions, and we pronounce as follows: Whether socialism be considered as a doctrine or as a historical fact or as a movement, if it really remain socialism it cannot be brought into harmony with the dogmas of the Catholic church, even after it has yielded to truth and justice in the points we have mentioned; the reason being that it conceives human society in a way utterly alien to Christian truth.

"And if society is to be healed now"—we use the words of our predecessor—"in no way can it be healed save by a return to Christian life and Christian institutions," for Christianity alone can apply an efficacious remedy for the excessive solicitude for transitory things which is the origin of all vices. The fundamental cause of this defection from the Christian law in social and economic matters, and of the apostacy of many workingmen from the Catholic faith which has resulted from it, is the disorderly affection of the soul, a sad consequence of original sin, the source of these and of all other evils. By original sin the marvelous harmony of man's faculties has been so deranged that now he is easily led astray by low desires, and strongly tempted to prefer the transient goods of this world to the lasting goods of heaven.

Hence comes that unquenchable thirst for riches and temporal possessions, which at all times has impelled men to break the law of God and trample on the rights of their neighbors; but the condition of the economic world today lays more snares than ever for human frailty. For the uncertainty of economic conditions and of the whole economic regime demands the keenest and most unceasing straining of energy on the part of those engaged therein; and as a result, some have become so hardened against the stings of conscience as to hold all means good which enable them to increase their profits, and to safeguard against sudden changes of fortune the wealth amassed by unremitting toil. Easy returns, which an open market offers to anyone, lead many to interest themselves in trade and exchange, their one aim being to make clear profits with the least labor. By their unchecked speculation prices are raised and lowered out of mere greed for gain, making void all the most prudent calculations of manufacturers.

The regulations legally enacted for corporations, with their divided responsibility and limited liability, have given occasion to abominable abuses. The greatly weakened accountability makes little impression, as is evident, upon the conscience. The worst injustices and frauds take place beneath the obscurity of the common name of a corporative firm. Boards of directors proceed in their unconscionable methods even to the violation of their trust in regard to those whose savings they administer. In the last place must still be mentioned the unscrupulous but well-calculated speculation of men who, without seeking to answer real needs, appeal to the lowest human passions. These are aroused in order to turn their satisfaction into gain.

With the leaders of business abandoning the true path, it is not surprising that in every country multitudes of workingmen too sank in the same morass: all the more so, because very many employers treated their workmen as mere tools, without any concern for the welfare of their souls; indeed, without the slightest thought of higher interests. The mind shudders if we consider the frightful perils to which the morals of workers (of boys and young men particularly), and the virtue of girls and women are exposed in modern factories; if we recall how the present economic regime and above all the disgraceful housing conditions prove obstacles to the family tie and family life; if we remember the insuperable difficulties placed in the way of a proper observance of the holydays.

All those versed in social matters demand a rationalization of economic life which will introduce sound and true order. But this order, which we ourselves desire and make every effort to promote, will necessarily be quite faulty and imperfect unless all man's activities harmoniously unite to imitate and, as far as is humanly possible, attain the marvelous unity of the divine plan. This is the perfect order which the Church preaches with intense earnestness and which right reason demands; which places God as the first and supreme end of all created activity and regards all created goods as mere instruments under God, to be used only in so far as they help towards the attainment of our supreme end.

Present circumstances, therefore, indicate clearly the course to be followed. Nowadays, as more than once in the history of the Church, we are confronted with a world which in large measure has almost fallen back into paganism. In order to bring back to Christ these whole classes of men who have denied Him, we must gather and train from amongst their very ranks auxiliary soldiers of the Church, men who know their mentality and their aspirations, and who with kindly fraternal charity will be able to win their hearts. Undoubtedly the first and immediate apostles of the workingmen must themselves be workingmen, while the apostles of the industrial and commercial world should themselves be employers and merchants.

Let us not permit the children of this world to seem wiser in their generation than we, who by God's goodness are children of light. We see these men cunningly select and train resolute disciples, who spread their false doctrines daily more widely amongst men of every station and of every clime. And when it becomes a question of attacking more vehemently the Church of Christ, we see them lay aside their internal quarrels, link up harmoniously into a single battle line, and strive with united forces towards this common aim.

No one indeed is unaware of the many and splendid works in the social and economic field, as well as in education and religion, laboriously set in motion with indefatigable zeal by Catholics. But this admirable and self-sacrificing activity not infrequently loses some of its effectiveness by being directed into too many different channels. Let, then, all men of good will stand united. Let all those who, under the pastors of the Church, wish to fight this good and peaceful fight of Christ, as far as talents, powers, and station allow, strive to play their part in the Christian renewal of human society, which Leo XIII inaugurated in his immortal encyclical *Rerum Novarum*. Let them seek, not themselves and the things that are their own, but the things that are Jesus Christ's. Let them not urge their own ideas with undue persistence, but be ready to abandon them, however admirable, should the greater common good seem to require it: that in all and above all Christ may reign and rule, to whom be honor and glory and power forever and ever.

Given at Rome, at St. Peter's, the fifteenth day of May, in the year 1931, the tenth of our pontificate.

PIUS PP. XI.

ON CHRISTIAN MARRIAGE
Encyclical Letter *Casti Connubii* of His Holiness
Pope Pius XI

HOW GREAT IS THE DIGNITY of chaste wedlock may be judged best from this, that Christ our Lord, Son of the eternal Father, having assumed the nature of fallen man, with His loving desire of compassing the redemption of our race, not only ordained it in an especial manner as the principle and foundation of domestic society and therefore of all human intercourse, but also raised it to the rank of a truly great sacrament of the New Law, restored it to the original purity of its divine institution, and accordingly entrusted all its discipline and care to His spouse the Church.

In order, however, that amongst men of every nation and every age the desired fruits may be obtained from this renewal of matrimony, it is necessary first of all that men's minds be illuminated with the true doctrine of Christ regarding it; and secondly, that Christian spouses, the weakness of their wills strengthened by the internal grace of God, shape all their ways of thinking and of acting in conformity with that pure law of Christ so as to obtain true peace and happiness for themselves and for their families.

And to begin, let it be repeated as an unchanged and inviolable fundamental doctrine that matrimony was not instituted or restored by man but by God; not by man were the laws made to strengthen and confirm and elevate it but by God, the author of nature, and by Christ our Lord by whom nature was redeemed, and hence these laws cannot be subject to any human decrees or to any contrary pact even of the spouses themselves.

By matrimony, therefore, the souls of the contracting parties are joined and knit together more immediately and intimately than are their bodies, and that not by any passing affection of sense or spirit, but by a deliberate and firm act of the will; and from this union of souls by God's decree, a sacred and inviolable bond arises. Hence the nature of this contract, which is proper and peculiar to it alone, makes it entirely different both from the union of animals entered into by the blind instinct of nature alone in which neither reason nor free will plays a part, and also from the unions of men which are far removed from all true and honorable union of wills and enjoy none of the rights of family life.

Therefore the sacred partnership of true marriage is constituted both by the will of God and the will of man; from God comes the very institution of marriage, the ends for which it was instituted, the laws that govern it, the blessings that flow from it, while men, through the generous surrender of their persons one to another for the whole span of life, become, with the help and co-operation of God, the authors of each particular marriage, with the duties and blessings annexed thereto from divine institution.

Now when we come to explain what are the blessings that God has attached to true matrimony, and how great they are, there occur to us the words of that illustrious Doctor of the Church whom we commemorated recently on the occasion of the fifteenth centenary of his death. "These," says St. Augustine, "are all the blessings of matrimony on account of which matrimony itself is a blessing: offspring, conjugal fidelity, and the sacrament."

Thus amongst the blessings of marriage, the child holds the first place, and indeed the Creator of the human race Himself, who in His goodness wished to use men as His helpers in the propagation of life, taught this when, instituting marriage in Paradise, He said to our first parents and through them to all future spouses: "Increase and multiply, and fill the earth." How great a boon of God this is and what a blessing of matrimony is clear from a consideration of man's dignity and of his sublime end, for man surpasses all other visible creatures by the superiority of his rational nature alone. Besides, God wishes men to be born not only that they should live and fill the earth, but much more that they may be worshipers of God, that they may know Him and love Him and finally enjoy Him forever in heaven. From this it is easily seen how great a gift of divine goodness and how remarkable a fruit of marriage are children born by the omnipotent power of God through the co-operation of those bound in wedlock.

But Christian parents must also understand that they are destined not only to propagate and preserve the human race on earth, indeed not only to educate any kind of worshipers of the true God, but children who are to become members of the Church of Christ, to raise up fellow citizens of the saints, and members of God's household, that the worshipers of God and our Savior may daily increase. For although Christian spouses, even if sanctified themselves, cannot transmit sanctification to their progeny—nay, although the very natural process of generating life has become the way of death by which original sin is passed on to posterity —nevertheless they share to some extent in the blessings of that primeval marriage of Paradise, since it is theirs to offer their off-spring to the Church in order that by this most fruitful mother of the children of God they may be regenerated through the laver of baptism unto supernatural justice and finally be made living members of Christ, partakers of immortal life, and heirs of that eternal glory to which we all aspire from our inmost heart.

The blessing of offspring, however, is not completed by the mere begetting of them, but something else must be added, namely, the proper education of the offspring. For no one can fail to see that children are incapable of providing wholly for them-selves, even in matters pertaining to their natural life, and much less in those pertaining to the supernatural, but require for many years to be helped, instructed, and educated by others. Now it is certain that both by the law of nature and of God this right and duty of educating their offspring belongs in the first place to those who began the work of nature by giving them birth, and they are indeed forbidden to leave unfinished this work and so expose it to certain ruin. But in matrimony provision has been made in the best possible way for this education of children that is so neces-sary, for since the parents are bound together by an indissoluble bond, the care and mutual help of each is always at hand.

The second blessing of matrimony is the blessing of conjugal honor which consists in the mutual fidelity of the spouses in fulfill-ing the marriage contract, "so that what belongs to one of the parties by reason of this contract sanctioned by divine law, may not be denied to him or permitted to any third person, nor may there be conceded to one of the parties that which, being contrary to the rights and laws of God and entirely opposed to matrimonial faith, can never be conceded." Wherefore conjugal faith, or honor, demands in the first place the complete unity of matrimony which the Creator Himself laid down in the beginning when He wished it to be not otherwise than between one man and one woman. And although afterwards this primeval law was relaxed to some extent by God, the supreme legislator, there is no doubt that the law of the Gospel fully restored that original and perfect unity and abro-gated all dispensations, as the words of Christ and the constant teaching and action of the Church show plainly.

This conjugal faith blooms more freely, more beautifully, and more nobly when it is rooted in that more excellent soil, the love of husband and wife which pervades all the duties of married life. For matrimonial faith demands that husband and wife be joined in an especially holy and pure love, not as adulterers love each other, but as Christ loved the Church. This precept the Apostle laid down when he said: "Husbands, love your wives as Christ also loved the Church," which of a truth He embraced with a boundless love, not for the sake of His own advantage, but seeking only the good of His spouse.

This outward expression of love in the home demands not only mutual help but must go further—indeed, must have for its primary purpose that man and wife help each other day by day in forming and perfecting themselves in the interior life, so that through their partnership in life they may advance ever more and more in virtue, and above all that they may grow in true love towards God and their neighbor, on which indeed "dependeth the whole law and the prophets." This mutual inward moulding of husband and wife, this determined effort to perfect each other, can in a very real sense, as the Roman Catechism teaches, be said to be the chief reason and purpose of matrimony, provided matrimony be looked at not in the restricted sense as instituted for the proper conception and education of the child, but more widely as the blending of life as a whole and the mutual interchange and sharing thereof.

Domestic society being confirmed therefore by this bond of love, it is necessary that there should flourish in it 'order of love,' as St. Augustine calls it. This order includes both primacy of the husband with regard to the wife and children, and the ready subjection of the wife and her willing obedience which the Apostle commends in these words: "Let women be subject to their husbands as to the Lord, because the husband is the head of the wife, as Christ is the head of the Church." This subjection, however, does not deny or take away the liberty which fully belongs to the woman both in view of her dignity as a human person and in view of her most noble office as wife and mother and companion; nor does it bid her obey her husband's every request even if not in harmony with right reason or with the dignity due a wife; nor, in fine, does it imply that the wife should be put on a level with those persons who in law are called minors, to whom it is not customary to allow free exercise of their rights on account of their lack of mature judgment or of their ignorance of human affairs. But it forbids that exaggerated license which cares not for the good of the family; it forbids that in this body which is the family, the heart be separated from the head to the great detriment of the whole body and the proximate danger of ruin. For if the man is the head, the woman is the heart, and as he occupies the chief place in ruling, so she may and ought to claim for herself the chief place in love.

These, then, are the elements which compose the blessing of conjugal faith: unity, chastity, and honorable, noble obedience. But this accumulation of benefits is completed and, as it were, crowned by that blessing of Christian marriage which, in the words of St. Augustine, we have called the 'sacrament,' by which is denoted both the indissolubility of the bond and the raising and hallowing of the contract by Christ Himself whereby He made it an efficacious sign of grace.

In the first place, Christ Himself lays stress on the indissolubility and firmness of the marriage bond when He says: "What God hath joined together let not man put asunder," and "Everyone that putteth away his wife and marrieth another committeth adultery, and he that marrieth her that is put away from her husband committeth adultery." Therefore, although before Christ the sublimeness and the severity of the primeval law was so tempered that Moses permitted it to the chosen people of God on account of the hardness of their hearts that a bill of divorce might be given in certain circumstances, nevertheless Christ, by virtue of His supreme legislative power, recalled this concession of greater liberty and restored the primeval law in its integrity by those words which must never be forgotten: "What God hath joined together let not man put asunder."

And if this stability seems to be open to exception, however rare the exception may be, as in the case of certain natural marriages between unbelievers, or if amongst Christians in the case of those marriages which though ratified had not been consummated, that exception does not depend on the will of men nor on that of any merely human power, but on divine law, of which the only guardian and interpreter is the Church of Christ. However, not even this power can ever affect for any cause whatsoever a Christian marriage which is valid and has been consummated; for as it is plain that here the marriage contract has its full completion, so, by the will of God, there is also the greatest firmness and indissolubility, which may not be destroyed by any human authority.

How many and how important are the benefits which flow from the indissolubility of matrimony cannot escape anyone who gives even a brief consideration either to the good of the spouses and the offspring or to the welfare of human society. First of all, the spouses possess a positive guarantee of the enduringness of this stability which that generous yielding of their persons and the intimate fellowship of their hearts by their nature strongly require, since true love knows no end (I Cor. 13:8). Besides, a strong

bulwark is set up in defense of a loyal chastity against incite-
ments to infidelity, should any be encountered either from within
or from without; any anxious fear lest in adversity or old age the
other spouse would prove unfaithful is precluded, and in its place
there reigns a calm sense of security. Moreover, the dignity of
both man and wife is maintained and the mutual aid is most satis-
factorily assured, while through the indissoluble bond, always en-
during, the spouses are warned continuously that not for the sake
of perishable things nor that they might serve their passions, but
that they might procure one for the other high and lasting good
have they entered into the nuptial partnership, to be dissolved only
by death. Nor do lesser benefits accrue to human society as a
whole, for experience has taught that unassailable stability in matrimony is a fruitful source of virtuous life and of habits of integrity. Where this order of things obtains, the happiness and
well-being of the nation are safeguarded.

But considering the benefits of the sacrament, besides the firmness and indissolubility, there are also much higher benefits as the
word *sacrament* itself very aptly indicates. Christ, by raising the
matrimony of His faithful to the dignity of a true sacrament of
the New Law, made it a sign and source of that peculiar internal
grace by which "it perfects natural love, it confirms an indissoluble union, and sanctifies both man and wife" (Trid. Concil., sess.
xxiv). And since the valid matrimonial consent among the faithful
was constituted by Christ as a sign of grace, the sacramental nature is so intimately bound up with Christian wedlock that there
can be no true marriage between baptized persons "without it being by that very fact a sacrament" (Cod. Iur. Can. 1012). By the
very fact, therefore, that the faithful with sincere mind give such
consent, they open up for themselves a treasure of sacramental
grace from which they draw supernatural power for the fulfilling
of their tasks and duties faithfully, holily, perseveringly even unto
death. Hence this sacrament not only increases sanctifying grace,
the permanent principle of the supernatural life in those who place
no obstacle in its way; but it adds particular gifts, dispositions,
seeds of grace, by elevating and perfecting the natural powers in
such a way that the parties are assisted not only in understanding
but in knowing intimately, in adhering to firmly, in willing effectively, and in successfully putting into practice those things which
pertain to the marriage state, its aims and duties. It gives them,
in fine, a right to the actual assistance of grace, whensoever they
need it for fulfilling the duties of their state.

When we consider the great excellence of chaste wedlock it appears all the more regrettable that particularly in our day we
should witness this divine institution often scorned and on every
side degraded. For now, alas, not secretly nor under cover, but

openly, with all sense of shame put aside, now by word, again by writings, by theatrical productions of every kind, by romantic fiction, by amorous and frivolous novels, by motion pictures, by addresses broadcast by means of the radio, in short, by all the inventions of modern science, the sanctity of marriage is trampled upon and derided. Divorce, adultery, all the basest vices, either are extolled or at least are depicted in such colors as to appear to be free of all reproach and infamy. Books are not lacking which dare to pronounce themselves as scientific, but which in truth are merely coated with a veneer of science in order that they may the more easily insinuate their ideas. The doctrines defended in these are offered for sale as the productions of modern genius, of that genius, namely, which is considered to have emancipated itself from all those old-fashioned and immature opinions of the ancients, and to the number of these antiquated opinions they relegate the traditional doctrine of Christian marriage.

And since, in order that the deceits of the enemy may be avoided, it is necessary first of all that they be laid bare, since much is to be gained by denouncing these fallacies for the sake of the unwary, even though we prefer not to name these iniquities "as becometh saints," yet for the welfare of souls we cannot remain altogether silent.

To begin at the very source of these evils, their basic principle lies in this, that matrimony is repeatedly declared to be not instituted by the Author of nature nor raised by Christ the Lord to the dignity of a true sacrament, but invented by man. How grievously all these err and how shamelessly they leave the ways of virtue is already evident from what we have set forth here regarding the origin and nature of wedlock, its purposes, and the good inherent in it. The evil of this teaching is plainly seen from the consequences which its advocates deduce from it, namely, that the laws, institution, and customs by which wedlock is governed, since they take their origin solely from the will of man, are subject entirely to him, hence can and must be founded, changed, and abrogated according to human caprice and the shifting circumstances of human affairs. Armed with these principles, some men go so far as to concoct new species of unions, suited, as they say, to the present temper of men and the times, which various new forms of matrimony they presume to label 'temporary,' 'trial,' and 'companionate.' These offer all the indulgence of matrimony and its rights without, however, the indissoluble bond, and without offspring, unless later the parties alter their union and mutual association into a matrimony in the full sense of the law.

Indeed, there are some who desire and insist that these practices be legitimatized by the law or at least excused by their general acceptance among the people. They do not seem to suspect that these proposals partake of nothing of the modern 'culture' in which they glory so much, but are simply hateful abominations which beyond all question reduce our truly cultured nations to the barbarous standards of savage peoples.

And now we shall explain in detail the evils opposed to each of the benefits of matrimony.

First consideration is due to the offspring, which many have the boldness to call the disagreeable burden of matrimony and which, they say, is to be carefully avoided by married people, not through virtuous continence (which Christian laws permit in matrimony when both parties consent), but by frustrating the marriage act. Some justify this criminal abuse on the ground that they are weary of children and wish to gratify their desires without their consequent burden. Others say that they cannot on the one hand remain continent nor, on the other, can they have children because of the difficulties, whether on the part of the mother or on the part of family circumstances.

But no reason, however grave, may be put forward by which anything intrinsically against nature may become comformable to nature and morally good. Since, therefore, the conjugal act is destined primarily by nature for the begetting of children, those who in exercising it deliberately frustrate its natural power and purpose sin against nature and commit a deed which is shameful and intrinsically vicious.

Since, therefore, openly departing from the uninterrupted Christian tradition, some recently have judged it possible solemnly to declare another doctrine regarding this question, the Catholic church, to whom God has entrusted the defense of the integrity and purity of morals, standing erect in the midst of the moral ruin which surrounds her, in order that she may preserve the chastity of the nuptial union from being defiled by this foul stain, raises her voice in token of divine ambassadorship and through our mouth proclaims anew: Any use whatsoever of matrimony exercised in such a way that the act is deliberately frustrated in its natural power to generate life is an offense against the law of God and of nature, and those who indulge in such are branded with the guilt of a grave sin.

Holy Mother Church very well understands and clearly appreciates all that is said regarding the health of the mother and the danger to her life. Who would not grieve to think of these things; who is not filled with the greatest admiration when he sees a mother risking her life with heroic fortitude, that she may preserve the life of the offspring which she has conceived? God alone, all bountiful and all merciful as He is, can reward her for the fulfillment of the office allotted to her by nature, and will assuredly repay her in a measure full to overflowing (Luke 6:38).

We are deeply touched by the sufferings of those parents who, in extreme want, experience great difficulty in rearing their children. However, they should take care lest the calamitous state of their material affairs should be the occasion for a much more calamitous error. No difficulty can arise that justifies the putting aside of the law of God which forbids all acts intrinsically evil. There is no possible circumstance in which husband and wife cannot, strengthened by the grace of God, fulfill faithfully their duties and preserve in wedlock their chastity unspotted.

But another very grave crime is to be noted, which regards the taking of the life of the unborn offspring. Some wish it to be allowed and left to the will of the father or the mother; others say it is unlawful unless there are weighty reasons which they call by the name of medical, social, or eugenic 'indication.' Because this matter falls under the penal laws of the state, these people demand that the 'indication' which in one form or another they defend, be recognized as such by the public law and in no way penalized. There are those, moreover, who ask that the public authorities provide aid for these death-dealing operations; a thing, which, sad to say, everyone knows is of very frequent occurrence in some places.

However much we may pity the mother whose health and even life is gravely imperiled in the performance of the duty allotted to her by nature, nevertheless what could ever be a sufficient reason for excusing in any way the direct murder of the innocent? This is precisely what we are dealing with here. Whether inflicted upon the mother or upon the child it is against the precept of God and the law of nature: "Thou shalt not kill." The life of each is equally sacred, and no one has the power, not even the public authority, to destroy it.

It is of no use to appeal to the right of taking away life, for here it is a question of the innocent, whereas that right has regard only to the guilty; nor is there here question of defense by bloodshed against an unjust aggressor, for who would call an innocent child an unjust aggressor? Again, there is no question here of what is called the 'law of extreme necessity,' which could never extend to the direct killing of the innocent. Upright and skillful doctors strive most praiseworthily to guard and preserve the lives of both mother and child; on the contrary, those show themselves most unworthy of the noble medical profession who encompass the death of one or the other, through a pretense of practicing medicine or through motives of misguided pity.

Those who hold the reins of government should not forget that it is the duty of public authority by appropriate laws and sanctions to defend the lives of the innocent, and this all the more so since those whose lives are endangered and assailed cannot defend themselves. And if the public magistrates not only do not defend them, but by their laws and ordinances betray them to death at the hands of doctors or of others, let them remember that God is the judge and avenger of innocent blood which cries from earth to heaven (Gen. 4:16).

Finally, that pernicious practice must be condemned which closely touches upon the natural right of man to enter matrimony, but affects also in a real way the welfare of the offspring. For there are some who, over-solicitous for the cause of 'eugenics,' not only give helpful counsel for more certainly procuring the strength and health of the future child—which, indeed, is not contrary to right reason—but put 'eugenics' before aims of a higher order. By public authority they wish to forbid marriage to all those who, even though naturally fit for marriage, they consider, according to the norms and conjectures of their investigations, would through hereditary transmission bring forth defective offspring. And more, they wish to legislate to deprive these of that natural faculty by medical interference despite their unwillingness; and this they do not propose as an infliction of grave punishment under the authority of the state for a crime committed, nor to prevent future crimes by guilty persons, but against every right and good they wish the civil authority to arrogate to itself a power over a faculty which they never had and can never legitimately possess.

Those who act in this way are at fault in losing sight of the fact that the family is more sacred than the state and that men are begotten not for the earth and for time, but for heaven and eternity. Public magistrates have no direct power over the bodies of their subjects. Therefore, where no crime has taken place and there is no cause present for grave punishment, they can never directly harm or tamper with the integrity of the body, either for the reasons of eugenics or for any other reason.

We may now consider another class of errors. They are destroying mutual fidelity who think that the ideas and morality of our present time concerning a certain harmful and false friendship with a third party can be countenanced, and who teach that greater freedom of feeling and action in such external relations should be allowed to man and wife, particularly as many (so they consider) are possessed of an inborn sexual tendency which cannot be satisfied within the narrow limits of monogamous marriage. Such unworthy and idle opinions are condemned by that noble instinct which is found in every chaste husband and wife, and that even by the light of the testimony of nature alone, a testimony that is sanctioned and confirmed by the command of God, "Thou shalt not commit adultery." The force of this divine precept can never be weakened by a merely human custom, bad example, or pretext of human progress. The same false teachers who try to dim the luster of conjugal faith and purity do not scruple to do away with the honorable and trusting obedience the woman owes to the man. Many of them even go further and assert that such a subjection of one party to the other is unworthy of human dignity, that the rights of husband and wife are equal; wherefore they boldly proclaim that the 'emancipation' of women has been or ought to be effected. This, as they wish it, must be threefold: in the ruling of the domestic society, in the administration of family affairs and in the rearing of the children. It is to be "social, economic, physiological": physiological, for the woman is to be freed at her own good pleasure from the burdensome duties properly belonging to a wife as companion and mother (we have already said that this is not an emancipation but a crime); social, inasmuch as the wife being freed from the cares of children and family; should, to the neglect of these, be able to follow her own bent and devote herself to business and even public affairs; finally, economic, whereby the woman even without the knowledge and against the wish of her husband may be at liberty to conduct and administer her own affairs, giving her attention chiefly to these rather than to children, husband, and family.

This, however, is not the true emancipation of woman, nor that rational and exalted liberty which belongs to the noble office of a Christian woman and wife. It is rather the debasing of the womanly character and the dignity of motherhood and indeed of the whole family, as a result of which the husband suffers the loss of his wife, the children of their mother, and the home and the whole family of an ever-watchful guardian. More than this, this false liberty and unnatural equality with the husband is to the detriment of the woman herself, for if the woman descends from her truly regal throne to which she has been raised within the walls of the home by means of the Gospel, she will soon be reduced to the old state of slavery, if not in appearance, certainly in reality, and become, as she did among the pagans, the mere tool of man.

We have so far shown the excellency of the first two blessings of Christian wedlock which the modern disturbers of society are attacking. And now considering that the third blessing, which is that of the sacrament, far surpasses the other two, we should not be surprised to find that this, because of its outstanding excellence, is much more sharply attacked by the same people. They put forward in the first place that matrimony belongs entirely to the profane and purely civil sphere, that it is not to be committed to the religious society, the Church of Christ, but to civil society alone. They then add that the marriage contract is to be freed from any indissoluble bond, and that separation and divorce are not only to be tolerated but sanctioned by the law; from which it follows finally that, robbed of all its holiness, matrimony should be enumerated amongst the secular and civil institutions. The first point is contained in their contention that the civil act itself should stand for the marriage contract (civil matrimony). Moreover, they want it to be no cause for reproach that marriages be contracted by Catholics with non-Catholics without any reference to religion or recourse to the ecclesiastical authorities. The second point, which is but a consequence of the first, is to be found in their excuse for complete divorce and in their praise and encouragement of those civil laws which favor loosening the bond itself.

Even by the light of reason alone it is sufficiently obvious that there is a certain sacredness and religious character attaching even to the purely natural union of man and woman. This sacredness of marriage arises from the divine origin we have just mentioned, from its purpose, which is the begetting and educating of children for God and the binding of man and wife to God through Christian love and mutual support, and finally from the very nature of wedlock, whose institution is to be sought for in the far-seeing providence of God, whereby it is the means of transmitting life, thus making the parents the ministers as it were of the divine omnipotence. To this must be added that new element of dignity which comes from the sacrament by which the Christian marriage is so ennobled and raised to such a level that it appeared to the Apostle as "a great sacrament, honorable in every way."

They, therefore, who rashly and heedlessly contract mixed marriages, from which the maternal love and providence of the Church dissuades her children for very sound reasons, fail conspicuously in this respect, sometimes with danger to their eternal salvation. This attitude of the Church to mixed marriages appears in many of her documents, all of which are summed up in the Code of Canon Law (canon 1060): "Everywhere and with the greatest strictness the Church forbids marriages between baptized persons, one of whom is a Catholic and the other a member of a schismatical or heretical sect, and if there is added to this the danger of the falling away of the Catholic party and the perversion of the children, such a marriage is forbidden also by the divine law." If the Church occasionally on account of circumstances does not refuse to grant a dispensation from these strict laws (provided that the divine law remains intact and the dangers above mentioned are provided against by suitable safeguards), it is unlikely that the Catholic party will not suffer some detriment from such a marriage.

Whence it comes about not infrequently, as experience shows, that deplorable defections from religion occur among the offspring, or at least a headlong descent into that religious indifference which is closely allied to impiety. Assuredly, also, will there be wanting that close union of spirit which, as it is the sign and mark of the Church of Christ, so also should be the sign of Christian wedlock, its glory and adornment. For, where there exists diversity of mind, heart, and will, the bond of union of mind and heart is wont to be broken, or at least weakened. From this comes the danger lest the love of man and wife grow cold and the peace and happiness of family life, resting as it does on the union of hearts, be destroyed.

But especially, as we have pointed out, the daily increasing facility of divorce is an obstacle to the restoration of marriage to that state of perfection which the divine Redeemer willed it should possess.

The advocates of the neo-paganism of today have learned nothing from the sad state of affairs, but instead day by day, more and more vehemently, they continue by legislation to attack the indissolubility of the marriage bond, proclaiming that the lawfulness of divorce must be recognized, and that the antiquated laws should give place to a new and more humane legislation. Many and varied are the grounds put forward for divorce. Thus, in the first place, they maintain that it is for the good of either party that the one who is innocent should have the right to separate from the guilty. In the second place, they argue, the good of the child demands this, for either it will be deprived of a proper education or will too easily be affected by the discords and shortcomings of the parents, and drawn from the path of virtue. And thirdly, the common good of society requires that those marriages should be completely dissolved which are now incapable of producing their natural results, and that legal separation should be allowed when crimes are to be feared as the result of the common habitation and intercourse of the parties. Others, taking a step further, simply state that marriage, being a private contract, is like other private contracts to be left to the consent and good pleasure of both parties, and so can be dissolved for any reason whatsoever.

Opposed to all these reckless opinions stands the unalterable law of God, fully confirmed by Christ, a law that can never be deprived of its force by the decrees of men, the ideas of a people, or the will of any legislator. "What God hath joined together let not man put asunder." Let that solemn pronouncement of the Council of Trent be recalled to mind in which, under the stigma of anathema, it condemned these errors: "If anyone should say that on account of heresy or the hardships of co-habitation or a deliberate abuse of one party by the other, the marriage tie may be loosened, let him be anathema."

In certain circumstances imperfect separation of the parties is allowed, the bond not being severed. This separation, which the Church herself permits and expressly mentions in her Canon Law removes all the alleged inconveniences and dangers. It will be for the sacred law and to some extent also the civil law, in so far as civil matters are affected, to lay down the ground, the conditions, the method, and the precautions to be taken in a case of this kind in order to safeguard the education of the children and the well-being of the family, and to remove all those evils which threaten the married persons, the children, and the state.

It is, then, fitting that with all paternal solicitude we should turn our mind to seek out suitable remedies whereby those most detestable abuses which we have mentioned may be removed, and everywhere marriage may again be revered. In order, therefore, to restore due order in this matter of marriage, it is necessary that all should bear in mind what is the divine plan and strive to conform to it. And since the chief obstacle to this study is the power of unbridled lust, which indeed is the most potent cause of sinning against the sacred laws of matrimony, and since man cannot hold in check his passions unless he first subject himself to God, this must be his primary endeavor, in accordance with the plan divinely ordained. For it is a sacred ordinance that whoever shall have first subjected himself to God, shall, by the aid of God's grace, happily find subject to himself his own passions and concupiscence, while he who is a rebel against God will, to his sorrow, experience within himself the violent rebellion of his worst passions.

Consequently, as the onslaughts of these uncontrolled passions cannot in any way be lessened unless the spirit first shows a humble submission of duty and reverence towards its Maker, it is above all and before all needful that those who are joined in the bond of sacred wedlock should be wholly imbued with a profound and genuine sense of duty towards God, which will shape their whole lives and fill their minds and wills with a very deep reverence for the majesty of God.

They are greatly deceived who, having underestimated or neglected these means which rise above nature, think that they can induce men by the use and discovery of the natural sciences (such as those of biology, the science of heredity, and the like) to curb their carnal desires. We do not say this in order to belittle those natural means which are not immoral, for God is the author of nature as well as of grace, and He has disposed the good things of both orders for the beneficial use of them. The faithful, therefore, can and ought to be assisted also by natural means. But they are mistaken who think that these means are able to establish chastity in the nuptial union, or that they are more effective than supernatural grace.

This conformity of wedlock and moral conduct with the divine laws respecting marriage supposes, however, that all can discern readily, with real certainty, and without any accompanying error, what those laws are. But everyone can see to how many fallacies an avenue would be opened up and how many errors would become mixed with the truth, if it were left solely to the light of reason of each to find out, or if it were to be discovered by the private interpretation of the truth which is revealed. On this account it is necessary that a filial and humble obedience towards the Church should be combined with devotedness to God and the desire of submitting to Him. For Christ Himself made the Church the teacher of truth in those things also which concern the ruling and regulation of moral conduct, even though some things are not of themselves impervious to human reason. Hence they ought to show this due obedience, not only when the Church defines something with solemn judgment, but also, in proper proportion, when, by the constitutions and decrees of the Holy See, opinions are proscribed and condemned as dangerous or distorted.

Wherefore let the faithful also be on their guard against the overrated independence of private judgment and that false autonomy of human reason, especially in those present-day discussions about marriage. For it is quite foreign to everyone bearing the name of Christian to trust his own mental powers with such pride as to agree only with those things which he can examine from their inner nature, and to imagine that the Church, sent by God to teach and guide all nations, is not conversant with present affairs and circumstances, or even that they must obey only in those matters which she has decreed by means of solemn definition as though her other decisions might be presumed to be false or to put forward insufficient motive for truth and moral goodness.

Thus will it come to pass that the faithful will whole-heartedly thank God that they are bound together by His command and led by gentle compulsion to fly as far as possible from every kind of idolatry of the flesh and from the base slavery of the passions. They will in a great measure turn and be turned away from these abominable opinions which to the dishonor of man's dignity are now spread about in speech and in writing and collected under the title of 'perfect marriage' and which indeed would make that perfect marriage nothing better than 'depraved marriage,' as it has also been called with good reason.

Even the very best instruction given by the Church, however, will not alone suffice to bring about once more conformity of marriage to the law of God. Something more is needed in addition to the education of the mind; namely, a steadfast determination of the will on the part of husband and wife to observe the sacred laws of God and of nature in regard to marriage. In fine, in spite of what others may wish to assert and spread abroad by word of mouth or in writing, let husband and wife resolve to stand fast to the commandments of God in all things that matrimony demands; always to render to each the assistance of mutual love; to preserve the honor of chastity, nor to lay profane hands on the stable nature of the bond; to use the rights given them by marriage in a way that will be always Christian and sacred, more especially in the first years of wedlock, so that should there be need of continency afterwards custom will have made it easier for each to preserve it.

All these things, however, venerable brethren, depend in large measure on the due preparation, remote and proximate, of the parties for marriage. For it cannot be denied that the basis of a happy wedlock and the ruin of an unhappy one is prepared and set in the souls of boys and girls during the period of childhood and adolescence. There is danger that those who before marriage sought in all things what is theirs, who indulged even their impure desires, will be in the married state what they were before; that they will reap that which they have sown; that within the home there will be sorrow, grief, mutual contempt, strifes, estrangements, weariness of common life; and, worst of all, that such parties will find themselves left alone with their own unconquered passions. Let, then, those who are about to enter on married life approach that state well disposed and well prepared, so that they will be able as far as they can to help each other in sustaining the vicissitudes of life, and yet more in attending to their eternal salvation and in forming the inner man unto the fullness of the image of Christ. This will also help them to behave towards their cherished offspring as God wills, that is, that the father be truly a father, and the mother truly a mother.

To the proximate preparation of a good married life belongs very specially the care in choosing a partner. And so, that they will not deplore for the rest of their lives the sorrows arising from an indiscreet marriage, those about to enter into wedlock should carefully deliberate in choosing the person with whom henceforward they must live continually. Let them diligently pray for divine help, so that they will make their choice in accordance with Christian prudence, not indeed led by the blind and unchecked impulse of lust, nor by any desire of riches or other base influence, but by a true and noble love and by a sincere affection towards the future partner; and then let them strive in their married life toward those ends for which this state was constituted by God. Lastly, let them not fail to ask the prudent advice of their parents with regard to the partner, and let them regard this advice in no light manner, in order that by their mature knowledge and experience of human affairs they may guard against a baneful mistake, and on the threshold of matrimony may receive more abundantly the divine blessing.

Since it is no rare thing to find that the perfect observance of God's commands and conjugal integrity encounter difficulties because the married parties are oppressed by straitened circumstances, their necessities must be relieved as far as possible. So in the first place an effort must be made that in the state such economic and social agencies should be set up as will enable every head of a family to earn as much as, according to his station in life, is necessary for himself, his wife, and for the rearing of his children, for "the laborer is worthy of his hire." To deny this or to make light of what is equitable is a grave injustice and is placed among the greatest sins by Holy Writ; nor is it lawful to fix such a scanty wage as will be insufficient for the upkeep of the family in the circumstances in which it is placed. Care, however, must be taken that the parties themselves for a considerable time before entering upon married life should strive to dispose of or at least to diminish the material obstacles in their way. Provision must be made also, in the case of those who are not self-supporting, for joint aid by private or public guilds. When these needs which we have pointed out are not fulfilled, the needs particularly of a larger or poorer family, Christian charity toward our neighbor absolutely demands that those things which are lacking to the needy should be provided. Hence it is incumbent on the rich to help the poor, that having an abundance of this world's goods they do not expend them fruitlessly, but employ them for the support and well-being of those who lack the necessities of life.

If, however, private resources do not suffice for this, it is the duty of the public authority to supply for the insufficient resources of personal effort. If families, particularly those in which there are many children, have not suitable dwellings; if the husband cannot find employment and means of livelihood; if the necessities of life cannot be purchased except at exorbitant prices; if even the mother of the family, to the great harm of the home, is compelled to go forth and seek a living by her own labor; if in the ordinary or even extraordinary labors of childbirth she is deprived of proper food, medicine, and the assistance of a skilled physician—then it is evident to everyone that, if husband and wife lose heart, home life and the observance of God's commands will be rendered difficult for them. Indeed, great is the evil that can arise to public security and to the welfare and very life of civil society itself when such men are reduced to such a condition of desperation that, having nothing which they fear to lose, they are emboldened to hope for chance advantage from the upheaval of the state and of established order.